IN SEARCH OF THE ROMANOVS

A Family's Quest to Solve One of History's Most Brutal Crimes

PETER SARANDINAKI

With editorial assistance by Rob Suggs

Potomac Books | *An imprint of the University of Nebraska Press*

 Potomac Books is an imprint of the University of Nebraska Press. Manufactured in the United States of America.

∞

Library of Congress Cataloging-in-Publication Data
Names: Sarandinaki, Peter, author.
Title: In search of the Romanovs: a family's quest to solve one of history's most brutal crimes / Peter Sarandinaki; with editorial assistance by Rob Suggs.
Other titles: Family's quest to solve one of history's most brutal crimes
Description: Lincoln: Potomac Books, an imprint of the University of Nebraska Press, [2024] | Includes bibliographical references and index.
Identifiers: LCCN 2023043109
ISBN 9781640121560 (hardback)
ISBN 9781640126244 (epub)
ISBN 9781640126251 (pdf)
Subjects: LCSH: Nicholas II, Emperor of Russia, 1868–1918—Assassination. | Nicholas II, Emperor of Russia, 1868–1918—Death and burial. | Nicholas II, Emperor of Russia, 1868–1918—Family. | Dom Ipat'eva (Ekaterinburg, Russia) | Romanov, House of. | Russia—History—Nicholas II, 1894–1917. | Human remains (Archaeology)—Collection and preservation. | Human remains (Archaeology)—Analysis. | Forensic anthropology. | BISAC: HISTORY / Russia / General | TRUE CRIME / Historical
Classification: LCC DK258.6 .S27 2024 | DDC 947.08/30922—dc23/eng/20240108
LC record available at https://lccn.loc.gov/2023043109

Set in Garamond Premier Pro by A. Shahan.

Dedicated to Anna

1900–1989

The voice of thy brother's blood
crieth unto me from the ground.

—GENESIS 4:10

Contents

Illustrations

Acknowledgments

First, I must acknowledge my grandmother, Anna Sergeyevna Rozanova-Naryshkina. Hearing so many stories about her life prompted me to ask her to write them down, and her notes became the basis for part 1. Thank you for your bravery and strength, Baba (as we called her).

I thank my wife, Masha (Maria Vladimirovna Tolstaya-Sarandinaki), for putting up with me all these years, as well as encouraging me to keep going even after so many returns without results. And my children, Deacon Alexandre, Tatiana, and Sergey, as well as their spouses, I thank them all for their support.

I thank the late Dr. William R. Maples, director of the C. A. Pound Human Identification Laboratory, University of Florida, Gainesville, for introducing me to Dr. Alexander Avdonin and his wife, Galina, and for encouraging me to meet the U.S. Army scientists at the Central Identification Laboratory, Hickam Air Force Base, in Honolulu, Hawaii, and to get them to help search for the remains of Tsarevich Alexei and one of his sisters (Maria or Anastasia).

Our search for the remains of Tsarevich Alexei and his sister Grand Duchess Maria in 1998–99 and 2004 was only possible due to Dr. Avdonin, Dr. Sergey Nikitin, and Vladimir Soloviev. I thank them for their friendship and trust. It was Dr. Nikitin who introduced me to Col. Vladimir Konstantinov, who told me about Grand Duke Mikhail Romanov.

After Dr. Maples passed away, Dr. Anthony Falsetti took the helm of the University of Florida Human ID Lab. Tony was instrumental in introducing me to Dr. Diane France of NecroSearch International in Denver, Colorado, who, together with geologist Jim Reed, traveled to Yekaterinburg in February 1998 to plan future searches for Tsarevich Alexei's and his sister Maria's remains. This trip, of course, did not work out well, but it was a beginning, and I'm grateful.

In 2007 Dr. Anthony Falsetti introduced me to Col. Louis Finelli, director of the Armed Forces DNA Identification Laboratory, who agreed to perform DNA studies of the remains of the two Romanov children found at the site of Porosenkov Log (Pig's Meadow). Thank you, Dr. Michael Coble, section chief, and Dr. Odile Loreille for your excellent work.

I do thank NecroSearch International forensic experts forensic geophysicist George Clark Davenport, investigator Brook Thomas Schaub, geologist Jim Reed, forensic botanist Crystal Strouse, and historian Steven Jackson for their great effort from 2013 to the present in traveling to Perm, Russia, and methodically searching for the remains of Grand Duke Mikhail Romanov and his secretary, Nikolai Johnson. Thank you for your trust and friendship.

Search Dogs UK's Michael Swindells, our search team manager, braved the high seas and traveled countless hours to reach Perm with his two dogs, border collie Sam and later his black lab, Ronnie, to direct our thorough and methodical searches for the remains of Mikhail Romanov and Nikolai Johnson. I thank you, Mick, for all your work.

Forensic archaeologist John R. Hunter, OBE, PhD, MCLFA, FSA, FCSFS: your expertise in search methods and procedures was greatly appreciated. Thank you.

Our Russian team was instrumental in getting proper permits and logistics. Thank you, Luba Markova, Larissa Baletova, and Nelli Zenkova for your historical knowledge of the case, and Col. Andrey Bezmaternykh of the Russian Police for your participation, leadership, and for helping to make our searches possible.

I would like to thank my friend Nicholas B. A. Nicholson for introducing me to Fabergé expert Nikolai Bachmakov, who provided the hairs from the locket and the frame to the FBI DNA Laboratory for DNA testing. I thank Dr. Odile Loreille, Jodi Irwin, and Anthony Onorato for their trust and hard work, and for developing new techniques and protocols that improved the science of DNA and helped give closure to the Romanov case.

I wouldn't have been able to work on the Romanov case without the trust, acknowledgment, and support of Col. Vladimir Soloviev and Gen. Marina Victorovna Molodsova.

Thank you, Toten and Nadja Bacardi, for your friendship, support, and encouragement to continue my searches.

I also would like to acknowledge and thank our friends George and Christine Sosnovsky for their belief in me and strong financial support, which made the expeditions to Perm possible.

I was able to go to Russia with the late author Robert K. Massie as his interpreter in 1994 and was able to get the lay of the land at Four Brothers and Pig's Meadow. We met the many scientists involved in the Romanov identification case—thank you, Bob.

Margarita Nelipa, thank you for helping me finish the first draft of this book and for doing all the needed translations. You are a true friend.

I thank the Board of the Search Foundation, Inc., for their support and fund-raising that made the searches possible, and Peter Y. Malyshev for providing extremely valuable legal advice all these years, which helped make this book a reality.

A big thank you to Tanya Penkrat and Marina Poutiatine for reading the manuscript and making edits and corrections.

And finally, thank you, Rob Suggs, for turning this into a wonderful book that my grandchildren and future generations will be proud to read and talk about. You added so much style and eloquence. I highly recommend Rob to anyone who would have need of an editor or ghost writer: "he is a virtuoso of the written word."

IN SEARCH OF THE ROMANOVS

Prologue

LETTING THE WORLD KNOW

Yekaterinburg, Russia, December 5, 2008

It was a restless room, packed with reporters, scientists, government representatives, and one Russian Orthodox priest. This was a historic day. The Romanov family DNA results would finally become public.

Nine sets of remains had been found under a bridge of old rail ties along the Koptiaki Road. Would the mystery of the imperial family—their fate and their burial—finally be put to rest?

After nearly a century of rumors, legends, fantasies, and questionable claims, modern science would finally speak. And as the scientists reviewed their findings, the answers came forth with a clear and definitive "yes": Here were the earthly remains of Nicholas, the last of the Romanov emperors. And here was his family—at least some of them.

Dr. Nikolai Nevolin, forensic scientist, capped his presentation by introducing Capt. Peter Sarandinaki. He was the man who had worked behind the scenes for long, patient years, encouraging investigation and finally gathering scientists from three continents to study the DNA of what might or might not be the Romanovs.

The captain had waited many years for this moment, but he had no idea what the results would show. Emperor Nicholas II; his wife, Empress Alexandra; their children, the Grand Duchesses Olga, Tatiana, and Anastasia; the family's doctor; and three servants would eventually be identified and even acknowledged by the church as saints.

As Captain Sarandinaki stood to speak, the image of his grandmother, Anna, came to the forefront of his memory. How much would this day have meant to her?

Anna had been no more than a child when she witnessed the turbulence of the years leading up to 1917. She'd seen and had explained to her the rising contempt by the Russian peasant class. Her father, Sergei Rozanov, had been a soldier in eastern Siberia during the Russo-Japanese War—and *his* great-grandfather had been a war hero who defeated Napoleon in 1812. Service to the mother country ran deep in the family blood.

When the Great War came in 1914, Anna's father had fought the Austrians and risen to commander of the army.

During all that time, it was Anna's mother who was left to care for the family and defend their land, even as starvation stole across the countryside. The revolutionary crowd had little trouble spreading unrest throughout the population.

By March of 1917, there was a new threat from within. Tsar Nicholas was forced to abdicate the Russian throne. He and his family had been placed under house arrest, and by April of the following year, they were sent to Yekaterinburg, their ultimate place of execution, by the Bolsheviks, who were now seizing power.

Lieutenant General Rozanov, taking the side of the White Russians (the anticommunist faction) escaped to the east. His wife and his teenage daughter Anna fled just in time to evade arrest. By horseback, carriage, and camel, they made a harrowing journey to freedom. Anna's father gave her a pistol. "Seven bullets," he said grimly. "The last of them for you," he said. Peter grew with these stories.

The White Army and Czech troops liberated Yekaterinburg only seven days after the Romanovs were murdered there. Anna's father was among the first to approach the House of Special Purpose, where the royal family had been kept.

He stood for a few moments in the house, guessing at the horrors that had transpired there. As he couldn't bring himself to enter the basement, he sent an aide, who saw fresh traces of blood but no bodies.

Where were the emperor and his family? Could any of them be yet alive? For the rest of his life, Rozanov would wonder without receiving an answer. So would the rest of the world.

Anna's father introduced his good friend Nikolai Sokolov to the White Army general staff, and Sokolov was given the task of tracing the imperial family and its potential murderers.

Sokolov was worthy of his friend's trust. His detective work led him to an open pit at the Four Brothers Mine, fifteen kilometers north of Yekaterinburg. The best sources pointed to this site as the final destination of the bodies. There Sokolov found traces of three bonfires, scraps of burned clothing, a set of dentures, a few broken gemstones, and even a few bullets. Beneath a flooded open shaft, a false floor was found. And beneath that, a dog—surely Anastasia's dog, Jimmy. In the cold water, the body had never decomposed.

Hundreds of searchers paced through the forest, a few meters apart, looking for anything indicating a grave, but nothing emerged. Sokolov examined maps and tried to think like someone concealing a crime. He should have paid more attention to Pig's Meadow, on the Koptiaki Road, where the Bolsheviks had spent much time and even built a bridge of rail ties, only four miles from the mine. Here was the very spot where the Reds' truck had gotten mired in the mud; why would they take the time to build a bridge in such an unpromising location?

There was no more time to consider these things; the Red Army was drawing nearer. Sokolov fled to Vladivostok to join his friend Rozanov, Anna's father.

In January of 1920 Lieutenant General Rozanov and his family were evacuated to Japan, where they waited for a ship to take them to Europe. Meanwhile, his friend Sokolov, who had unearthed evidence of the murder of the imperial family, sought refuge in China. Later, Sokolov and his wife boarded the same French passenger ship, *Andre Lebon*, and ended up sharing a cabin with Rozanov's daughter, Anna, and her husband, Kirill Naryshkin.

Anna would remember that voyage quite well, particularly the small suitcase containing proof of the murder that Sokolov placed under her bunk. He kept a strict eye on that suitcase; it was to be guarded at all times.

One day, Anna lifted the lid and peeked inside. There she saw, among other things, pieces of bone and a scrap of wallpaper on which was scrawled, "Belsatsar was killed this night by his own servants."

She puzzled over those words, taken from German poet Heinrich Heine, who in turn was loosely quoting ancient scripture. Belsatsar was a Babylonian king. But the poet's spelling was *Belsazar*. The extra *t* introduces the word *tsar* into the quotation. No one knows who scribbled those words.

Anna had many talks with Sokolov and knew he'd concluded that all the remains of the bodies had been burned. Four years later, he published his book *Judicial Inquiry on the Assassination of the Russian Imperial Family*.

The world, of course, wasn't satisfied. What became of the bodies? And what about the rumors of at least one survivor?

Forty-one years later, Anna's ten-year-old grandson Peter entered the United States as his parents emigrated from Argentina. He was left in the care of his grandmother, along with his brother and sister. And thus began the stories the old woman told him about life in Russia at the beginning of the twentieth century; about the terror of revolution, with the sounds of distant firing squads; about a tense escape to France.

Peter's childhood was haunted by these stories. Over and over, he would ask to hear one more time about the suitcase on the ship, about the time she opened the box and saw a finely manicured finger and a few bones. In his mind's eye, he staged the scene in the basement, picturing how the strange words on the wallpaper came to be written.

The Bolshevik leader of the execution squad in 1918 was a man named Yakov Yurovsky. He was a member of the Cheka (the secret police), and he'd been in that half-cellar room when the walls were wet with blood. He'd done one good thing: he'd left behind a detailed statement of his actions.

In 1978 retired geologist Dr. Alexander Avdonin of Yekaterinburg and filmmaker Geli Ryabov of Moscow used Yurovsky's statement to make a search of their own. Beneath a soil-covered wooden bridge, they came up with three human skulls. They knew this had to be the site of the Romanov graves. But the Soviets were still in control, and such a discovery was highly dangerous, worthy of imprisonment. So the two men swore an oath of silence for as long as communism lasted in their homeland—which turned out to be until 1988, the year that system's collapse began.

A few months later, the filmmaker Ryabov offered a blockbuster revelation in *Rodina*, a popular Russian magazine. The burial site of the Romanovs, he said, had been found. The bones of Tsar Nicholas had finally emerged.

In 1991 the local government gave permission to exhume the remains of eleven people thought to be buried together: Emperor Nicholas II, his wife, Alexandra, their five children, court physician Yevgeni Botkin, and three servants.

There was great interest across the world when the careful digging began. The bodies were there, just as the skulls had indicated they would be, with the exception of two sets of remains that were mysteriously absent: Tsarevich Alexei, heir to the throne, plus one of his sisters, either Maria or Anastasia.

So, for now, the mystery endured. Two Romanovs were still unaccounted for.

On the eightieth anniversary of the murders, July 17, 1998, the nine sets of remains were interred at the Saint Catherine's Chapel of Saint Peter and Paul Cathedral in Saint Petersburg. The burial service was conducted by four priests. But there was no acknowledgment of royalty or significance in the burials; these departed souls were to be taken simply as individuals who happened to be named Nicholas, Alexandra, Olga, Tatiana, and Anastasia.

It may have seemed fairly ludicrous, but the discovery had collided with ecclesiastical politics. The Moscow patriarchate did not—could not—accept these remains as belonging to the Romanovs. There was too much controversy attached to this iconic, tragic family.

Watching on television from far away, I, Peter Sarandinaki, grandson of Anna Naryshkina, couldn't believe what I was seeing. I swore an oath to myself that somehow, some way, I would see the church confess the truth to the world. These were the Romanovs, Russia's last imperial family. They had died cruelly, brutally, their remains treated like the carcasses of animals.

They were also the first victims of the notorious Soviet communism. The homeland and even the world owed them at the very least the acknowledgment of their true identity. History demands unflinching honesty. As saints of the Russian Orthodox Church, the family's burial deserved the presence of the patriarch, along with all his metropolitans and bishops.

Ninety years after the executions, I became the first of my family to return to Russia. I played a part in solving the crime and identifying the remains, constantly pleading with forensic scientists and governmental authorities to investigate. Surely now the church would hear my case on its merits.

So once again, I laid it all out for those who would listen: the story of my family; the harrowing details of their flight from certain death; my participation in three searches for the two missing Romanov children. Where I could, I made use of the advocacy of influential friends.

I felt it extremely important to recount to all who were interested how it felt to sift through a pile of stones left by Sokolov himself and to find in my hands a bullet fired from a Nagant pistol that fateful day. I shouted, "I found a bullet!" and everyone in the party quickly surrounded me, elated.

It was an amazing moment, after which Dr. Avdonin, leader of the expedition, awarded me a shot of good Russian vodka in celebration.

The next day yielded nothing. But on the third day, as I sifted through a pile of stones with a small garden shovel, something glimmered in the corner of my eye. I picked up a small stone, wiped away the dust, and saw a jewel of white topaz with a hole in the middle.

Again, I shouted in elation, for everyone knew the emperor had given each of his daughters a white topaz stone for her necklace on each birthday. So many years ago, Sokolov had found fourteen of these; here was a fifteenth, and it earned me another shot of vodka.

From the dusty debris of history, such Old World jewelry still gleams. I felt it was worth the search, because the past deserves our homage, and because the future deserves the lessons we learn.

This is the story of a quest of one family, relentlessly searching for the truth about another, about a past that has faded but must never be forgotten.

PART 1

Anna's Story

1

Distant Fire

It was sometime in the middle of the night, and Anna was wide awake.

This was where the story inevitably began, the story she would tell her young grandson so many years later, from the other side of the world. The old world, the one in her story, would by then be long gone: a dream shared by a few elderly people, like herself, and a matter for the history classes.

Anna was four on that frightening evening, and noises had jolted her awake. What monsters were prowling the darkness beyond her window? She could hear explosions and shouting voices; she could see the light of flames flickering on the windowpane.

It was people. Ordinary people from the country—that's what she was told.

Anna's family lived on a fine estate in Saratov, on the Volga, in southwestern Russia. She gathered, with a child's tentative grasp, that these country people were upset with families such as hers—the families that lived in the larger homes.

It was comforting to hear the footsteps of Abram the watchman outside, circling the grounds. Abram would protect them.

But somehow the noises were louder, closer tonight. The cries were shrill, like the cries of beasts. Mama came into the room to hold Anna until she drifted back into slumber.

The next morning, she rose to find quite a commotion. It was all about those noises and cries she'd heard. Mama and the servants hurried through the household, packing things and preparing meals for travel. The family would be moving northwest, to Penza, a safer haven for a family. There were soldiers in Penza. If only Papa were here—but he was away, with the army. Mama said he was very important, that he commanded many soldiers, that they should be proud of him. And she was certain they would see him soon, and Anna could give him as many hugs and kisses as she wanted.

As the horses carried them to Penza, Anna looked out upon the scenery and saw things that made her hide her eyes: the ashes of buildings she had known; cows and oxen lying dead on the ground, often skinned, with halos of flies. Who would do these things? Why were these people so angry? She knew many of them, and they had always been kind to her.

Mama said these were "disturbances," that people were angry at the tsar and all the leaders. They were angry about many things, mostly about their lives and their daily work. She said the problems were too large for a little girl to think about, and there were too many people shouting and destroying things. It would all calm down, she assured Anna, with a comforting kiss on the cheek; things always calm down.

Anna remained curious about the forces that were at work tearing apart her homeland. In the cities, particularly Saint Petersburg, the laborers were seeing their wages grow smaller as the price of living climbed ever higher. Strikes were beginning to shut down the factories, and leaders such as the priest Father Georgy Gapon began to call out to the tsar for relief. He demanded an eight-hour workday and better conditions, including for women workers. They too should have some of the freedoms that were appearing in other parts of the world: freedom of the press, freedom of speech, freedom of religion. And everyone wanted this new war with Japan to be over with.

The first week of January 1905, more than one hundred thousand workers were on strike in Saint Petersburg. The men and women were banding together, joining workmen's associations, to find the only strength available to them: strength in numbers.

Tsar Nicholas II was becoming nervous. What answers could be found? He called in the army to surround and protect his palace.

Gapon created a petition that read, "We workers, our children, our wives, and our old, helpless parents have come, Lord, to seek truth and protection from you. We are impoverished and oppressed, unbearable work is imposed on us, we are despised and not recognized as human beings. We are treated as slaves, who must bear their fate and be silent. We have suffered terrible things, but we are pressed ever deeper into the abyss of poverty, ignorance, and lack of rights."

He included his demands for freedoms, privileges, and improved conditions. More than 150,000 signees gave the petition gravity and urgency. Then, on January 22, he led a procession of workers to the Winter Palace to present the great document. This was a Sabbath event with solemnity attached. It was not meant to be a threatening or intimidating march; people wore their Sunday clothes and carried religious icons and pictures of the tsar. Women, children, and the elderly participated. At the palace, these people stood in the snow for two hours, anticipating the tsar's appearance and words. Like all those before him, he was referred to as "our father the tsar." In Russia, a tsar wasn't seen as a government officer; he was *Papa*, Father. When you were hurting, when you needed something, you went to your father.

So they waited. But only the horsemen came.

Cossack forces descended upon the crowds, their swords brandished. It all happened so swiftly, the crowd had no way to defend itself. The horsemen encircled the crowd, striking from all positions, as screams filled the winter air.

Bloody Sunday changed everything. Father Gapon, the heart and soul of the movement, survived to renounce the tsar, the church, even God. His anger radiated out through the thousands of factory workers who paid heed to him.

And still, the tsar was confused about what had happened and what could be done. He was a devout, committed family man, always absorbed by his wife, his daughters, and his little son, and many felt that it was Tsarevich Alexei, the heir, the boy struggling with hemophilia, who thoroughly distracted his father. This, too, was a boy who needed Papochka.

The next day, more strikes were announced—at electricity stations this time. The walkouts were spreading like a fever across the cities, and too late, Nicholas began to look into freedoms and peace offerings for the working class. From Geneva, the communist Vladimir Lenin paid close attention, beginning to realize that these events in Russia were opening up real questions for the future. A true revolution was possible. Printing presses were churning out pamphlets full of incendiary language and calls to action.

In February there was an attempt to assassinate Grand Duke Sergei Alexandrovich, governor-general of Moscow. He was the tsar's uncle. As the grand duke's carriage approached the Bolshoi Theatre, the assassin stood ready to hurl a bomb, but he relented when he saw the grand duke's wife and children. Instead, he threw his bomb two days later.

From prison, he told the grand duke's wife he had committed the murder because Sergei Alexandrovich was "a weapon of tyranny. I was taking revenge for the people." He then used his trial to play up the "two warring camps," the imperial government and the people. "You have declared war on the people," he said. "We have accepted your challenge."

The fever even spread to the high seas. On the battleship *Potemkin*, sailors were angry about the rotten, maggot-filled meat on their table. There was a protest, and the captain ordered the ringleaders to be executed. But the firing squad would not comply. They joined with the rebels and threw the officers overboard. With the captain and many of the officers gone, a committee was organized to guide the ship. It was difficult for the newspapers of the time to avoid depicting the *Potemkin* as a metaphor for the "ship of state." It was a season for overthrow: autocratic leaders were out, and the people would create their own government.

The crew's ringleaders certainly made the connection. When they traveled to Geneva, they delivered a message to Father Gapon. And soon, there were uprisings in the army and elsewhere in the navy.

By October, with a complete strike of the railway network, Russia was all but incapacitated as a functioning nation.

The tsar's chief minister boiled the options down to two. The tsar must either join the people's movement and give in to its demands, bringing on profound change—or he must declare a military dictatorship and use brute force and mass executions to maintain control.

The minister recommended something along the lines of the first option, and that was the direction Nicholas II chose. For a few years, the bandage held.

Even if Anna had been older and known more of the world, she couldn't have realized the depth of the problems. Few did. The revolution wound down with a new constitution, an October Manifesto, and a new system allowing for political parties, including the State Duma, a lower house of the legislature. Emperor Nicholas II would support a host of new policies—at least in the beginning—supporting civil rights, free speech, a free press, and the people's participation in their government. These ideas were working elsewhere in the world. Why not Russia? In retrospect, it was too little, too late.

All Anna knew was the joy she felt when her father came home—though in truth, she could hardly remember his face. He seemed weary and distant, as if his war was only beginning. He would lift his daughter into his lap and tell her stories of distant lands and odd sights, of soldiers in their finery and regiments, of the sounds of galloping stallions and approaching cannons. He asked her if she would like to move again, to see other places and homes. It sounded like a cheerful thing as he explained it, but Mama was silent and sad as he spoke of more packing, more travel.

Late autumn brought the rains, day after day, and Anna was confined to the rooms and halls of the old house. Many of her things were packed away; her mother said they must always be ready for the road. Anna couldn't understand why, nor would even her grandmother explain it to her. Anna adored her grandmother, who shared her name.

Babushka (Grandmother) Anna lived in a nearby cottage. She was a baroness, always accompanied by Matriona, her servant, who fussed over her and cared for all her needs. Even a small child could understand this was a woman of some importance. She saw to the needs not only of her home but the homes of everyone nearby.

"We share this name, you and I," Babushka Anna told the little girl. "It speaks to the world of our family, so you must carry it with grace and honor. And you, little Anna, have your special place—you were born in the first year of the new century and have brought in a new age. It appears to be a troubled age, but perhaps you can make it a healthier one. You will grow up to a world much different than the one I've known. You may travel the world and see things I will not."

The travel part seemed certain. Just as Father had predicted, the time came to move again. Anna was always upset and a bit fussy when these mornings came, and all her things were placed into trunks, but once they all boarded the troika, there were many things to see and wonder about. The family boarded a train to Saint Petersburg, and this was an adventure in itself. There was a comfortable compartment, a fine, bright window, and endless villages filing by in procession.

In the station at Ryazhsk, a lengthy table was set, and dinner was served. Passing through Moscow was wonderful as well. This was the most exciting trip Anna had experienced.

After two days, the family arrived Saint Petersburg and took an apartment at 17 Spassky Street. City living was different but had many charms. Anna could visit the Summer Garden, gaze into the windows of shops, and stare at all the remarkable faces. Anna hadn't realized the world held so many people, and of so many varieties.

Mademoiselle Lane, who cared for her, showed her the proper way to walk in public. Scampering, skipping—these things were strictly forbidden. Young ladies from respectable families stepped forward elegantly, with dignity. "You must set yourself apart, Anna," she said. "You are a Rozanov."

Anna wanted to stop and study the more interesting people, such as the round, jolly woman with the apples. But Mademoiselle wouldn't tolerate such lapses.

There was music in cities. A street organist would play, and there would be a monkey or a bird on his shoulder. It was almost unbearable for Anna to retain poise and elegance at times like these. The bird drew tickets for fortune-telling. The monkey danced, chattered, and took coins from the people.

Springtime arrived, even in a city of pavements and brownstones. Flowers bloomed in little gardens and on window boxes. Trees spread their leaves majestically as if to say, "We, too, are of proud lineage." And every day was a fine one for walking—even of the elegant, stately type. Maslenitsa was a week of festivals and celebration before Great Lent. It was filled with color, music, and laughter. For a while, Anna and all those around her forgot about unrest and violence.

She had heard talk about Bloody Sunday, just recently, in this very city. It was impossible to miss—the description of vast numbers of people standing quietly in the snow, simply wanting to make their requests, only to have Cossack soldiers descend on them with swords. It was hard for Anna to imagine such frightening things on sunny streets such as these. Perhaps there was no safe place, and the anger and violence were everywhere.

Anna looked forward to the day when she could attend school with other children. She was told this was a place of wonderful learning, where the world would be opened up before her. But to be admitted to first grade, she was required to pass a test. This was a frightening affair: a little child standing before a great, long table covered in green cloth. The women who sat at this table seemed hostile and accusatory as they shot their questions at her, one after the other.

Anna was frightened; was this what school was like? At the end of the interview, she was informed her examination was unsatisfactory, and she was escorted unceremoniously out to the street with Mademoiselle. For the rest of that day, she hid beneath her family's dining room table, afraid she would be punished or scolded.

But her parents made little comment. They seemed preoccupied with other things. Soon they would be leaving Saint Petersburg anyway, so school enrollment was of no consequence.

The sad news was that her father would be staying behind in the city, where he still had important matters to attend to. The more cheerful news was that the rest of the family would rejoin Babushka Anna in the country, at her estate.

Again, they made the long and interesting journey. This time Anna felt herself a woman of the world, however, because she knew these villages. She was accustomed to these sights and experiences. She had lived in town and country, and what stories she could tell the other children. Of course, there were fewer of them in the country.

She missed the round woman with the apples, the man with the birds and monkeys, the grand church ceremonies at Easter. On the other hand, there were woods to explore, a river in which to fish. One day, the family made a picnic of their fishing trip to the Sura. The river was delightful, presenting a beach on which the children could run and play. Anna didn't want to go home; there was too much fun to be had.

But as the horses plodded home along that same narrow road—now gloomier, as the sun retreated—a group of peasants turned up, standing in the road and peering at their carriage. To Anna, they seemed stern and a bit threatening. The coachman climbed down, and there was a tense conversation.

One of the peasants carried a yardstick, and he was pointing to the places where the horses had trampled the grass. This wasn't a wide road, but one intended for travelers on foot. The villagers were measuring the inches of trespass in hoofprints and complaining. The coachman, hands on hips, retorted that this was a silly matter, and they should take their yardsticks and go home.

But Anna hated the quarreling voices and worried that something terrible would happen. After that, Babushka Anna decreed there would be no more fishing trips to the Sura. This was peasant land, including the road, and there was no wisdom in increasing the tensions.

2

Country Life

In the long weeks of winter, the charm of country life faded with the leaves. Staying warm was serious business, though it didn't seem to bother the local people as much. But this season, Anna was told, was cold even beyond Russian memory. The hearth was the magnet of every room. Firewood must be kept in full supply; it was a matter of survival, as explained to Anna.

At night, the winds moaned and wept, and Anna's family drank tea and shared old stories. When the firewood needed to be replenished, a servant opened the door to the porch to bring in more logs. The wind would come rushing indoors, furious and insistent.

There was talk about a hut in nearby Klyuchi, where peasants had huddled around the fire, nursing their tea to warm their hands and faces. In the early evening, when one of them opened the door to slip out for fresh kindling, there was the unmistakable sound of a human voice, crying out for help. The winds could impersonate people in distress quite well, but everyone knew what they'd heard was real.

When the man returned with his wood, he said, "I could not find this poor man. It's impossible to see or hear out there. I took a few steps and called out, but I couldn't tell the direction."

"Let me try," said one of the other men. He and several others in their group hurried outdoors, shouted, and listened, but it was hopeless, and after a while, the man was lost and confused, then quiet.

The rest of the evening, the group was anxious. And sure enough, when morning came, a poor soul was found no more than a few hundred feet away, frozen in the snow.

The greatest misery of the story was that somehow, during the commotion, no one had thought to fetch a lantern. Such a sad tale might have come from the pen of Tolstoy. Perhaps a speck of light would have saved a life, but who could know?

On long, cold nights, Anna burrowed deeply into her blankets, as haunted by the man as if she'd heard him herself, his ghostly cries returning in the angry winds of the night.

She was more than delighted in the springtime, when she could venture outdoors again. She'd learned how to find Dedushka (Grandfather) Trofim and his wonderful bees. It was necessary to walk past her family's apple orchard, find her way through a forest of oaks, then proceed two kilometers to the little valley where Dedushka kept his apiary. For him, bees were the most important matter in the world. He loved telling Anna all about the events of their lives, how they cared for their queen, how they made delicious honey, and he even added a few fairy tales about bees.

The old man was always happy to see her, always ready with a slice of bread and honey and a new tale from the insect world. But only for a while. After an hour or two, he would grow tired, and say, "Run home now, little Anna. I'm sure they're out looking for you."

Thanks to Dedushka, there was always plenty of honey. And Anna could eat her fill of apples from the orchard, along with perch, pike, and crawfish caught in the river. There were mushrooms, strawberries to be eaten with cream, and so many other wonderful foods.

She also enjoyed tagging along with Babushka Anna. It was the best way to learn new and surprising things. In some ways, her grandmother was the queen bee of these lands. Peasants came to her with their problems on Sundays. Babushka Anna would sit on the porch, holding court, offering advice and commands that would solve everyday problems. The people came to her with a respect that she reciprocated.

"Madam," said one of the local women, "I have a husband who loves the bottle more than he loves his family. He earns very little money, but he takes most of that and throws it away on drunkenness at the tavern. Meanwhile, our children go hungry, and he ignores my pleas for food and clothing."

Babushka Anna listened carefully, then sent for her property manager. "Give this woman flour," she instructed, "and whatever basic goods she needs. Then go to this husband and instruct him that henceforth, his wife will manage his earnings. All the money must be placed in her hands."

Anna listened raptly. She couldn't wait for word of what transpired next—did the woman's husband howl in anger? Did he accept the decree? But most of the time, that was the end of it. Apparently, Babushka Anna's word was law. She ruled with the wisdom of King Solomon.

On other occasions, their day would be interrupted by some emergency. One of the people had been bitten by an animal or cut his foot. More and more, the younger Anna was allowed to help the older woman dress wounds and apply bandages. It felt very important, very adult. The hospital in town was a fine one, but still, there were few doctors, very little medicine, and who could afford such things? The queen bee must care for the workers. It was a world of mutual respect, if not always without tension.

Anna was confused by the idea of these farmers and everyday people, and how her family fit into their world. She liked the men and the women who came to see her grandmother, sometimes bringing their children. Anna's dearest friends were the children of the servants, for with children, there are no social differences.

But sometimes her mind drifted back to the night terrors, to those faceless people in the dark who started fires and slaughtered cattle. Did they have no Babushka Anna to whom they could present their grievances? The world was a perplexing place. It seemed to Anna that people just needed to listen to one another and get along. Why didn't someone tell the angry ones?

As Anna grew older, these views became more nuanced and better informed as she learned more about her country and her family. It was always stressed to her that her family had a proud heritage, and on both sides. Her father, Sergei Rozanov, was a colonel who commanded a regiment. And her father's great-grandfather was Marshal Mikhail Illarionovich Kutuzov, a name everyone knew. He was the general who had saved the Russian army from Napoleon almost a century earlier, using attrition warfare.

Kutuzov was considered a national hero, a name never to be forgotten by Russian children. His painted portrait showed a serious and determined man, a leader at the height of his power. Though Anna was still young, she understood that a great name brought with it responsibility—something to uphold. And this included kindness and a patience with the people of the villages and towns.

Anna's father, Sergei, understood his legacy as a career soldier, but he had come to it not so much by inheritance as by sorrow. His own father had been a doctor in Moscow. When Sergei was six, just beginning school, his mother had left them and run away to Rome. Her abandoned husband, feeling incapable of raising a son, sent the boy to military school, and in that world Anna's father had come of age. He'd met his wife, Marie Skuratov, Princess Belsky, and they had married. Anna was their child, entering the world in 1900.

Marie had two sisters—Anna's aunts—who had married a pair of brothers from France. Anna understood them to be prestigious men in their own country. As it happened, they had a business interest in a cotton factory in Sudan, and invited their brother-in-law, Rozanov, to invest and perhaps add to his family's wealth. He placed some money in the factory but paid little attention to it afterward; Russia's many problems absorbed his time.

He was appointed commander of the Venden Regiment, and the first thing he did was purchase a house in Penza, where he was based. The family enjoyed having a house in town, and Anna was now able to register as a student at Penza Lyceum.

But in the winter, the family debarked to their country home, and Anna had to do her studying at home. Another Anna, Anna Ivanovna, served as the teacher for three villages at the school in Alferievka, which was larger and had its own church, and was a good friend for Anna's mother as well.

This teacher spoke of a talented and intelligent student she'd met at that school. His name was Vasya, and he had real potential. "He needs much more opportunity than our three-year program can offer him," she said. Marie, Anna's mother, was happy to learn about the opportunity for a good deed. She found a family in Penza that was willing to house Vasya while he attended the Penza High School. He graduated successfully, and the time came when he returned the favor to Marie and her family by saving their lives.

Life takes odd turns. The gift to Vasya seemed like a small thing at the time, and the Sudan cotton factory investment by Rozanov was almost forgotten—yet both circumstances would take on the appearance of saving gifts from heaven.

One of Anna's playmates brought her a wonderful gift when she was eleven. The boy had rescued two baby owls in the woods. Anna quickly fashioned a home for them by her windowsill, where they could be fed yet enjoy the nearness to their native sky and trees.

Somehow, one of the baby owls swallowed the key to a door and died almost immediately. The other became Anna's constant friend. Each day, she brought her fresh bits of meat from the family table; the owl quickly accepted the windowsill as her restaurant of choice.

During the day, the little owl would sleep as Anna went about her day, mostly studying her lessons. When the sun vanished over the trees, it was time for the owl's dinner. If Anna fell asleep before feeding time, her mother would steal into the room and see that the little bird was fed. Mama, too, had become attached to the young orphan.

The owl grew quickly and soon relocated to a linden tree branch beside the window. Now she could spread her wings and fly where she wished, but she continued appearing at the windowsill, always on time for dinner.

The girl and her pet remained good friends. As Anna approached the house on a horseback ride, the owl would fly from branch to branch, keeping pace. Everyone on the premises marveled over such a friendly owl, and the family went so far as to lock up the dogs at dinnertime, to avoid frightening her.

One evening, however, no dinner for birds was forthcoming. Guests were visiting the home, and Anna wasn't able to reach the windowsill with the evening meal. The owl scouted the perimeter of the house, peering through windows, searching for her hostess and friend. Then, spotting a table set for the family's own dinner—surely a tempting feast—she glided in through the open window and was immediately blinded by the lighting. She laid waste to the table and its trappings, sought quick refuge in the pantry, and emerged with sticky flytraps affixed to her feathers.

It was a pitiful sight. In shame, before the startled household could rescue her, the bird leaped back out the window. No one was upset by the mess, just heartsick with worry for the owl, who, with hindered wings, might not survive.

Late that night, Anna stepped outside, whistled, and to her wonder, the owl appeared, miserable with glue she was helpless to remove. Some of the servants came and placed the bird in a basin of warm water, washing and trimming damaged feathers. As soon as she was free from the probing hands and blades, she took flight once more, angrier than ever.

Anna wondered if their friendship was irretrievably broken. But after a few days, the owl returned, and in the fall, a handsome male owl had joined her on the linden tree branch. He lacked the courage to eat from the windowsill, but Anna's owl brought bits of food to him, bite by bite, from Anna's hand.

Winter came in, and the owls disappeared, never to return. After all, they had their own family to build, their own legacy. Living near woods, trees, and a river, Anna was beginning to identify with the cycles of life and seasons. She was fortunate enough to appreciate the joys around her—fishing, picking berries, galloping along on a beautiful horse, discovering fascinating creatures. Perhaps her life would continue on in the country. She would lodge no complaints.

Yet the seasons taught her one more lesson: nothing stays the same. There is growth, budding, blooming, and beauty in its time. Between the winters, there is life, and life is change. In 1912 she traveled with her father to France; met her cousin, a countess; and saw their astounding family castle, the Château du Bouchet, located in the Loire Valley region of France—so different from her simple life in the country.

She was coming to understand the vast differences between the wealthy classes and the common people in the little towns that paraded by her carriage and train windows. And she was gaining a better understanding of the tensions that were growing between the possessors and the dispossessed.

Anna herself was growing, becoming a smart and self-confident young woman. Like the flowering trees of the countryside, she would come into her own. Perhaps, like her owl friend, she would take flight and leave her small surroundings behind.

She wondered what the changing seasons of the world held for her family.

3

Revolution

In August of 1914 the whole world seemed to go up in flames. Archduke Ferdinand of Austria-Hungary was assassinated. Serbia, which was held responsible, was a Russian client-state, and Russia was expected to defend it from Austria-Hungary's angry response.

But Nicholas II and Russia were not inclined toward all-out war. Russia was slowly gaining advantages over its rival, Germany, anyway; a war might throw everything off-balance. But France backed Russia, France wanted war, and the Russians didn't want to appear weak.

Seeing no other way out, Nicholas II mobilized the Russian troops to defend Serbia from the Austro-Hungarians. Almost immediately, Germany itself declared war.

Anna's father was caught up in this whirlwind. Sergei Rozanov commanded the Second Brigade of the Forty-Fifth Infantry Division, but his rank continued to rise. Within two years, he was promoted to major general. Leadership was a desperate need; Russia's vast army included nearly 1.5 million soldiers, but there were organizational and logistical problems.

Yet domestic challenges continued to rival those on the front lines of battle. Saint Petersburg was now known as Petrograd, because *-burg*, it was realized, was too German. The city was filled with strikes, protests, and clashes. There was every possibility of a civil war, even as a world war raged. The Bolsheviks were coming into power by stirring up the peasants against the upper class, the intelligentsia, military officers, the church—anyone considered to be part of the ruling establishment. And what greater symbol of that than the emperor? After a time, Nicholas II would surely have to abdicate or face overthrow.

The Duma—the governing body created after the 1905 riots—wasn't faring any better. Russia was on the verge of the unimaginable. If the tsar was forced out and the Duma dissolved, chaos and anarchy would take their place.

On March 2, 1917, Tsar Nicholas agreed to sign a document abdicating the Russian throne, including the rights of Alexei, his thirteen-year-old son and heir. Tsarevich Alexei was hemophiliac, and his health was an issue, but he represented the future of the regime. The tsar named his brother, Grand Duke Mikhail, as his successor.

A week later, a provisional government was formed. On March 10 Nicholas and his family were placed under house arrest in the Alexander Palace. For five months they remained under guard there.

Grand Duke Mikhail saw the futility of his position and abdicated as well. He released a statement advising the people to trust the provisional government. For a while, his movements were confined to Petrograd. Then he, too, was placed under house arrest, along with his secretary, Nikolai Johnson.

Russia had been a monarchy since Prince Rurik took the throne in AD 862. More than a thousand years of royalty had been pushed to the side. To be replaced by what, exactly?

In April a sealed train arrived at the Finland Station in Petrograd, and out stepped a man known as Vladimir Lenin. His passage had been arranged by the Germans, and he had a number of singular ideas on a Russian future. They were ideas very much of the moment; ideas sparked by his encounter of the book *Das Kapital* by Karl Marx. And he was bringing these ideas, along with a ruthless strategy to impose them, into a society that, after three hundred years of tradition, was now in utter chaos. There was turmoil to be exploited.

How had it come to this?

The year was 1547—close to the midpoint of the sixteenth century. So much was happening. It was the year Henry VIII of England died, and with him, it seems now, the long medieval slumber of Western Europe was coming to an end. Indeed, historians agree that this was the decisive century, the period when Western civilization emerged.

In Europe the Renaissance was now in full swing, characterized by art, scholarship, science, and, for the first time, world exploration. The Protestant

Reformation, sparked by Germany's Martin Luther, reflected the democratization even of religion and the decline of the church's utter dominance of culture.

Ideas of politics were rapidly changing as states made allies, found strength in union, and became nations. Machiavelli's idea of *The Prince*—an ambitious, centralized ruler willing to take ruthless action—was also taking hold. Yet as nations became larger, the world became smaller. Copernicus insisted that the sun, moon, and planets didn't revolve around the earth after all; the earth was just another sphere in endless orbit, tiny in relation to what was out there. And this globe could be circumnavigated. European ships were now crossing oceans, finding lands previously unknown to those in their homeland.

That year of 1547, Ivan IV, known to history as Ivan the Terrible, became the first tsar of Rus, also called the Tsardom of Muscovy, a centralized, Moscow-based state that, for the next century and a half, grew by thirty-five thousand square kilometers per year. Ivan the Terrible was from the house of Rurik and reflected the more brutal times from which he came, yet he also played out the Machiavellian idea of the powerful leader spurring on his nation at whatever cost.

His reign began with a beauty pageant of sorts, much like in the biblical story of Esther. A number of eligible women were brought to the Kremlin from some of Russia's most prominent families. This was actually a Byzantine and Russian tradition to find the most beautiful and gifted bride for the emperor. Seventeen-year-old Anastasia Romanovna Zakharyina-Yurieva was chosen. Tradition states that Anastasia made Ivan a little less terrible. She was a calming influence for an impulsive and sometimes reckless leader. And when she died, he lashed out in every direction, executing the boyars (nobles) he was certain had poisoned his wife. Time vindicated his suspicions, if not his actions; in 1990 neutron activation analysis of Anastasia's remains showed she had ingested a large amount of mercury.

Ivan the Terrible organized a standing army and centralized the state administration. He defeated all challengers on the battlefield and won out in power struggles with the nobility. Russia under Tsar Ivan IV began to look less like a medieval region and more like an organized, modern nation. Almost symbolically, he died while playing a game of chess. His only heir was a weak-minded son who ended Ivan's line, slowly lost control of the system his father had built, and left the legacy of a miserable era of chaos known as the Time of Troubles. This was the final act of the Rurik Dynasty, and the curtain rising for a new one. Mikhail I—Mikhail *Romanov*—became the next tsar, and the first of the Romanovs. His great-aunt was Anastasia Romanovna.

Emerging from the political chaos of the Time of Troubles, Mikhail I was in position to become an icon and a national hero. During his time, Russia added most of Siberia to its expanding borders. The nation was now bounded not by the Urals but by the Pacific Ocean, making Russia a power to be reckoned with. Yet Mikhail I was no Ivan the Terrible. Instead of being impulsive and wrathful, he was known to be cautious, pious, and even gentle. When he took the throne, no music had been allowed in Russia since a twelfth-century bishop's decree. Yet Mikhail I invited musicians from European nations. It was the baroque period, and now melody, orchestra, and chorus filled the air again.

For these and other reasons, the Romanov name became a dynasty. Eighteen Romanovs took the throne and held it for a period longer than the history of the United States as a nation. It came to feel like a permanent thing, as if God would always have a Romanov available to take leadership when needed. Some were more popular than others, but the greatest of them seemed legendary, larger than life.

Mikhail I's grandson, Peter I, is known to us as Peter the Great for good reason. He all but finalized the expansion of Russia's borders that transitioned it from a nation to an empire, which he proclaimed in 1721. He was not the gentle or pious type his grandfather had been, however. He could be ruthless, and he had his son tortured to death on the accusation of involvement in an overthrow plot. But Peter also traveled all across Europe, learning about the cultures and breakthroughs of other nations. This opened his country to greater influences from abroad and modernized Russia, giving it a progressive character to keep up with the expansion of its borders. He decreed that the children of nobility deserved education, and he made it compulsory. He founded the city of Saint Petersburg, which remained the national capital until 1917.

The Romanovs were not infallible and not invariably popular. Peter III was overthrown in the mid-1700s—only to have his wife ascend to the Russian throne. We know her as Catherine the Great, and she was far more successful. She began her rule in 1762. These were the years of the Enlightenment in Western

Europe, but also years of great struggle and bloodshed. The Seven Years' War began the same month Catherine became empress. She reigned for thirty-four years, introducing to Russia a period of progress in science and art, new cities and new universities. All the great culture—novels, music, theater—we associate with Russia were possible because Catherine emphasized the importance of the arts. By then immigrants were arriving from other nations in Europe. Russia was a stylish, modern, glamorous place.

Perhaps the peak of Russian glory came a few years after her tenure, when the army of Alexander I defeated Napoleon Bonaparte of France at Waterloo. He was far from the great leader Peter or Catherine had been, and he could be arbitrary, suspicious, and even paranoid. In the end, there were also terrible losses on the battlefield. But he was another progressive leader during a liberal period.

The Romanovs carried on at the helm of Russia for another hundred years. Through their three-century hold on the throne, the greatest of them had one thing in common: they all expanded Russia's borders and claimed new regions until Russia was the largest country in the world by land mass. New leaders knew this was a key to their legacy. Did the nation grow? Did it retain its territorial dominance? Much later, in the twentieth century, understanding this value makes it easier to comprehend why premiers and presidents, after the fall of communism, continued to cast covetous eyes on Czechoslovakia, Georgia, or Ukraine. Russia also needed land with useful resources.

But during the final century of Russian tsars, the leaders and the old ways began to fail, and the ruling class model didn't wear so well as people became better educated and more conscious of the great disparity between the aristocracy and the working class. Two ideas clashed: the love of tradition, including the Romanov family who had brought the nation through so much change and growth, even glory; and resentment of the autocracy of the royals, the arrogance of the aristocrats, amid the poverty of so many others. There was even resentment against the Russian Orthodox Church, which seemed to offer no help to the masses during food shortages, the problems of urbanization—the poor were flocking to the cities—and military failure in the 1905 Russo-Japanese War, for which Nicholas II received most of the blame.

At the worst of times, the fate of Russia came down to a fairly unpopular tsar, Nicholas II, and his young heir, Alexei, who was too medically challenged to symbolize a powerful future for the Romanov dynasty. Robert K. Massie has written, "Along with the lost battles and sunken ships, the bombs, the revolutionaries and their plots, the strikes and revolts, Imperial Russia was toppled by a tiny defect in the body of a little boy."

But of course, it was a lot more than that. An unprecedented war—a world war—added to the chaos. In 1917 World War I was still crawling, bloody and battered, to its final ending in the muddy fields of Germany. At home in Russia, peasants were rioting. Nicholas II wasn't another Peter the Great, but his wife from Germany was seen as intolerable. Her entanglement with the strange mystic Rasputin translated into widespread rumors that damaged the popularity of the imperial family almost beyond repair.

Conditions in Saint Petersburg were near boiling point, and the Bolsheviks found their window of opportunity.

Vladimir Lenin had read his Marx. He understood all these forces and the political ideas and remedies suggested. But he also understood the psychology of anger, and he knew how to stoke those fires until a flame raged out of control. He vilified the church, the Romanovs, and particularly the aristocracy. They were the problem, he shouted—they have stolen from you, the good people, the salt of the earth.

And when the riots broke out, the lynching began, and the old estates began to burn, Lenin and his people would be there to step in and take charge.

Major General Rozanov was not among the angry and riotous. He was a disciplined military man, a lover of order, but also a member of the landed aristocracy. Though he and his family had always gotten along well in their community, people began turning against them. He was personally a royalist who supported the Romanovs and the standing traditions, but he understood times were tense. This was a time to be shrewd and cautious. He huddled with the other military leaders and signaled his allegiance to the provisional government. To do anything else wasn't a good way to avoid arrest and execution.

At this time, Anna and her mother were back near Penza, where Rozanov was based and where he could look after them. But things were not the same. The Bolsheviks and their terror squads had been at work, and the peasants were stirred up, energized, ready to express their anger, in Penza as elsewhere.

The constant refrain was that rich people were the problem; they needed to be stripped of all they had. Towns and villages were awash in the false promises of the Bolsheviks, who were infiltrating every town and city. Dreams were floated before the people—promises of the wonderful things they'd be given if they supported the revolution.

Anna felt her life and opportunities had slipped out of her grasp. She was on the verge of adulthood. This would have been her final year of school, but she couldn't think about formal education in the wake of all this chaos. She worried about her father and of course her family; her personal future held no guarantees and few hopes.

One day she heard the sound of hoofbeats rushing toward the house. The clip-clop of trotting would have meant everyday business; this was a full-on gallop.

Anna hurried to the door, expecting some kind of word from her father. In moments like these, she could only whisper a prayer and hope for the best. It was Fouget, an Austrian prisoner of war who tended the Rozanovs' stallions, and he was extremely agitated, bearing a note from Babushka Anna.

"We need help, immediately!" cried Fouget, and he handed over the note. In Babushka's hand, it said an angry mob had surrounded her house. The people wanted to know the whereabouts of Anna's mother, Marie, so they could kill her. She was the latest target from the landed classes, apparently; her husband, as a military leader, was beyond their reach.

There may have been soldiers in the crowd, returned from the front. Some were known to have killed their officers and come to seize their land.

According to the note, Anna's younger sister, Olga, had ventured outside to reason with these people. Her governess and two fox terriers had also emerged, but their efforts backfired. The governess had been beaten and dragged away.

Babushka Anna, shaken, was desperate for help to arrive.

Fouget wasn't in much better shape. It looked as if his escape had been a close call. Anna's immediate concern was for her mother, who was out in public and might easily be seized. Hurrying into Penza, Anna found Marie safely accounted for at the office of the chief of police, where news of the mob had arrived.

Two carriages filled with soldiers were soon dispatched, and the governess was found and taken to a clinic for medical care. The ring leaders of the mob had slipped out of sight.

Back at home, Marie and Babushka Anna decided the estate was no longer a safe haven. Babushka Anna would be moved to town, where ruffians were less likely to strike. There was a military presence, with Anna's father present as well.

In Babushka Anna's absence, Anna's mother, Marie, made her way to the estate to prepare to move their possessions. Ten soldiers were assigned to guard her. Marie loaded up eight sleds, along with the family's stable of thoroughbreds, and set out for Penza. Anna rode in a small sled along the snow-covered road.

The village of Khamaika had more than its share of rabble-rousers, and sure enough, when the procession came to this town, a crowd of peasants pounced immediately. One of them grabbed the reins of the lead horse.

Marie's guards quickly surrendered, throwing down their weapons. Whatever feelings of safety Anna had enjoyed quickly evaporated.

Some of the ruffians grabbed the coachman and dragged him into the mob. Marie just had time to take the reins from his hands. Her courage was startling. Marie, now every inch Princess Belsky, stood boldly and defiantly as the mob began shouting, brandishing their fists. At any second, they would grab her and drag her away, and Anna might never see her again.

A woman came up to Marie and called out to her, "Mistress, go away! They've sent for the Klyuchevsky people. They won't hesitate to kill you!" These were the angriest peasants from nearby Klyuchi, and they were known to be bloodthirsty indeed.

Anna's mother pulled hard at the reins, and some of the horses reared up. This caused the man holding their bridle to slip, lose his grip, and fall into the snow, and the horses took off running. The family and their belongings were safe, for now, and the Klyuchevsky group, upon arriving, were furious that the general's wife had slipped from their fingers.

Anna's father was with them in Penza. More than ever, it was clear to him that his family was as much at risk as he was. Was there any safe place in Russia? How far had the terror groups penetrated?

The next morning, a delegation of visitors arrived at the house. They described themselves as the "elders of Khamaika," the village where the ambush had occurred. They wished to speak peacefully to Rozanov. They appeared calm, and he went out to talk with them. They offered an apology for the hotheads who had endangered the major general's family. They wished their village to be forgiven.

Rozanov invited them all in for tea and vodka. It was the wisest response, as angry as he may have been. Calm discussion and meetings of the mind might be the only thing that could soothe the destructive emotions that were being manipulated by the Bolsheviks. For quite some time, the two groups visited and enjoyed pleasant conversation.

Alexander Kerensky was the socialist leading the new provisional government. In August he told the tsar and his family he was moving them to Tobolsk in the western reaches of Siberia. The July Days, a series of riots in Petrograd, had made it clear that the imperial family wasn't safe in such a high-tension area. Kerensky would have known that he, too, was in a difficult position. The provisional government was bound to be seen as one more obstacle to the Bolsheviks.

Nicholas, his family, and forty-seven other people made the lengthy journey to the desolate house in Tobolsk, a safer place, at least from the general disturbances. The conditions were acceptable; a priest was allowed to come and hold services, since the family couldn't go freely in public.

It was October when Lenin seized power. The power of the Bolsheviks was near absolute by this time, and Kerensky had to flee for his life. He briefly attempted to raise an army to retake power, but his efforts were ultimately futile. Lenin and his disciples were already setting up a new Soviet government.

Not that this brought calmer conditions across the countryside. The anger remained at a boiling point, enough so that at Rozanov's home, the servants and workers quietly disappeared. At this time, Babushka Anna, Baroness Anna von Rosen, was ill, and Anna and Marie were left to watch over her at the country house. Rumors reached them that the house might be set on fire some evening, so there was no period when the few left in the house could relax. Anna kept one of the fox terriers on one side of the house, and Marie guarded the other side with the other fox terrier. Rozanov, of course, was still with the army.

Occasionally, a woman would come running from the village with a warning: "The angry ones are making threats again," she'd say. "They want to attack your family." Once the soldiers were assigned, Anna felt the villagers were less likely to make good on their threats. But during the days before, when it was just the three women and a couple of dogs, Anna and Marie took turns keeping watch at night, as Rozanov had trained them to do.

There was an apple tree on a hill that offered a good view across the orchard and toward the village. It was the best vantage point for the vigil. One night, when the darkness was particularly impenetrable, Anna lay beneath her black cape and simply tried to listen; nothing could be seen, at least until a tiny point of light appeared under the nearest tree. It was joined by another flicker, then several more. Anna counted as many as twenty cigarette lights.

She was invisible to them, at least for the moment. She began to crawl toward the house, slowly and stealthily, hoping and praying no twig snapped or bush rustled. When she arrived at the house, she woke her mother, and every light in the house was turned on. Those hiding in darkness eventually left, and eventually the morning light offered a welcome reprieve. Anna and her mother each let out a weary sigh and reflected on just how exposed and vulnerable they were. "What can we do?" asked Anna.

"You and your grandmother and the others can go live in town," said Marie. "You need to finish your education anyway."

"But why can't you come with us? You'll have no safety at all by yourself."

"We'll see. But I will not abandon our stallions. This is our home, our life."

She began to transfer horses, a few at a time, into town, and ten soldiers were also assigned to protect Marie and the home. Anna would visit her mother on horseback by night whenever possible. Upon arrival, she'd leave her horse with the Austrian servant in the stable. The Russian army had brought home many thousands of prisoners of war, most of them from Austro-Hungary, and about twenty of them were attending to the family stud farm. These men behaved well, wanting to do nothing that might jeopardize their chances of returning to their home. Anna found them to be decent, kind men who responded to kindness like anyone else, and she trusted them.

Everyone assured each other that these things would pass. Surely there would be a return of peace and calm, and people from all stations could work together again. As Anna and one of the officers took a few colts out for exercise, she enjoyed the Penza forest, and it felt as if the violence and disturbances were already fading in the past. Russia was the greatest of countries; it would rise above these troubles.

But the officer with Anna, and many of his peers, would be shot by the Bolsheviks. In truth, the atrocities were only beginning. And some of the peasants were coming to realize they'd been used simply to help a new party seize power. The family cook confessed to Anna and Marie that she'd supported the Bolsheviks for the promise of new rubber boots. A simple thing, but of course no such boots were forthcoming.

There was a period when Rozanov was ill with typhus, contracted at the front. During the days of Kerensky's rule, Rozanov's Polish orderly turned up at the home, helping Rozanov through the door. They'd taken backroads to get to the house. There, he spent some time recovering and regaining his strength. Then one day, he left for Moscow, and this time he took his daughter with him.

Rozanov told his family that this remained a very dangerous time. The Bolsheviks had taken control during the October Revolution, and they were brutally removing any shred of resistance they could find. Bloodshed was everywhere, and the more prominent one's position, the more closely they were scrutinized. Leon Trotsky was by Lenin's side directing foreign affairs, and he had approached Rozanov to come join the Red Army—that is, the Bolshevik forces.

Rozanov had said yes.

However, this was only part of the truth, he explained to his family. In secret, he was working with the anti-Bolsheviks in both Moscow and Petrograd in a movement to rescue as many good military officers as possible from Bolshevik firing squads.

Remarkably, he brought Anna to work with him. By this time, he knew his daughter was up to the task. She seemed to have no fear—this was a young lady who, with her mother, had already seen and handled deadly situations. She had guarded their home. And now he involved her in espionage. Anna visited Lubyanka prison in the guise of a laundry girl who could walk past the guards, collect dirty laundry whose folds contained the names of endangered officers, and walk out again. She carried out this mission repeatedly, helping to save these officers.

The Red Army held the power, but in the shadows a White Army was taking shape and beginning to grow. Its base was in the south. The idea was to meet officers as they returned from the front and redirect them southward, where they could help organize the new resistance. It wasn't always successful; there were arrests and shootings.

Anna saw fighting in the streets on a daily basis, often over some bit of food. Finally, Rozanov had seen enough. He decided to take his daughter home to Penza. They arrived only to learn that Babushka Anna had finally succumbed to illness. On her final day, the Bolsheviks had pulled her out of her bed, searching for gold; they found none. These searches were becoming commonplace after the sun went down. There would be a loud banging at the door, soldiers would barge in, and rooms would be laid waste during searches as the family watched in their nightgowns.

A commissar found Rozanov's medals in a drawer, including his Cross of Saint George, a medal awarded for undaunted courage. He examined them, then tossed them to a soldier. "Why do you care about those?" Marie asked. "You were not the one who earned them." Her words must have hit home, because the cross was found under the bed the next day.

"Why do you torture us?" asked Marie as the men left.

The commissar stopped and smiled coldly at her. "And why do you tolerate us?"

4

Darkness in Penza

One night the Bolsheviks showed up for another search. This time, they were demanding to be told the location of General Rozanov. Anna and her mother remained calm and composed, but they knew he wasn't far away. He was in town, walking around in plain sight!

The men searched the house thoroughly and left, angry they hadn't caught their prey. Then, as the first light of morning broke through the trees, Marie opened the door, and there was the general, as if it were an ordinary day. She all but fainted. "You can't be seen!" she said. "They came for you in the night."

She hurried him to the one location that had evaded every previous search: the attic. Apparently, they'd missed that space.

Rozanov did his best to get comfortable among the dust and darkness. He remained there for two days, knowing, of course, he couldn't hide forever. But these two days gave Maria Lysova, née Zakharchenko, a family friend, time to work out a plan of escape. Maria was thirty-four and an agent dedicated to fighting the Bolsheviks however possible.

The Hussars had a proud tradition as elite cavalry, reflected in their colorful uniforms. The rise of the Bolsheviks would spell the end of their tradition, and most of the officers were disbanding without any affirmation of the new Red regime. But the Bolsheviks began arresting and shooting them. Maria had planned to go home, but now, like Rozanov, she devoted herself to helping officers gain safe passage from Penza to the south, where resistance was strong.

Maria came to the door late at night, and Rozanov emerged from hiding. He was carefully dressed in peasant clothes and taken to the train station, with Maria and Anna beside him. Even in his disguise, he was well known to the soldiers, and one of them spotted him. He smiled and whispered, "Don't worry, General—I won't say a word. We have collected too many memories together through the war years." He handed Rozanov a piece of black bread, knowing there would be little to eat on such a journey.

General Rozanov nodded to show his gratitude and stepped onto the train, which was headed toward Siberia where a provisional government had already been formed.

He knew that if they were searching for him near his home, they'd also be on the lookout in Moscow. So many of his friends and fellow officers had already been executed, shot unceremoniously one by one or in firing squads after torture and interrogation, that it was no small miracle to be alive and headed for safety.

Maria and her husband were headed south through Persia to fulfill other missions. Later, Anna and her father would meet Maria again, this time in Paris, working for Gen. Alexander Pavlovich Kutepov, who had worked with Rozanov to help form the White Russian Army of the South at the outset of the Russian Civil War. Like many others, Maria became relentless, willing to do anything to fight the despised criminals who had destroyed her homeland. She took on terrorist missions into Moscow, and inevitably, she was captured and executed on her way over the Polish border. She wouldn't be forgotten, by Rozanov, his family, or any of the countless people she helped to rescue.

By January 1918 Penza was fully under Soviet control. The war across the continent was grinding into its final months, but the Bolsheviks had already taken a chokehold over the key cities of Russia. Within a month, victory would be complete.

The first detachments of the Red Guard and combat worker squads were established in Penza. Every measure was taken to suppress peasant uprisings.

Marie Rozanov had few options after her husband's departure. She decided to bring her daughters into their home in Penza and prepare for hard times. Food and supplies were now hard to come by. Soviet officials were always watching everything and everyone, and mere suspicion of counterrevolutionary sentiments was enough for arrest, imprisonment, or execution. Women and children weren't spared. No one trusted neighbors anymore because informants were turning in names to the secret police to curry favor with the new leaders—or simply to gain a measure of revenge against someone who was the subject of an old grudge.

At night, Anna, Olga, and their mother could hear gunfire from the Communist Party headquarters, no more than a few buildings away. The firing squads never seemed to run out of targets. The clamor of the rifles was a constant reminder that no one was safe. The time for unrest and disturbances had been replaced by a time of sheer terror and fear.

One day there was word the White Army was approaching, and the Bolsheviks took flight. Apparently, their control wasn't complete yet. As they fled, they left all their documentation out in the open at their headquarters.

It was an opportunity for some anti-Red mischief. Anna and a few of her friends climbed over a wall, entered the headquarters, and set all the files aflame. This included a waiting list of names set for execution. The approaching army rumors turned out to be false, and when the communists returned the next day, they were enraged at what had been lost.

But Anna worried about being found out. Any of her friends, protecting their respective families, could offer her name to the Bolsheviks. To oppose the new regime was to court disaster; to do nothing was unacceptable. One day, Anna was sent out for a newspaper, and she was recognized by a communist soldier. "Aren't you the daughter of General Rozanov?" he asked.

"Yes, I am," she could only reply.

"I served with your father in the war," smiled the soldier. "And I liked him very much. Go on your way; I won't report you."

One night a young soldier appeared at a window, knocking on the pane. Marie was frightened for a moment, then her face lit up. "Vasya!" she said.

"Yes, it's me," he smiled. He was the gifted student she'd been told about some time back. She had gotten him the opportunity to extend his studies, and he had never forgotten the kindness. Now, he dressed in the attire of the communists, but he wouldn't turn against his friends. "I've come to let you know—your family is in danger," he said. "You've been denounced by some neighbor as enemies of the new regime, and tomorrow they'll come here to arrest you. It's important that you leave quickly and quietly."

Marie and Anna realized that Vasya had risked his life to bring this message. He could have been spotted. He could be linked to the Rozanovs through his past, once it was clear they'd been tipped off. While this was a time of treachery and distrust, it was also a time of risk and sacrifice for people with integrity who cared about one another.

Marie and her two daughters carried a change of clothing and a blanket and relocated to the home of a friend.

The house was then taken by the Bolsheviks, who were nothing if not opportunistic. One commissar immediately claimed Babushka Anna's Empire-style mirror, which was quite a prize. He had it ported to his girlfriend's lodging. Anna knew this because Matriona, their servant, followed from a distance to keep track. She and the governess stayed in the house and reported on the goings-on. The dining room was full of Bolshevik typewriters, according to Matriona.

But there was no time to fixate on such things. Life was complicated. One of Marie's friends had asked her to care for her three-year-old boy while she, the friend, searched for her husband in Petrograd. But the friend did not return, so it seemed that Anna and Olga had a new young sibling, and a small child was a challenge. Anna had to slip into a neighboring village to find milk and other supplies.

Any such mission had to be planned out because there were patrols all through the day. In the end, it was determined the little boy should be cared for by family, so he was taken to live with his aunt and grandfather. Three years later, his mother returned to claim him.

Marie took stock of the family's situation. Her husband, the father of her daughters, was away helping to organize and command the White Army. But he wouldn't like the conditions into which Penza had fallen. It was time for Marie to escort the two girls to safety in the direction of Siberia. But the idea of such a journey sent a shiver up her spine. The three of them would have to cross villages and towns that may or may not be sympathetic to their imperial loyalties. There would be no easy way to determine it.

But there was no other option, not even a place to live. The three women moved around between the homes of friends, always feeling they were endangering those friends. Sometimes they were split up between houses, and at great distance. There was no safe way to see each other.

On one occasion Anna rose from the bear rug on which she was sleeping on a friend's floor. One of the Austrian prisoners of war who worked on area farms had come with a note. "Come with this man," said the note, in Marie's handwriting. "He will take you to me." Anna rose the next day and braced herself against the cold. On the way, her feet froze, and she had to stop and let them warm up by a fire.

Crossing the Sura, they came to a house whose hostess was a friendly woman. But the house was occupied by Bolsheviks and their families. Marie was using her cook's passport for identification, and Anna's passport was that of the cook's niece, so the two had to pretend this was their relationship. Anna served as the landlady's governess while they were there, and she and her mother had to watch their words at all times. Anna actually enjoyed caring for the children; what an escape, to take part in the innocent worlds of children.

Everyone slept in one great room. Anna and Marie would meet to whisper a few honest words in the restroom. Even now, Marie was sending her daughter on small secret missions, meeting with friends and fellow loyalists. Anna took the train back to Penza, three or four stations away, and received money for the coming journey from a good friend who had sold Marie's ruby ring for them. On the way, she crossed paths with their old governess and the two fox terriers, who of course knew nothing about keeping a low profile. They leaped on Anna and barked with pleasure, but nothing unfortunate came of the reunion.

Anna could have wept with pleasure to see the dogs one more time. The next day she would say farewell to Penza once and for all, knowing as she watched it fade into the horizon from the windows of the train it was unlikely she'd ever see it again.

As the long winter finally began to melt into the awakening earth, the time was approaching for departure to Siberia. On some mornings, Marie would whisper to Anna to go to the rail station and buy a newspaper. It was important to keep up with the rapidly changing tides of revolution. As she paid for her paper one day, she saw a soldier eyeing her closely. He questioned her, skeptical about her identity. The three women did what they could to obscure the nobility in their past, but sometimes, little things gave them away. Bolsheviks could sniff out nobility like dogs on the hunt for foxes.

The soldier came to the house and asked a number of questions of the landlady. "Who is this young lady? How long have you known her?" After a while, he left, but the woman was spooked. Marie knew it was time for her and her "niece" to leave. The landlady told them about a convent whose mother superior was an old friend. The road there still passed through snowy woods and across a still-frozen river, which was frightening to cross with a horse. But they arrived at the convent. Even here, there was a priest who had given himself over to Red sympathies, but the mother superior was kind and gave them warning.

The convent had a library, and this gave Marie an excellent idea. She consulted the books and found a list of villages between their location and the Volga, roughly five hundred miles away. Nuns made the rounds, collecting money, from villages to villages, and here was their itinerary. This map would prove very helpful. Marie copied the list down, and Anna realized the time for the arduous journey had finally come. Spring was arriving, and at any rate the mother superior was expecting the authorities to arrive for an inspection soon.

The prospect of it was frightening, but in journeys, there is always hope, always a chance to move away from the past. With the help of the nuns, Marie, Anna, and Olga prepared their clothing, sewing secret pockets into their corsets. What little money or keepsakes they carried could be hidden. Each woman had a blanket, a coat, and a small pillow. And then there was the general's parting gift.

The general had placed a seven-shot Nagant pistol in Anna's hands. He trusted his daughter's courage in the event of danger. At the age when other young ladies would be finishing school, perhaps considering marriage proposals, and enjoying the prime of life, Anna knew what it was like to face the most horrible potentialities without giving in to fear.

Seven bullets. The three women knew how those shots were to be distributed: four to ward off attackers, but three to be reserved, no matter what. If they faced rape or murder, there was a quick way out.

As their journey began, Marie told her two daughters she had recently passed by their beloved old estate house, the place of so many family memories. Nothing remained of it but ashes, a couple of ugly black poles looming over the rubble. The image made it all real to the women: their old home and way of life were no more. There could be no reclamation of better times.

The only future to be claimed was a harrowing journey away, in an unfamiliar setting, and with no certainties.

5

A Flight to Freedom

Russia is a vast nation—immense in its culture, ancient in its history, near infinite in its diversity. In its sheer size, it spreads for thousands of miles across two continents. A journey from Penza to Siberia can't be captured simply by imagining some two-thousand-mile trek. Neither will factoring in the travel conditions of 1918 paint an adequate picture. One must also imagine such a journey in which each outpost along the road may represent certain imprisonment or execution. This was the trial of the Rozanov women in the spring of 1918.

Marie, Anna, and Olga traveled by whatever means was available along the route ahead—one day by carriage, another on horseback, and on occasion even by camel. Whenever possible, they bypassed the larger towns, where it was more likely the Bolsheviks terror squads had already made their presence known.

Lenin's party was not taking its time. By March 1918 it had changed the national calendar to the Gregorian model, changed its name from Bolshevik to Communist Party, and moved the capital from Petrograd to Moscow.

In the beginning, the three women went from safe haven to safe haven, through the network of loyalist families who knew other families. They would sleep wherever there was room, expressing gratitude for meals and hospitality, and the next morning the host would walk them to the next village, where a sympathetic friend would take them on. Marie used information sometimes from the list she'd made and sometimes from the guidance of friends met along the way.

Wherever like-minded citizens could be found—people who opposed the new regime with every fiber of their souls—there was always kindness to be found. These were mostly peasants living in relative poverty, but they would accept no payment for the lodgings they offered. "You are with friends," they would say, waving off any offer. Still, Marie would find a way to slip a few coins to the children.

Each morning Marie would take her two daughters to the barn and see that they washed thoroughly with soap and water from a pail. Sleeping in all kinds of conditions, she worried constantly about lice, and they checked each other's hair daily.

Anna wondered what was happening in the cities. There was little news in these villages but plenty of rumors not to be trusted. The railroad stations would have been good sources for information, but these were swarming with soldiers and had to be avoided.

The Russian Orthodox monasteries were a saving grace. These were to be found throughout the countryside, and they nearly always remained loyal to the emperor. The party had announced it would seize all church lands. The church had enjoyed significant power in the imperial government, so the revolution was quick to strip it of all that. In the ensuing civil war, church officials naturally supported the White Army in most cases. There were 550 monasteries across the nation, and for the three travelers, each one seemed an oasis in the desert, a place of peace and security, at least for a day or two of rest.

By the time the women had moved hundreds of miles across the landscape, coming to the Volga River, they could no longer remember what it was like not to be travel-weary, not to have aching feet, not to spend only a few days under the same roof. But this was the first great milestone in the journey.

When they arrived, the river had overflowed and was wider than normal. No boats were in sight, but across the river, soldiers were visible. These were the front lines of the conflict. But the only path to freedom was straight through.

Marie found a man with a small rowboat, and he agreed to ferry the three women to the other side. The river current was running strong, and Olga in particular was terrified. They'd come too far, however, to be defeated by water.

Once they were on the other side, an inn wasn't hard to find. Naturally, it was filled with drunken soldiers and a perilous place for three unprotected women. They were around more communist soldiers then than at any time before. But the inn was their only choice. Sitting in their little room, Marie pondered strategy, and then she thought of finding a German priest. There were a great number of German colonists in this area, and a priest was certain not to be a Bolshevik.

Before parading past the soldiers, who were immersed in revelry, Marie covered her daughters with a blanket to obscure that they were young ladies. Then the three of them stepped outside the inn and made inquiries about a priest.

Sure enough, the priest they found was a decent man. He understood their sympathies and made arrangements for them. "Come at sunrise to the corner I'll tell you about," he said. "You'll find a German farmer, and he'll have a carriage. You can trust him with your lives."

The farmer was a gentle and kind man. He brought the three women to his farm, where his own wife and daughter were happy to receive them. Now, for the first time in weeks, they were able to wash themselves and their clothing properly. The wife and the daughter even provided fresh clothing. Marie, Anna, and Olga slept better than on any occasion in recent memory and ate a fine dinner with healthy appetites. Everyone was all smiles.

After dinner, the farmer's wife took Marie aside and said, "My husband is willing to take you farther down the road. Only you must give me your solemn promise that you will value his life, and that you won't say or do anything to compromise him before the authorities."

Marie took the woman's hands in her own and gave that promise. Then the farmer drove them through the steppe and came to a little Tatar village known as Altata, where they rested that evening. It seemed they had come through one of their most dangerous tests; perhaps they could begin to sleep better each evening.

During the night, a battle broke out. An army of White Cossacks attacked the village without warning. At least that's what people were saying. For the first time, Marie, Anna, and Olga had to worry about danger from the other army—the one on their side. No one knew who they were. Also, Marie had made a solemn promise that she would do nothing to put their friend the farmer into the line of fire. He was still with them. So the three women sat and waited for some idea of how to respond to the latest challenge.

At dawn they came to the outskirts of the village and met the German farmer, who was waiting with his carriage. He took them toward the Volga, then, once they were sure they weren't being watched, he turned eastward and drove off the road and through the mire. It was a scenic route to be sure—quails scrambled out of the path of the cart; wild ducks eyed them from streams.

Again, the women were moved by the lengths to which a stranger would go to help them. This farmer was simply the friend of a priest they had consulted, and their two countries, Germany and Russia, had been at war since 1914. When freedom is in question, people find common ground.

As the day wore on and the carriage bumped and splashed its way through the wilderness, a line of horsemen appeared on the horizon. They were too far away to identify. They could be Red or they could be White.

Marie turned to her two daughters and said, "If these men are Bolsheviks, this is the end of our journey. Forgive me for all of this." And she wrapped her arms around them and pulled them into an embrace. Anna reached inside her bundle and felt the cool metal of the pistol, and there was nothing else to do but sit and wait for the men to approach them.

They galloped up, surrounded the carriage, and their identity was clear: Ural Cossacks, identified by the yellow band on their caps. They had to be curious about a little carriage full of women so far from any road.

"Where are you from?" asked the leader. "What's your business in this area?"

Mother knew exactly how to handle such a situation. She had been around soldiers for the duration of her adult life. "Take us prisoner," she invited. "Lead us to your regiment."

The men looked at each other, shrugged, and did exactly that. Escorted by the riders, the group entered a big village. Cossack soldiers emerged from the huts, delighted and laughing. "Look, what a wonderful gift! Women as prisoners!"

Now they were interested in hearing Marie's full testimony. She told them her full name, knowing that *Rozanov* would get a reaction. "I am the wife of General Sergei Nikolaevich Rozanov, and these are my daughters."

The men watched her skeptically. "Where was he stationed in 1914?" the leader asked.

"He was with the Second Brigade of the Forty-Fifth Infantry Division," she quickly replied.

They continued to quiz her on her husband's activities and accomplishments, particularly battles in Austria, and after she achieved a perfect score on their test, they accepted that she was really who she said she was, and everyone relaxed.

The leader told her, "Your husband still lives. He is with Kolchak. We'll send him a telegram right away." Marie lifted a silent prayer of gratitude to heaven for this news that her husband had survived the escape to the east and was now with Adm. Alexander Kolchak, head of the anti-Bolshevik White forces in Siberia, and that she and her daughters had fallen into safe hands.

"If I may offer one request," said Marie, "it would be about my friend here. He has placed himself in every manner of danger to escort us here. I know my husband would consider it a personal service to him if our friend was allowed to go home."

"Of course. But he's welcome to rest and eat first." The relieved German farmer did that, and soon they were bidding him farewell with heartfelt words of thanks. Marie also handed him a letter to send to her aunt in Moscow to demonstrate his safe passage. And she indeed received the letter.

Anna, her mother, and her sister continued their journey, now with assistance from the Cossacks, who would enable a reunion with General Rozanov. They would reach safety in Siberia and from there find shelter beyond Russia.

Meanwhile, among the communist leaders, the time had finally come to determine the fate of the imperial family.

6

Royal Captivity

As winter gave way to spring, and Anna, her mother, and her sister prepared for their journey across Russia, Vladimir Lenin was changing the name of his party. As the Bolsheviks, they had risen up and eliminated opposition. As the Communist Party, they would rule. Among the many new questions they faced in this transition was, what should be done with the Romanovs?

The new regime was ruthless, but not reckless. The imperial family had to be handled with care. There was still a sentimental attachment to them, even among some of the workers and peasants. It had now been a year since the abdication, and the Romanovs themselves weren't certain where they could or should go. They were not welcome in France, and Great Britain was reluctant to accept them in its own tense political atmosphere. So the family remained for a time under house arrest at the Alexander Palace at Tsarskoye Selo, just south of Petrograd.

But after July's riots in the city, it was clear the family must be moved to a safer location. Tobolsk, beyond the Urals, was chosen by Prime Minister Alexander Kerensky. It was in a much more sparsely populated area, with no rail stations nearby. If troublemakers came, there would be sufficient warning. The family was placed in the great house that had once served as the governor's mansion. It was comfortable, and Tsar Nicholas and Tsarevna Alexandra were able to tell themselves that perhaps the troubles would pass, normalcy would return, and they could return to Petrograd.

But the tension grew. In February 1918 the new government made it known there would be no more funding for furnishing the Romanovs with servants, so many of their servants had to leave. Meals became more basic, luxuries began to vanish, but still the family clung to its hopes of rescue. Rumors regularly arose, suggesting that various groups would free them and take them to a friendlier country.

In late March two rival groups of Red Guards converged in Tobolsk. They were in competition for power and hostile to each other, and the city, remote as it was, suddenly seemed dangerous after all. The family had to be moved again, this time to Yekaterinburg. However, Tsarevich Alexei was too ill to travel. It was determined that for the time being, three of his sisters would keep him company in Tobolsk while Tsar Nicholas and Tsarina Alexandra made the move to Yekaterinburg with Maria, the remaining daughter. On April 25 the first group made the several-day trip in a convoy of nineteen carriages.

Mid-journey, new fears developed. Various Red Guard groups were eager to ambush the travel party and assassinate Nicholas II. Plots of all kinds were circulating, as were disturbing suggestions that perhaps Yekaterinburg's revolutionary leaders might act violently against the imperial family. At each stop, there was communication with Moscow through a Hughes teleprinter, a telegraph process of the time. Permission was now granted to change the destination from Yekaterinburg to Omsk.

But when the ruling party in Yekaterinburg caught wind of the detour, leaders interpreted this alteration as an attempted escape to exile. An army of two thousand quickly mobilized and hurried to cut them off. Once again, disaster was imminent.

The traveling group contacted Moscow again, and a compromise was adopted: the family would be taken to Yekaterinburg after all, but with a solemn promise from its leaders that the Romanovs would not be harmed in any way.

The convoy arrived at Yekaterinburg on April 30, and the family was admitted to Ipatiev House, a merchant's home that would come to be known as "the House of Special Purpose."

Later, in May, the rest of the family joined them, traveling by steamer since the river was no longer frozen. This journey proceeded without incident. Now the Romanovs were treated fully as prisoners. Most of the remaining servants were dismissed, and all family members were regularly searched.

Lenin's plan all along had been to prosecute Nicholas II in a show trial with a guilty verdict prearranged. It would be staged for the benefit of the public and involve trumped-up "evidence" of corruption and treachery, quieting any remaining support for the royals.

But Leon Trotsky, Lenin's commissar of foreign affairs, was having second thoughts. As the Bolsheviks faced the Czech troop revolt, including near Yekaterinburg, the idea of the Romanovs' being liberated posed a greater threat. Now there was a rebellious Czech force approaching the city; tomorrow and the next day there would be some other threat.

The Yekaterinburg leaders sought permission from Moscow to execute the imperial family. On July 16, as Lenin conferred with his inner circle, a firing squad was gathered.

Yet there was another Romanov who had concerned the Bolshevik leaders. Nicholas II's younger brother, Grand Duke Mikhail Alexandrovich, presented a threat, if only a theoretical one—in truth, becoming tsar was the one future he'd tried his best to avoid.

The younger Romanov was utterly devoid of any thirst for power. Perhaps this was the result of his country's history of assassinations. His grandfather was murdered after five failed attempts. That was the childhood Mikhail had known. Being the ruler made one a target.

His oldest brother, Nicholas II, had accepted his legacy without complaint, however. Another brother, Georgi, was also ahead of Mikhail in line, but when Georgi died at the age of twenty-eight, Mikhail became the heir apparent. Even after the emperor and empress produced a son, that son's health was precarious.

Perhaps that's why Mikhail, a quiet and pleasant man, seemed to go out of his way to disqualify himself from the royal line. He pursued romantic relationships that made him a regular item of gossip and scandal. First, there was a relationship with a first cousin; Nicholas II said no to marriage.

Next came his sister's lady-in-waiting, a commoner; Mikhail was sent to Denmark.

Finally, he became involved with the wife of a fellow officer, with whom he parented a son. Eventually, after her divorce cleared the way, they were married. Eventually, Nicholas II legitimized their son, Georgi (named after the dead brother), but the marriage was held in contempt at the Winter Palace.

Throughout Mikhail's romantic liaisons, he had to contend with being followed and spied upon by his older brother's secret police. It can't have been a happy life. By the time the Great War came, in 1914, Mikhail seemed eager to struggle with an enemy other than his own royal lineage.

By all accounts, Mikhail was a success on the battlefield, even in the eyes of the tsar. He earned the Order of Saint George for his leadership in the Carpathian Mountains. Even so, the horror of this world war affected him in the same way it did so many others, regardless of national allegiance. He'd been a soldier most of his life, yet he came to the conclusion that war was a policy carried about by those in power at the full expense of those who lacked it.

Still, he carried out his leadership responsibilities and was popular with those in his command. As the war finally played out, Mikhail must have wondered what possibilities life still held for him. He was a wealthy man, but he despised the aristocratic life of Petrograd. His relationship with the imperial family was ragged. And he was fed up with war and the soldier's life.

Yet in at least one way, he demonstrated political judgment superior to that of Nicholas II. He was much more in tune with the feelings of the time. He wrote his older brother and detailed his distress about the currents of rebellion he was observing in the circles he frequented. The most frightening element was that he was witnessing it in those usually counted upon for loyalty. The ruling class was dangerously out of favor. Those surrounding Nicholas II, the men making the decisions, were resented, even held in contempt. And to some extent, the emperor and empress were insulated from the worst of these expressions of bitterness.

The Romanovs were in a fragile position. Mikhail stated clearly that he feared for his extended family's safety, and even beyond that, the future of the Russian traditions. Ominously, he noted that right, left, and moderate forces were all beginning to unite with a common enemy. And this blinded them to a new, rapidly rising enemy: the Red threat.

Warnings notwithstanding, it was already too late. The storm clouds had gathered, the peasant revolts had reached fever pitch, and the Bolsheviks were growing more confident by the day. By the early months of 1917, Mikhail's travel was limited by mobs, which waited on all the busiest avenues, hungry to lay hands on anyone thought to be tied to the nobility or the current government.

There was no palace with a moat deep or wide enough to provide safety from the riots, which were only growing in intensity.

As a Romanov, Mikhail was called upon to endorse each new compromise. With reluctance, he placed his signature on petitions about temporary cabinets and changes in leadership. He knew none of these salves would be strong enough medicine—not even the new provisional government that came to power on March 1.

Yet the collapse of the monarchy still came as a shock. Nicholas II abdicated the throne the next day, March 2, 1917, without giving the grand duke advance notice.

The abdication covered father and son; young Alexei, in poor health, had to be protected. Mikhail thus awoke to the discovery that not only was the throne passing to him, making him Emperor Mikhail II, Tsar of All the Russias, but that he would be visited immediately that day by the Duma, the governing body.

On March 3 Mikhail announced he would not proceed to the throne but would defer to governmental decisions. He affirmed the provisional government as the final authority over these matters and urged all the people to do so as well. His public ambivalence was the wisest political move, though his older brother was shocked and called the declaration "rubbish."

Once again, however, his passivity wasn't going to be enough to keep the peace. No word or action from a Romanov at that point would have been enough. The arc of political affairs was highly charged, passionate, and it bent toward only one possible resolution: blood.

Mikhail had experienced a long, costly continental war of attrition that seemed as if it might have gone on forever. The war within his beloved country was worse in many ways. It was angrier, more chaotic. Unless one was a Bolshevik, there seemed no hope at all, no path that would achieve any end other than demolishing Russia's rich history and tradition. And how could his family possibly escape the consequences? Was there a route to exile, a path to safety within calmer borders?

Mikhail, along with other Romanov relations, was dismissed from military service, though still allowed to wear the uniform. His movements were confined to the Petrograd area, then to an apartment there. As the months went by, he briefly glimpsed hope of relocation to Finland. House arrest was lifted for a time, and he prepared to travel. But when the Bolsheviks caught wind of his plans, they tightened his confinement.

Mikhail knew that the more time went by, the firmer the Bolsheviks' grip would be on political power and the less cautious they'd be in his handling. On March 7, 1918, he was re-arrested and moved to the Smolny Institute—at the time, Bolshevik headquarters. Two days later, he was sent to Perm, near the Ural mountains, where the local revolutionaries would become his wardens. With him, as always, was his secretary, Nikolai Johnson.

Johnson dreamed of being an opera singer. He suffered from extremely poor health, particularly for a military man with a position of importance. He'd met Grand Duke Mikhail Alexandrovich at artillery school, the two had hit it off, and Johnson spent the last few years of his life in the service of his friend. He was present when Mikhail signed the manifest renouncing the throne. After that, the two were arrested together and sent to Perm. However, what was shown to the public was that he occupied a room in the finest hotel in the city, along with servants, a valet, and a chauffeur.

Neither of the two were in good health during their captivity; both had digestion problems and often were unable to eat. The only way to pass the time was reading, and often Johnson would read aloud to the grand duke.

Meanwhile, a complicating factor was the revolt of the Czechoslovak Legion. Beginning in May, the Czechs increased their opposition against Bolshevik forces all along the Trans-Siberian Railway, taking a number of cities along the line. Their ultimate goal was the creation of an independent Czech nation. For now, they joined the White Army as opposition against the Reds and were approaching Perm at an alarming rate. This gave Mikhail one more problem to solve.

7

The Death and Burial of a Dynasty

In June of 1918 a leader of the secret police in Perm planned the murder of Grand Duke Mikhail Alexandrovich. On June 13 four men, all former prisoners of the old government, used a forged document to enter the house in which the grand duke and his secretary Nikolai Johnson were being kept. Brandishing a pistol and a grenade, they commanded the grand duke to accompany them.

Grand Duke Mikhail was suspicious and asked to speak to someone in authority. He also explained that he was in ill health and incapable of travel. But the men wouldn't leave, and finally the grand duke—voluntarily accompanied by his faithful secretary—climbed into one of the carriages in which the men had come. "We are heading for a rail station," one of the men said. "We must travel through a forest to get there."

Mikhail recognized one of his captors and trusted him at first, but as they entered the forest, he came to realize the end was at hand. "Can it be true that I will be shot today?" he asked.

His secretary, in a separate carriage, asked his guard, "Why should you shoot me? I do not have wealth; I live on a salary. I have only an old mother. To shoot Mikhail Romanov is also for nothing. He is a liberal person; he is loved by the people."

The grand duke attempted to buy his safety. "If I can save myself, I will shower you with gold and wealth," he offered in desperation. He even pulled out his notebook to record his captor's name for arranged payments.

The carriages stopped, and the two men were commanded to climb out. The woods were dark, and rain was falling. As Mikhail stepped into the dirt, he heard a shot ring out. He saw that Johnson had taken a bullet to the head. A separate pistol had jammed.

Another shot was then fired at Mikhail, but it was a misfire; he was only wounded. When he hurried in panic toward his fallen friend, crying, "Let me say goodbye to him," he was shot again at point-blank range, and this time the bullet entered his head. Two different members of the party later took credit for the grand duke's kill shot.

Now came the matter of two corpses, with daylight beginning to cut through the trees. The men gathered brush and old wood to cover the bodies. Then they traveled to the police station and planned a cover-up in greater detail. Two men were assigned to dig holes about six meters deep and dispose of the bodies.

The next day, a local Perm newspaper reported the disappearance of the two men, saying an "energetic search" would continue. But rumors quickly circulated. The grand duke had escaped, according to one. Perhaps he'd been abducted by the White Army or some band from the nobility.

Workers were angry—how could such a thing happen under Bolshevik supervision? Perhaps Mikhail II was somewhere with his cronies even now, planning a restoration of the monarchy and the ruling class.

Meanwhile, the workers and peasants had seen exactly what they were intended to see: a royal aristocrat had been put up in a swanky location, with servants and bodyguards all around him. Now he was unaccounted for. They resented all these things.

As usual, the Bolsheviks had exploited class bitterness to cloak the new regime's own violence and bloodshed. But still there remained the question of the emperor and the family that symbolized, to all the people, the Russia of long tradition: Tsar Nicholas Romanov, his wife, and their children.

By this time, the Romanov family was in Ipatiev House in Yekaterinburg. A doctor and three family servants were present with them. As the month of June progressed, life in the house was miserable for the family. The guards bullied them at every chance, while nuns prayed for the family and brought food from the local monastery, though the guards ate most of the food. A priest held services for the full family twice. The windows were sealed, and newspapers covered them so that no sunlight was admitted. Two fences were constructed to surround the house.

As had happened with Grand Duke Mikhail, current events had sealed the family's fate. With the Czechs due to reach the city in a matter of days, all plans for a show trial were ditched in favor of an execution. The imperial family had to be removed. On June 29, two weeks after the killing of Mikhail, the Ural Regional Soviet came to the conclusion that an execution must take place. A meeting in Moscow on July 3, with Lenin present, determined that the Ural group should plan and carry out the execution. The timing would depend upon military circumstances, and Moscow's go-ahead would be required. Philipp Goleschekin, Yakov Sverdlov, and Yakov Yurovsky, who led the execution squad, were conspirators in the killings.

Around midnight at the end of July 16, Dr. Botkin, the family physician, was awakened by Yakov Yurovsky, the Cheka (member of the secret police) who was now in charge of the House of Special Purpose. "Wake the family," he said. "There is unrest in town, and they would be in danger upstairs, with the shooting that could occur. They must take shelter in the basement." Indeed, everyone had heard shooting in the distance, and since the family was told to be dressed, it was easy to believe they'd be moved to a safer location.

Dr. Botkin saw that the family and servants were awakened, and one hour later, they all assembled on the ground floor of the house, a place where some of the guards slept each night and sometimes brought women. The emperor carried the tsarevich in his arms, and the empress asked for chairs. Two were brought, one for the sick boy and one for his mother, who also wasn't well.

Yurovsky told them to wait a few minutes for their truck. The family wasn't told the true reason for the truck; Yurovsky detected no signs of distrust among them. The group was herded into a smaller, semi-basement room.

Several minutes passed. Then a group of men came into the room behind Yurovsky, and they were all carrying pistols and revolvers. It was about two o'clock in the morning.

Yurovsky produced a document and began to read aloud an order from the Ural Executive Committee: "Nikolai Alexandrovich, in view of the fact that your relatives are continuing their attack on Soviet Russia, the Ural Executive Committee has decided to execute you." The emperor could only stammer, "What?"

The empress and the children made the sign of the cross just as the shooting began—loud enough but not very effective. The men had been told that each of them should target one of the prisoners. But most of the men were reluctant to shoot at young girls and were eager to seize the honor of killing the emperor and empress, so most of the shooting went in that direction. Besides, the girls had prepared for such a moment. They lined the inside of their blouses with jewels to create crude bulletproof vests.

The room quickly filled with smoke and burned gunpowder, dust cascaded from the ceiling, and it was difficult to see in any case once the shooting began. The cascading echoes of gunfire escaped the basement and woke up most of the neighbors who were in range. Dogs began barking and windows and doors were thrown open.

One of the men slipped outside to check the noise level and saw the commotion they'd caused. He ran back in and saw, according to his account, the younger daughters hunkered against the wall, covering their heads with their arms as two men fired at them.

The man who had run outside shouted, "Stop the firing! Use bayonets and the butt of your rifle to kill anyone left alive."

As the guns fell silent, the moaning of the wounded could be heard. A door was opened to disperse the smoke. Most of the family servants were dead, but the children were all still living; only Maria was injured. Demidova, the empress's maid, was still standing, huddled against the back wall as she was stabbed to death, trying in vain to defend herself with a pillow.

One of the men continued shooting Alexei, but he, too, had a layer of jewels sewn into his clothes. Finally, Yurovsky stepped up and finished the boy with a shot to his head.

The shooters killed the girls with their bayonets, then more gunshots, finally smashing their faces with the rifle butts to prevent identification. A lady-in-waiting screamed as she grabbed her shooter's bayonet with both hands and tried to divert it, but in the end, all were dead. Even the dogs were killed, except for Tsarevich Alexei's spaniel, which somehow survived and was later rescued by a British officer.

As the bodies were being placed on stretchers, one of the girls let out a final cry, still alive. Again, a bayonet failed to penetrate her vest, and she was shot in the head. A man named Peter Ermakov, who was drunk, walked through the room with his bayonet, checking for any sign of life.

By the time pulses were checked and all the sentences had been carried out successfully, about twenty minutes had passed since the family had gathered.

Someone, apparently a literature buff, left a cryptic line of poetry scribbled on the wall: "Belsatsar was, in this same night, killed by his slaves." It was one of any number of scrawls left by the guards who slept in the room. Most were insults to the imperial family. But this line was of particular interest, a biblical reference by way of German poet Heinrich Heine. Belsatsar was the last of the Babylonian kings (Balthazar in Western Bibles). But to quote the poet, the spelling should have been *Belsazar*. The added *t* on the wall scribble was a clear play on the word *tsar*.

Everything considered valuable, including diaries and papers from the family quarters, went into Yurovsky's office. And as he considered the poor quality of the hired men's work—a great many of whom were intoxicated—he decided he'd need to accompany the burial party. Everything else was shoved into the furnace and burned.

It was about half past two in the morning. For the first time in centuries, Russia had no emperor.

The bodies were placed on stretchers and loaded onto the truck. A cloth was spread because blood was everywhere. By three o'clock, the truck was on its way to the chosen gravesite for the imperial family.

Peter Ermakov, one of the leaders of the execution team, owned land near an open mine known as Four Brothers. Ganin's Pit seemed perfect for dumping bodies where they might never be found. He knew the area well, but few others did. He brought wood, kerosene, and acid with the intention of burning the corpses and then dumping the ashes. On the other hand, he brought only one shovel, which infuriated Yurovsky.

The truck arrived, after struggling through muddy ground, and the men loaded the bodies onto a *droshky* (cart). A crowd of hired men was waiting for them at the mine, though better described as a drunken mob. These men were infuriated. They wanted to take part in the royal execution. Grave digging was a menial task in comparison.

Most of them were ultimately dismissed, particularly after their attempts at looting and lewd behavior with the corpses.

At this point, the layers of jewels lining the corsets were found. Finally, the ineffectiveness of so much shooting made sense. The men began pocketing as many shiny stones as they could, until Yurovsky waved his gun and threatened to shoot anyone caught stealing. In the end, all the valuables were placed under his care with other items.

At this point, Yurovsky realized the pit wasn't as deep as he'd thought—only twelve meters. The muddy water didn't conceal the bodies. Hand grenades were thrown into the pit to collapse the walls and bury the contents, but unsuccessfully, like so much of the Bolsheviks' work that evening. He ordered the men to gather dirt, brush, and sticks and fill the hole. He then named three men to stand guard while he took the jewels back to Yekaterinburg and prepared to file his report with the Cheka.

The report didn't go over well. Yurovsky was told the bodies would be too easy to find and needed to be reburied. There was also displeasure about the great number of clumsy, undisciplined witnesses at Four Brothers. By now the location of the bodies was hardly a secret. A new burial place should be sought, at a deeper mine on the road to Moscow.

Early on the morning of July 19, the bodies were back on the truck and headed south. But only four and a half kilometers into the journey, the truck was once again mired in mud on the Koptiaki Road, not far from the railway line. It was the second such breakdown on this short trip. The men were irritable, tired, and near rebellion, and the sun would be coming up soon. An anxious Yurovsky decided the new burial site would be on this very spot. He found the railway watchman and asked for a few railroad ties, hoping they would help the truck move over the burial site.

A bonfire was also lit while the graves were being dug. Two small bodies were pulled from the group and incinerated, with the idea of burying them separately. The perception was that separating the groups would throw off those expecting to find the Romanovs, and the smallest were the easiest to identify. One was Alexei, the other a younger daughter, though in Yurovsky's mind there was some confusion between her and Demidova. The two graves were about seventy meters apart—not exactly the best disguise, but at this point everyone was ready to complete the misadventure.

The bones of the pair were deposited in the shallower hole, the soil was carefully evened out, and the tire tracks were covered with ashes from the two fires that had now been set.

Sulfuric acid was poured on the remaining corpses. Then, once they were in the grave, a second dose of acid was applied. The pit was filled in, railroad ties were placed across the top, and then the truck was driven back and forth over them, compressing the dirt.

Yurovsky felt the awful task was finally at an end. He gathered the men around and spoke to them of the importance of secrecy. The imperials should not become martyrs in the eyes of the Russian people. Not only that, but the team should consider that anyone who'd taken part in these acts would be in personal danger. This night's activities must remain a solemn secret.

Brushing the dirt from their hands, the men walked back to the truck.

8

Sokolov Investigates

The communists were right to worry about forces from the resistance closing in on Yekaterinburg. Less than a week after the Romanovs were executed in the basement of Ipatiev House, the White Army broke through and held Yekaterinburg for several months. They occupied the city and environs just long enough to get to the most basic truth about what happened to the Romanovs. The family indeed had been executed in the House of Special Purpose. These rumors of their survival were so much ill-founded propaganda—at best, a sentimental clinging to fantasy, at worst, the concealment of butchery.

Red Army forces took hold of the city by the end of June 1919.

Lenin dangled many empty promises before the people of Russia. One of them was that the Communist Party would create a high-minded, nonviolent society in a country sick of the high death count of the war and the assassination rate of its rulers. It wouldn't do for the public to find out that he'd approved the murder of the imperial family, including young girls, a sick boy, and even their dogs.

The party owned up to the execution of Nicholas II, whom it called, in one of its propaganda newspapers, "the personification of the barbarian landowner . . . this ignoramus, dimwit and bloodthirsty savage." The tsar was presented as the ultimate enemy of the worker and peasant class.

But the communists also endorsed rumors that the rest of the family had been taken from the house to a safer location. They wanted peace with the Germans, and one of Germany's demands was for the Reds to deliver Empress Alexandra and the children—which, of course was impossible.

So rumors were spread. Some claimed to have seen the family on a train leaving Yekaterinburg on July 17. Others insisted they'd seen the Romanovs in Perm. The story of Anastasia's escape also began to circulate. The claims of false heirs were becoming a problem.

Meanwhile, the House of Special Purpose still stood, still contained forensic evidence of murder. The house awaited a truth-driven investigation, and one became possible when the White Army took control of the area. Nikolai Sokolov was just the man to lead that investigation.

Sokolov was born and raised in Penza, where he was a court investigator with a law degree. He became good friends with General Rozanov and often visited the family estate for hunting. During the years leading up to the revolution, he became close to the whole family. In 1917 Sokolov was thirty-five and unwavering in his loyalty to the tradition and legacy of Russian monarchy.

As he watched the nation fall into ever-deeper chaos, he took sick leave from his post and made his way across the Urals and into Siberia, where imperial loyalists were not only welcome but quickly organizing. He worked for the prosecutors' offices at Irkutsk and then Omsk. And when the army of the Siberian government moved into Yekaterinburg several months after the Romanovs were murdered, he was in the right place at the right time to work out the puzzle of the imperial family's fate.

On February 5, 2019, Adm. Alexander Kolchak, who commanded the White Army, asked him to look into what had happened at Ipatiev House. Sokolov took this charge quite seriously. He wasn't solving a crime so much as filling in the historical record on a matter of profound importance. His discovery would tell the world a great deal about the new rulers of Russia.

Therefore, even when the Whites were driven out of the area, he held the evidence tightly, particularly important documents, and protected it for posterity by moving it out of the country.

General Rozanov and his adjutant, Capt. Kirill Mikhailovich Naryshkin, entered the city with the White Army. Since making his allegiance known as anti-Bolshevik and escaping from Penza, Rozanov had served under the commander of the Irkutsk Military District, then was appointed governor-general of the Yenisei Governorate and special commissioner for the protection of state order and public peace in the Yenisei Governorate. As the Russian Civil War was at its height, his military experience was invaluable to the loyalists, particularly because he'd been inside the Red Army during the revolution, before he'd made his allegiances known.

Now he approached the last known location of the royal family. As he cast his eyes on Ipatiev House, he noticed the ugly palisades that had been constructed to hide the windows and ordered them taken down. He and Naryshkin were among the first to enter the abandoned home, and he must have felt a deep sense of foreboding as he stepped into the darkness and silence of the large abode. He'd heard the rumors about basement executions, and he couldn't bring himself to walk down those steps—though surely if butchers had been at work, they would have made a thorough cleanup.

But at some point, there can be too much blood to wash away. Naryshkin inspected the rooms, and he reported that the tragic story was written on the walls—in the red ink of royal blood, the lead of smashed bullets, the bayonet-scarred floors, and the obscene scribbles on the wall, filled with the jubilant, taunting poetry of regicide. The attempt at mopping and obscuring had been halfhearted and rushed, even with a week to hide the evidence.

There had been bloodshed, but from how many victims? Were there survivors? Rumors had circulated of executions in this basement, and here was confirmation. Local families gave jumbled, conflicting accounts. A week ago, quite a racket had erupted in the dead of night. After that, all was quiet, and the royals (about whom there was a natural fascination) had not taken their daily fresh air.

The truth must be discovered, and the family must have a Christian burial. So, before Sokolov's involvement, a local investigator was assigned to discover whatever facts were available. He was quickly dismissed as untrustworthy and unenthusiastic. While a second appointee was taking over the case and making his first study of Ipatiev House, a group of officers searched the area of the Four Brothers Mine and brought back several pieces of evidence. A communiqué read,

> Herewith I am forwarding to you the following physical evidence: a human finger and two pieces of human skin, a gold earring with a pearl and a diamond, an upper denture, shrapnel from bombs, a male tie pin,

bird bones, glass vial fragments, iron piece off a boot and buttons and an iron shovel, found by mining engineer Alexander Nikolayevich Kuznetsov and noncommissioned officer of the volunteer army, Alexander Andreyevich Sheremetyevsky, in a mine near Koptiaki [*sic*] village, Yekaterinburg District.

By my authority, Dr. A. I. Belogradsky bottled the finger and the two pieces of skin with alcohol and sealed it with my stamp.

The letter created a sensation. It had been a month since the murders; decay was a relentless enemy whose weapon was time. Yet here was a discovery: potential evidence that the bodies of the imperial family and entourage might have been dumped in a nearby mine. There were plenty of stories of trucks heading in that direction, late at night and on the following morning.

At this point, Alexander Nametkin, the original investigator, had provided a few possible witnesses. Ivan Sergeyev, his successor, had searched the upper floor of Ipatiev and produced Tsarevich Alexei's diary. Everyone agreed with his report concluding that all members of the family, along with their loyal servants, were dead. Now, with the findings at the mine, the final destination of the bodies was clear.

What was lacking was a story, a narrative of how and why the family came to be executed. Sergeyev's theory was that the Bolshevik Ural military and civil authorities had given the order. He refuted theories of international conspiracies or the Bolshevik insistence that that the family was safe, intact, and in hiding.

But Nametkin and Sergeyev were viewed as insufficient. A sturdier, more wide-ranging investigation was needed, and in times when allegiances were crucial, General Rozanov wanted someone trustworthy, capable, and efficient. He thought of his friend Sokolov and sought permission to appoint him. He wrote:

Your honor,

The presenter of this letter: the Judicial Investigator for Highly Important matters in the district of the Penza court, Nikolai Alekseyevich Sokolov.

Gospodin Sokolov has long been known to me, both personally and through his official social activities.

In his specialty, he conducted many complex cases that aroused public interest, and enjoyed the reputation of an experienced investigator. As chairman of the Penza Court of Judicial Investigators, Gospodin Sokolov, since the Bolshevik coup, suffered all sorts of oppression from the Soviet government for his decisive refusal to serve in judicial Bolshevik colleges and for his refusal to impact the morals of his comrades in this direction.

Gospodin Sokolov served as a part of those who arose in Penza as a junction for military public organizations aimed at the revival of the motherland, personally led by me, and actively helped establish communications, sending out officers and so on. Thanks to his excellent knowledge of the places adjacent to the front, he provided necessary routes that needed to be taken, sometimes serving as a personal guide for couriers with responsible assignments.

Recently, staying on Soviet territory has become positively impossible and he, almost at the same time as me, broke through the front, walking the distance from Penza to Syzran on foot under the guise of a beggar.

In view of the foregoing, I consider myself morally obligated to ask you, Mr. Minister, to render Gospodin Sokolov all possible assistance on your part to get him a proper place in the judicial department.

Accept my assurance of perfect reverence and devotion.

Chief of Staff of the Supreme Commander in Chief
Lieutenant General S. Rozanov

On January 25, 1919, all the existing evidence, along with relevant paperwork, was gathered and transferred to Omsk for safekeeping. And on February 5, Admiral Kolchak, leader of the Provisional All-Russian Government, in Siberia, asked Sokolov to review the case and offer a report. Two days later, Sokolov was officially given full responsibility for investigating the death and burial of the Romanovs.

The two previous investigators, Nametkin and Sergeyev, were later arrested and executed by the communists, but Sokolov took hold of the case; though he never completed his work, neither did he let go within his lifetime, only five more years. Not only did he gather physical evidence and interview local witnesses; he also pursued documents, many obscure and hidden, that would give any level of guidance to untangling the mystery set before him. All the while, he knew that no matter what he found, it could never be offered in a true and objective Russian court, because the guilty party controlled that court.

Sokolov was dismissive of the earlier investigations, particularly in regard to what he felt was their failure to investigate Four Brothers. In truth, the mine had indeed been explored, and Tovarish Prosecutor Nikolai Magnitsky of the Yekaterinburg District Court excavated the open pit and discovered a number of belongings of the Romanovs. In the end, however, Magnitsky said, "The area we searched—was not searched," meaning he recommended that any successive investigations begin anew, taking nothing for granted.

Sokolov made his own trip to Four Brothers Mine and mobilized hundreds of volunteers to search the vicinity. This time the search produced fourteen topaz stones from a necklace worn by one of the daughters. He also gathered bones, melted fat, hair, and the carcass of Anastasia's dog, Gemmy.

Until the winter snow vanished from the ground, there was no more to be done. But from May 23 through June 17, Sokolov made further progress. He continued gathering testimonies from locals. For example, he discovered that on July 17, the date in question, a local pharmacy supplied a total of 190 kilograms of sulfuric acid to Bolshevik officials. Witnesses testified about trucks and mounted soldiers, and what times they were observed along the road and near the house. They observed drivers heading toward the Koptiaki forest, drivers who had made it known that no one should follow them to that location.

The most insistent evidence was that trucks with men carrying rifles seemed to have been in transit at an odd time of night. Some of these soldiers knocked on doors, woke up the local folks, and made demands, rudely threatening anyone who dared to object.

Sokolov worked on the assumption the bodies were taken toward the forest and to the abandoned iron ore mine, then burned with sulfuric acid and then utterly incinerated in flames set with gasoline. The resulting ashes would tell no story.

As for the lies about family members being safely moved, a telegram was found in Yekaterinburg after the desertion of the communists. It stated, "The whole family has suffered the same fate as the head."

On June 17 it became evident that the communists were drawing near. Sokolov was now pressured by their approach, just as the communists had been pressured when the Czech forces closed in. He had no choice but to abandon his on-site investigation. He understood that his work was far from complete, with far too many sites left unexamined; one of them was Grade Crossing No. 184. Included in his files was a photograph labeled "Small bridge, built by the Bolsheviks on the Koptiaki Road, where the heavy vehicle transporting the corpses of the Imperial Family to the mine, got stuck."

The possible significance of that location, of the railroad ties ("sleepers") and planks placed there to build a bridge, was never considered, either for lack of time or imagination. Most likely, the area around Ganin's Pit, which was obviously the most promising site, was the only one thoroughly examined in the time available.

Either way, it was simply impossible to come to a firm conclusion about what had happened to the bodies. Sokolov was only certain there was no scenario by which any members of the family could have escaped execution. The bones of Anastasia's dog testified to the thorough brutality of the killers.

Ultimately, Sokolov's investigation was hindered on several fronts. For one thing, a civil war was in progress. There were other more immediate priorities, and time was extremely limited, especially with the need to wait for the winter ground to thaw. He received little official support or assistance from the provisional government. And in the chaos, he worried about key documents being lost or scattered, so he was in the habit of having them duplicated for preservation. Then he gave them not only to official authorities but also to a few acquaintances for safekeeping. In fact, in July 1921 Sokolov's apartment in Berlin was raided by communist agents posing as burglars. They grabbed many of the documents, but fortunately, Sokolov had made copies.

The surviving Romanovs, including Grand Duke Nikolai Nikolaevich Romanov and the bereaved dowager empress Maria Fyodorovna, were unsympathetic with any investigation of a crime they wouldn't acknowledge. They still cherished foolish hopes that Tsar Nicholas, Tsarevna Alexandra, and the family had somehow survived. Neither would receive Sokolov, though the grand duke did arrange for the creation of a special committee for the maintenance of case evidence and materials. But that was the extent of Romanov support.

Sokolov worked almost in solitude, disappointed by the lack of support for his defense of a cause he believed in deeply: the integrity of the Russian monarchy. He trusted his friends, did his work, and held onto his documents for dear life. On January 6, 1920, he addressed a report to Maria Fyodorovna. Only after nine months was she shown the report, which read,

> The area where the corpses of the August Family were transported, is absolutely certain and precisely established in the provisional investigation. It all underwent the most thorough inspection and search, with the participation of especially trusted persons of military rank. . . . Taking the inspection data of this area into account and the range of locations found here, the investigative authority has no doubt and is completely convinced that the corpses of the August Persons and all the others who died with Them, were initially dismembered into parts, near one of the mines, and then burned in the fires with the aid of gasoline. The difficulty of succumbing to the action of fire, the parts were destroyed with the aid of sulfuric acid.

In 1925 Sokolov published his book, *The Death of the Imperial Family*, in French and later in Russian. Criticism followed; the subject was inherently controversial. Many complained that the author was too committed to the theory that the bodies had been burned (which in fairness, turned out to be true). But since, at the time, the background evidence was scattered across Europe, no one could put forward a version of the story with any greater substance.

That changed in 1946. The Soviet Special Services discovered in Berlin eight original volumes of Sokolov's inquiry. The Nazis had removed them from Paris during occupation. The most valuable source is surely the three-volume group of files known as Sokolov's "Bedside Register," which includes all the essential documents. We now have a full inventory of all the paperwork documenting Sokolov's investigation; practically speaking, nothing is missing.

Sokolov understood that he had gone farther than the two investigators before him, but still not far enough. Nor could he convince the surviving relatives that the victims were even dead. In March 1920 he left the country after sending his documents to France in two sections: by packet with diplomatic seal and by warship. From exile, he published his book and, like the frustrated detectives of any cold case, wondered if the final truth would ever be known. Four years later, he was dead at age forty-two.

Among those left to mourn the loss was General Rozanov, who had taken Sokolov hunting back in Penza, in the last days of the older. Another was his adjutant, Capt. Kirill Mikhailovich Naryshkin, who had entered Ipatiev House by his side and inspected the rooms where the murders occurred.

Naryshkin, however, was a married man by that time. His bride was none other than Anna Sergeyevna Rozanova-Naryshkina, the daughter of General Rozanov. And she had just traveled the length of Russia to escape terrorism and to meet her husband. The Sokolovs and Naryshkins left the Far East together as a party of four. They boarded a ship called the *Andre Lebon*, bound for Italy. A special military box was in their possession. It contained forensic evidence of the murders Sokolov had investigated.

The two couples shared a cabin, and many years later, my grandmother, Anna Naryshkina, would tell me about that voyage and the mysterious box that contained the most intriguing forensic evidence of the Romanov executions.

9

Expatriates

The Trans-Siberian Railway was, and is, the longest railway line in the world—four thousand miles. On one end lies Moscow; on the other is the city of Vladivostok, which sits on the Sea of Japan. The vast distance between the two cities mattered strategically in 1919. It mattered deeply.

At the time of the October Revolution in 1917, the power of the railway and the obedience of Vladivostok's people passed to the new Soviet government. But the Bolsheviks couldn't easily manage the allegiance of a city four thousand miles away. The White Army, allied with the Czechoslovak Legion, wrested control of the area from the Soviets. Japan, the United States, and China then used the city as a staging area for intervention against the revolutionary forces.

As in Yekaterinburg and elsewhere, however, the anticommunist forces in Vladivostok couldn't hold on. The White Army was falling apart, the civil war was coming to an end, and by the end of 1920, most White Russians had left. That included the Rozanovs, along with the general's adjutant, Capt. Kirill Naryshkin, and his young new wife, Anna.

The three Rozanov women had made the long, dangerous journey safely. Once they'd met the Cossack troops along the road, things became easier. The farther they traveled from the seat of Soviet power, the safer they felt. And now they were under the protection of friendly forces, loyal to General Rozanov.

Most of the remainder of the journey was made by train. Just before leaving their country forever, they managed to see a great deal of it from west to east, from the European side to eastern Asia, close to what is now North Korea—everywhere the Trans-Siberian Railway took them, including Harbin, China.

Already the substantial Russian community in Harbin was taking steps to preserve the culture of the old, imperial Russia. It was comforting to see these pockets of conservative resilience along the route, and it was no wonder the railway was such a military prize in the war being fought between Red and White.

In Vladivostok Anna could only offer a sigh of relief. It felt as if the Bolsheviks were half a world away. Culturally, this was a different place than the Russia she knew, though the city had been founded by the Russians as a military outpost only seventy years before.

Her time as a young lady of a country estate seemed like some other lifetime. She knew by now she would never return. She'd been involved in espionage, embroiled in politics and clandestine travel, and she hardly knew what normal felt like anymore.

Yet in Vladivostok she met a man who changed everything. Her father introduced her to his adjutant, and the two were attracted to each other quickly. Kirill Naryshkin was from a background similar to her own. His family name was prominent in Russian history; Peter the Great's maternal grandfather bore the name of Kirill Naryshkin in the seventeenth century. And Anna's young husband had a cousin, Prince Felix Yusupov, who had led the assassins who killed Rasputin in 1916. It was a small world—within a vast country.

As Kirill courted the general's daughter, he rowed her in a boat through Vladivostok Harbor. It might have been a romantic outing but for the sight of the American Expeditionary Fleet training its guns on the Japanese fleet, foreshadowing hostilities that would lead to war twenty years in the future. The couple grew more attached even as discouraging reports came from the various cities and battlefronts and as the Amur region itself slipped more and more from the hands of the White Army. Whatever the future brought, they would face it together.

On June 21, 1919, Anna and Kirill married. For Anna's father, it was a rare day of joy and celebration. He was still heavily involved in defending the railway, fighting against the Red partisan groups of the Kansk-Tayshet Front. Outnumbered, he led a successful attack against the enemy base and destroyed it, eliminating most of the opposition and keeping the Trans-Siberian Railway safe for the time being.

With this done, Admiral Kolchak transferred the general to Vladivostok, the end of the rail line, where he became the military governor-general of the vast Amur region until January 1920, when hopes were finally dashed.

Vladivostok hosted an international military multinational force comprised of American, British, French, Japanese, Italian, and Czechoslovak troops. This was an alliance against the communists, but that didn't mean relationships were particularly smooth. American Maj. Gen. William S. Graves disliked General Rozanov, seeing him as a merciless leader because of what he saw as barbaric tactics during his time as governor of the Yenisei and Irkutsk Military Region. Graves called him "the worst character known to me in Siberia."

His observations were accurate factually but represented the perspective of an outsider, not a Russian fighting for the survival of his nation. Rozanov's enemy was an unrelenting, murderous party that had seized his beloved government. He had spent just enough days in the Red Army at the beginning of the revolution to know the Bolsheviks would destroy everything in their path to achieve their goal, including the church itself and every sacred tradition associated with Russia's heritage. He believed fire must be fought with a fire no less raging. The old, civilized rules of war meant less than nothing to the Bolsheviks. Russians must adapt or perish.

Rozanov had already watched too many of his closest friends and best soldiers from his army executed simply for their affiliation. Like most bitter civil wars, atrocities mounted up on either side. Through American eyes, all of it was distasteful; through Russian eyes, there were no other options.

Col. William "Wild Bill" Donovan, the hero of the recent world war as commander of New York's Fighting Sixty-Ninth, visited Omsk and wrote a report in basic agreement with Graves on the character of Kolchak's regime. He couldn't endorse American support of it; one side was as bloodthirsty as the other, and the corruption he saw in the White government doomed it to failure. In his eyes, Lenin's party would soon win the favor of the people, who were coming to resent White as much as Red. Donovan reported on the chaos he saw—disease, disorganization, and the lack of any viable choice for a Russian future.

As the United States and other powers from the West cooled in their support of Kolchak, Rozanov, and the traditionalists, the futility of the cause became obvious all the faster. It was also true that the worst war in world history, up to that time, was only a few months in the past. No one wanted more fighting, more casualties, more expensive aid. The military tactics in Russia served as a viable excuse for other nations to look away, to tend their own fires.

In the end, Kolchak lost Siberia to the Bolsheviks and was executed.

The White Army lacked many things—time, organization, position, and particularly weapons. It was rich in one resource: gold. Admiral Kolchak's forces managed to transport more than five hundred tons of gold across the country to Siberia. The gold could be leveraged against the arms shortage. From Japan, the Whites could go to market for the guns and munitions they needed.

The United States quickly turned down a rich offer of gold for guns. General Rozanov loaded fifty-five tons of it on a Japanese cruiser and took it to Japan. As the gold continued to be parceled out in various deals and as gifts, some of it ended up in bank basements in Japan and Korea, and much of it simply vanished into obscurity, even as the cause of resistance itself was evaporating.

In January 1920, as a new decade arrived, General Rozanov had to begin thinking about the future and his family. He formally approached the Japanese government to ask for asylum for himself and his loved ones. He turned over some of the White government's gold reserves for safekeeping, and the empress of Japan granted his wish. He, his wife, his two daughters, and Anna's husband boarded a Japanese minesweeper and made the short trip across the water to Japan.

From there, they watched as the last elements of resistance fell in Russia and the Soviets took full hold of the largest nation in the world. He could only give thanks that he and his son-in-law—not to mention the women he loved—were spared the executions he knew were waiting for so many valued friends. And he wondered what the future might hold for him, as an old Russian warrior who belonged to a land that existed only in memory. Now, at fifty-one, he was a man without a country.

The Rozanovs and Naryshkins lived in a hut in Japan for a short period of time. They would remain grateful to these friends who saved their lives, but their long-term plan was always to make at least one more voyage by sea, this time to the west. When the opportunity came, the small Russian group boarded a ship called the *Andre Lebon* in Yokohama.

At a docking in Shanghai, they were joined by Nikolai Sokolov and his wife, Maria. There was a pleasant reunion between the general and the investigator he'd recommended back in Yekaterinburg. They spoke of Ipatiev House, speculated on the details still left unexplained, and they thought together about their plans for the future. Their first destination should be Italy, where they could make their case to the tsar's uncle.

In their hands was their treasure, Sokolov's box—surely the most mysterious military box in history. In it the investigator had gathered assorted pieces of evidence found at the burial site, from a human finger to the famous scrap of wallpaper with the Belsatsar inscription. These small pieces, clustered in a box that was then packed in a leather suitcase, symbolized the last shreds of hope for justice for the Romanovs and the Russian legacy.

Lenin's agents had done all they could to erase from history the inhuman brutality that had taken place in the House of Special Purpose, because that violence illuminated the lies undergirding sunny Bolshevik promises. There had been a royal family, and all that was left of its rich bloodline were the dark stains in this box. But perhaps these contents could be placed in the hands of the Romanov relatives, or even of the rulers of England or France.

With that hope, Sokolov preserved his papers, his findings, and the evidence in the box within the suitcase—which, during the voyage, was placed beneath Anna's bunk. The Naryshkins were sharing a cabin with the Sokolovs. For the rest of her life, Anna would speak of those days in the presence of these men who were at the center of the greatest crisis in Russian history. As a girl, she'd seen them as hunting partners on the family estate. Now they were figures of global significance. She lay awake nights with the knowledge of those things that lay in the dark, in a box beneath her bed.

The box was never to be left alone. Someone, a Sokolov or a Naryshkin, must have it in clear view at every moment, as if this was the wealth of a nation, rather than scraps of a lost heritage.

The ship took them only so far as Colombo at Ceylon (now Sri Lanka), but after that, they joined another ship bound for Venice. There they settled for a while, marveling, as all people do, at the curiosity of canal-based streets. Without wasting a day, the Sokolovs and Naryshkin sought and attained an audience with Grand Duke Nikolai Nikolaevich, the tsar's uncle. He was visiting Italy and listened quietly to the story of their adventures, particularly what they'd seen in Yekaterinburg.

They wished to present their box of evidence to the family through the grand duke so that through it, the family might seek the truth to be known to the world. But the grand duke wouldn't receive it. The feelings of the tsar's mother were well known. She persisted in the belief that her son and his family were yet alive. Couldn't these two visitors see? It wouldn't do to upset the great lady with this box and the disgusting bits within it. So the small delegation left in disappointment.

What now? Sokolov in particular was surely discouraged. He had traveled across Russia and several seas with his evidence held tight, only to be rebuffed for the petty purposes of spared feelings. It was time to settle somewhere and continue the fight.

The next port of call was France, where Russian expatriates were beginning to gather and create a community. There they settled, the Naryshkins and Sokolovs choosing different towns but maintaining their friendship. Rozanov and Naryshkin, however, got their wives and daughters settled, then slipped back into Russia to fight for Gen. Pyotr Wrangel on the Southern Front. This was the last-ditch effort of the White Army, holding on in Crimea, and many of their former officers and troops were there fighting.

By late in 1920, most of the troops had evacuated, and Rozanov and Naryshkin returned to France. At one point, a Japanese delegation approached Rozanov, asking him to become their viceroy after the Japanese took control of a section of Siberia. The general declined; he couldn't imagine fighting against his own people on Russian soil for another nation. Indeed, the request was an odd one, though it showed the deep respect the general had earned.

France was a good distance from the turmoil, but the expatriates weren't entirely removed from danger. The Soviets were known for using agents to reach across international lines to silence enemies past and present. They were known to have kidnapped and murdered two Russian generals.

In 1925, at the age of forty-two, Nikolai Sokolov died from cardiac arrest while working in his garden. He was known to have a weak heart and was thin, nervous, and prone to headache. His body and mind had borne a heavy load of stress over the past seven years, and heart attacks are possible even at a young age. With chilling prescience, he had recently written to a friend that he was tired and hadn't long to live.

Even so, the death was mysterious. Many in the Russian community believed poison was involved. There was no investigation of the event, and no cause was recorded on the death certificate. Sokolov had continued his investigation, traveling to Germany, then to the United States at the invitation of Henry Ford. He'd also signed a book contract. Sokolov's account of the investigation had appeared in 1924. Did it render him a target? Two weeks after his return from America, he was dead.

What would happen to Sokolov's box? The Russian Orthodox Church ended up with its contents, promising they'd be kept safe, while the box and Sokolov's many notes—plenty of them excised from the final published manuscript—stayed with the family. My grandmother told me that when Sokolov returned from America he visited his friend General Rozanov and showed him his new book. This was a second book; he asked Rozanov to read it and if he should publish it. Rozanov answered: "Only you can decide that." After Sokolov died, his wife kept the book under her bed.

When I visited Sokolov's grandson Jean-Michel Rullon-Sokolov in France, I saw what was left of a possible second unpublished book or perhaps some of the information the publisher had forced him to cut from the original edition. Many photos weren't used because of the reproduction costs at that time, and much of the information was discarded because French audiences weren't interested in the minutiae of the investigation. Perhaps Sokolov had planned a more exhaustive account.

The expatriates had left most of their wealth and property behind them when they fled. But General Rozanov had invested in Sudanese cotton mills years earlier, at the request of his brothers-in-law in France. Now it meant something to have money outside Russia. He used it to buy a small farm in Brittany for the Naryshkins. Kirill and Anna settled there and had a daughter, Anastasia, in 1921. The child was named after the grand duchess, though no one could have foreseen the notoriety that name would attain with the public.

For a while, Kirill worked as a farmer and a carpenter, but he couldn't find contentment in the simpler pleasures of country life. He continued to dream of the glamour and luxury some of his friends continued to enjoy. His cousin Prince Serge Obolensky had married the socialite Lady Astor. In 1928 Kirill served divorce papers to Anna and left for southern France, where the more flamboyant and aristocratic expatriates could be found. Kirill enjoyed music, the social scene, and fine wine, but he also remained involved with fighting Russian communism.

A decade passed, and in October of 1939, just as Europe was once again descending into the flames of all-out war, Kirill's body was found, strangled to death by his own necktie, tied to the bedpost. The ruling was accidental suffocation, but this time the signs of murder were far more obvious. His efforts against the Soviets weren't appreciated by secret police. Years later, Anna heard a rumor that found its way from a German concentration camp. Supposedly a prisoner, just before execution, confessed to Naryshkin's murder. Who knew whether there was truth to the story? Anna had to live with the mystery of a husband who had been with her only for a short time before a questionable death.

He left behind a daughter, Anastasia, who was too young when he left to retain any memories of him. At the age of eighteen, just before her father's death, she determined to travel to the south of France and finally get to know him. But friends counseled against it. Leave it alone, they said; you won't like what you find. He can no longer control his drinking; he's in a sad condition. It would make you very unhappy. Anastasia took the advice. Her father was buried at the Russian cemetery in Nice.

After Kirill left his family, it would have been difficult for Anna to manage a farm on her own, particularly with her daughter. She still had relatives in Russia, but the idea of returning there and submitting to Soviet rule wasn't appealing. Anna finally decided to sell the farm and move to Paris, where she bought an apartment on Rue Pergolèse and took up work as a seamstress.

Anastasia knew the adventure of growing up in Paris, even traveling to England during summer vacations. There she learned the English language, which would be a strong benefit to her future.

By the time World War II came, Anastasia was as practical as her mother, making ladies' shoes out of cork and cloth while supplies were hard to come by. She was a tremendous fan of the music of America's George Gershwin, turning up the volume on her gramophone, even knowing the German SS officer across the street would become angry and slam the windows shut. Perhaps Gershwin's melodies weren't the latest thing in Berlin.

Anastasia reflected the undercover work her mother had done in Russia by assisting the French underground, helping them with train schedules. Courage ran in the blood of Rozanov women, though they surely longed for times when so much of it wasn't necessary.

In 1945 Anastasia met a tall, handsome young man with a wonderful laugh. His name was Alexander Sarandinaki, and he, too, had a dramatic family story of survival during the Bolshevik Revolution. The name Sarandinaki is Greek. Alexander's ancestors had fought the Turks in the eighteenth century, then joined the Russian navy in the time of Catherine the Great—after which they served as captains under John Paul Jones, the American admiral, against the Ottoman Turks. In reward, they were granted land in Russia and became part of the landed gentry.

That was one side of his family. Another great-great-grandfather was a famous Greek pirate who also fought the Turks on behalf of the Russians. His colorful story is depicted in a movie called *Pirate*, in which he is seen traveling an enormous distance on foot to receive his prize from Catherine the Great. He later made a fortune selling caviar, which he'd worked out a way to transport without damaging the delicate eggs. The former pirate used his wealth to assist the Greeks during the Greek Revolution.

Between Alexander and Anastasia, it was difficult to say who had the more heroic bloodline.

Alexander, however, probably had the most compelling personal story. He'd been born in Taganrog, Russia, a port city on the Sea of Azov, during the most desperate days of the Russian Civil War. When he was six months old, his mother decided to visit her husband, who worked on a Red Cross train operated by the White Army. She left her baby with the nanny.

Just after she left, the Red Army took hold of Taganrog. Though Elena, his mother, was aware of this, by then it wasn't safe to go back. She had to leave without her baby, knowing it would be impossible to return.

The nanny realized how much danger she and the child would face, so she took him to her village, where there was better food and shelter—though not much better. She fed him only at night, because no one could know she had food; it would surely have been seized, since she had no man to protect her.

So terrible was the starvation that cannibalism was occurring, but little Alexander was too small and frail to be taken away for that purpose. He nearly died of starvation several times, but somehow his nanny always found something for him and nursed him to health. Months passed, then years, and at age three, his hand froze while he begged for food at the entrance to a church. Alexander had known nothing but dire poverty, and all this time, no one knew where his parents were.

In 1924 a woman who was a friend of the Sarandinakis rushed to tell them their son was alive and in the nanny's home village. Somehow, she had come across this information, and now there was a reunion. Then, in 1927, Alexander was brought to France as a beneficiary of Lenin's New Economic Policy. His parents arranged for him to train as a woodworker at the age of sixteen, and he joined an old and distinguished guild of craftsmen. He became quite adept at his trade, and the excellent training saved his life once the Nazis invaded France.

By that time, Alexander had volunteered for the French Army Engineer Corps. He'd come forward in 1939, but when France quickly gave way to the Germans in 1940 he was sent home again. At first, he applied himself to the study of engineering, seeing this as his future direction. But then he watched what went on around him, and it became clear he'd end up serving the Nazis as a slave worker. He'd be sent to conquered areas to build their bridges and facilities.

So when he was asked for his occupation, Alexander said, "I am a carpenter." The Germans weren't interested; they said they had too many already, and that was good news for a young man who despised the Nazis. He was allowed to stay in France and quietly bide his time for five years, in hopes of liberation for the country.

It was in Tours that Alexander met Anastasia Kirilovna Naryshkina, as the war was finally winding down. The Nazi takeover had failed—the Germans knew it; the French knew it. And it seemed a safe time for a young man to fall in love. Alexander and Anastasia married in Paris the following year, and the joy of being together kept them going in the rubble that was postwar France.

The nation, of course, bore the terrible scars of modern combat, and jobs were few—particularly for a *sale étranger*, the French phrase for a "dirty foreigner."

No matter that he'd been loyal to France for twenty years and suffered with everyone else. This was a time when the French distrusted anyone from outside their borders.

With no job prospects, however, Alexander had an idea. Why not emigrate to Argentina, where Alexander's aunt Asya had lived since the Russian Revolution? Aunt Asya could afford to come to their aid. She had been married at least seven times. Somehow her husbands kept dying, each one leaving her with more wealth. At that point she owned a hotel she'd sentimentally named after her first three husbands: JOCARAL, for Jorge, Carl, and Albert. The name would have been too lengthy and confusing if she'd honored any more of the bunch.

She also owned quite a few farms and restaurants here and there. The possibilities for the young couple seemed endless. Argentina looked to be a promising destination for Alexander and Anastasia.

However, once they arrived in Mar del Plata on the South Atlantic coast, they weren't invited to live in her lovely chalet. Instead, she had a rather rude shack waiting for them. It was furnished with a kerosene stove that was soon hurled out the window because it was useless. The couple bought land and Alexander began building a house and a workshop. His mother-in-law, Anna, soon joined them, having sold her apartment in Paris. She bought a house across the street, delighting her daughter as well as the children who began to arrive.

In 1947 Anastasia gave birth to a daughter, Katherine. Then, in 1949, she carried twins but lost them in a miscarriage. A boy came along in 1950, and they called him Peter. Alexis, a second son, joined the family in 1953, and George in 1956. But heartache seemed inevitable during those years in Argentina. At three years of age, Alexis ran into the street and was killed by a truck. George, too, was hit by a motorcycle; he survived but with brain damage. After so many days of wartime danger for their respective families, it turned out that times of peace brought the most grief. The Sarandinakis again had thoughts of other places, other dreams, and their hopes and prayers were answered in a remarkable way.

The family cherished the story of how Alexander had been protected with love and perseverance by his nanny, during those hellish days in Russia—and how later, a friend found them and reunited the two with Alexander's parents. Now, that same woman, already a blessing to them, turned up to change their lives again. She lived in Sea Cliff, New York, and she found a sponsor to help the family emigrate to the United States.

After fourteen years, marred by the loss of three children and the accident that left another son mentally impaired, the family was again pulling up roots and heading for a new continent, a new culture, and a place that seemed like a suburb of heaven to many White Russians who'd left war-torn Europe. The United States was a nation that welcomed immigrants, and it was prospering. It was possible to build healthy businesses and families there. Anna came along with the Sarandinakis as they left for the United States and sought full citizenship.

Alexander held a Nansen passport, given to refugees who had no countries. He was a Greco-Russian who'd called France and Argentina home. Becoming an American citizen was everything to him; it meant solidity, permanence, and hope for his carpentry career, his wife, his children. On one occasion, he fashioned a beautiful birch conference table for a local hospital where he volunteered. In a newspaper interview, he was asked his age. "I am twenty-seven," he smiled. "I only started to live when I came to America."

Alexander and Anastasia came by themselves first, hoping to establish a foundation. After selling their home and farm in Mar del Plata, they had five thousand dollars to their name. They came through Customs at Miami, Florida, and headed immediately to the Fontainebleau Hotel—at that time, the finest in the city. America must have looked pretty attractive at first glimpse. In their minds, they were still covered with the dust of Argentina. They had struggled there, and they wanted to celebrate the promise of a new life. The money was well spent.

They arrived at their sponsor's home in Sea Cliff, New York, with three hundred dollars remaining but no worries at all. Alexander quickly found work as a carpenter, though an interpreter had to accompany him on jobs. Anastasia sold women's shoes at Lord & Taylor; she had learned English on her trips to England growing up. Many years later, she sold a pair to Svetlana Alliluyeva, the daughter of Joseph Stalin, conversing with her in the native language. Alliluyeva, too, had decided the United States might be a nice place to live. Soon the Sarandinaki children joined them, and the family began the enjoyable work of learning to live in improved conditions.

Anna was happy for them all. Upon entering the United States, she was soon to enjoy her sixtieth birthday. She thought back across her life and all the places she'd been, all the experiences she'd had, all the emotions she'd felt, from the time she'd been frightened as a little girl by the sounds of nighttime peasant unrest. She had come through revolution and civil war, times of danger and deliverance. She'd seen China and Japan, France and Argentina, and now this new destination, a land of freedom. She'd lost friends, relatives, a husband, grandchildren. Perhaps there were still a few sunny days ahead.

Anna's adventures, she knew, were drawing to a close. Now there was time for rest, for the telling of stories. Stories keep the past alive so that we can be instructed and inspired. They show us where we've been, that we may better comprehend where we're going. And all storytellers thrive on eager ears—people who are curious and willing to listen.

Anna found such a listener in me, her grandson, Peter. I couldn't get enough of the accounts she offered, particularly of Russia and the dangers she'd faced. None of my friends had such stories in their families. I asked a thousand questions. But what I wanted most to know about was that box—the one beneath her bunk on the sea voyage; the one bearing a human finger, melted fat, pieces of flooring and wallpaper, even a set of dentures. On one occasion, the box had been opened for her to see.

I saw it all through my imagination. How could a little boy not be fascinated by such things?

The politics seemed complicated and hard to follow—Bolsheviks, White Russians, Red Russians, ruling families, cities with odd names. But in the middle of it all was the image of a family like mine, a family in a little room posing as if for a portrait; a little boy, perhaps one I would have liked to know; and then, a cascade of bullets. Men shooting young girls and a little boy. There was the furtive rush to the woods for a botched burial; the mob of drunken peasants, tearing at the corpses; the mystery of what became of the bodies.

I was haunted by mental images of these things and the questions they raised. And I decided that, if I could find a way, I would be the one to help answer those questions.

Interlude

THE MYSTERY OF ANASTASIA

Public personalities—celebrities, artists, prominent leaders—are, in some respects, public property. They're the living faces of the current culture. When they die, we grieve. We feel we've lost someone we knew, and also something we cherish—something they symbolized. As with the loss of true acquaintances, though, we feel their absence, and we move on.

When such people simply disappear, however, we lack closure. Even if we're certain these people died, the abiding questions gnaw at us. We wonder exactly what happened, and sometimes, we entertain the notion that maybe they live on, in secret. Wouldn't that be wonderful? Maybe they're still out there somewhere, and perhaps they'll come forward, tell their story, and resolve all the questions. And some part of our past will live on with them.

Something of this type occurred with the death of Tsar Nicholas and his family. The idea of that family, those winsome daughters, and small, frail Tsarevich Alexei all being gunned down—surely such a thing couldn't have happened. To Russians of the old guard, to accept the Romanov deaths was to accept the death of the Old World, for these faces were its present and its future. To the public mind, the tsar was surely executed, and probably his family with him. But as for the others—the small ones—there was just room for a fragment of hope. For a miracle.

Nor did it help that Lenin's people refused to come clean. Given the kind of clear, humane leadership they promised, the Bolsheviks weren't going to admit to executing children. Plus, there was a treaty with the Germans, who were formally demanding "the safety of the princesses of German blood."

Thus, Lenin and Trotsky encouraged and even helped spread false rumors of the family's survival. Almost immediately sightings of various Romanovs were reported, and a great many of these rumors centered on the youngest daughter: Grand Duchess Anastasia Nikolaevna. Occasionally there were stories of the young heir Alexei living on, but surely an emperor in waiting wouldn't have been spared.

The year 1920 came. The world was finding its footing again after its most horrific war. In Moscow the Soviet government was falling into place, resistance all but eliminated. And in various countries of the West, Russian refugees were beginning new lives. It was then, two years after the executions, that an event occurred that didn't even register as a significant event. A German policeman pulled a freezing young woman from Berlin's Landwehr canal. Having attempted suicide, she was placed in a mental hospital. The woman refused to identify herself, and she was officially called Miss Unknown by the staff. For the remainder of her life, the title might have been an apt one.

No relative or friend stepped forward to claim her. She was seen and mostly ignored as a disturbed and disturbing patient, given to fits of anger and verbal abuse. But one day, someone in the hospital showed her a magazine with a feature on the Grand Duchess Anastasia, and the rumors of her survival. One of the many photographs of Anastasia was included, and Miss Unknown became fascinated with the picture. "Do you notice anything special about this?" she asked one of the nurses, showing it to her. The nurse shrugged. "Can't you see the similarity?" She held her face next to the picture, but no one saw any particular resemblance.

Miss Unknown began to use the name Anna Tschaikovsky, then Anna Anderson. In 1922 her claim as the last survivor of the tsar's family began to circulate, helped along by Harriet von Rathlef-Keilmann's book that appeared in 1928. Her story was that she had survived the first volley of bullets and had been thought to be dead along with the rest of her family—only to have a kind soldier notice her movements and smuggle her to safety. She married this soldier around the time of giving birth to their child, and when the soldier died in a brawl, she placed the child in an orphanage.

Over the next few decades, with her behavior somewhat erratic, she lived between Europe and America and between asylums and the homes of supporters—including the composer Rachmaninoff, for one. Quite a few Russians met her and came away convinced she was the real thing; others, including most of Nicholas II's relatives, were just as adamant this woman was an impostor.

For one thing, she failed to recognize friends and relatives of the grand duchess. In the early days, she refused to speak Russian, though she seemed to understand it. And why was her memory so selective? She seemed to recall certain details of the royal household well enough and could sound convincing. Yet when questioned in specifics on other simple matters, she became impatient and unwilling to respond.

Yet there always seemed to be the report of a peculiarity with her feet that matched that of Anastasia, or her knowledge of an obscure story that only the youngest daughter of the tsar would supposedly have known. There were constant comparisons of her ears with Anastasia's, and a seeming match.

The grand duchess's aunt, Olga Alexandrovna, who had known Anastasia well, fully accepted the identification, and she begged her relatives to join her in welcoming their prodigal daughter back to the family. It was true that Anna Anderson's memories were lacking, said Aunt Olga, and that her behavior could be questionable at times. But hadn't she been through an unthinkably traumatic experience? Would any of us have come through such an event without mental and emotional scars?

One of her most enthusiastic advocates was none other than the son of Dr. Botkin, who had attended the Romanovs in Ipatiev House and who had summoned them to the cellar room to die and be buried with them. Gleb Botkin first met Anna Anderson at Seeon Abbey in Bavaria, one of her many temporary residences. When she heard he was coming, Anderson asked him to "bring along his funny animals," which matched a memory of Botkin's. He was a true survivor of Ipatiev, having spent time with the royal family, played with the children, told them stories, then escaped the scene of terror via Japan. One year older than Anastasia, he was utterly taken with the idea that his friend could have survived, and he devoted much of his life to crusading for the world's acknowledgment of her true identity. Supporters such as these kept Anna and her story going.

There were also the other rumors adding flavor to the mystery—stories of enormous wealth stashed in London banks by the Romanovs just before the revolution. Where was the royal fortune, and could this claimant place her hands on it? In 1927 Ernest Louis, grand duke of Hesse and the brother-in-law of Nicholas II, funded an investigation of the woman who insisted she was the heir.

His detective identified her as a Polish worker named Franziska Schanzkowska. This woman had a history of mental illness and had disappeared with perfect timing to appear as another woman—at, significantly, a mental hospital. Schanzkowska's family members stepped forward to say that yes, this was their sister.

Miss Unknown said she'd never seen these people in her life.

What was known about the Polish woman? Franziska Schanzkowska was born to a large peasant family on December 24, 1896, in the village of Borovilhas between Pomerania and West Prussia. She seemed a bright child, a good student at school, and good with languages. Her father doted on her and proclaimed she'd be responsible for no household chores. It's not surprising, then, that Franziska had trouble getting along with her siblings. In 1914, still a teenager, she traveled to Berlin and took employment as a maid to a wealthy family. This would have given her a taste of the luxurious life—something more than simply avoiding housework. Afterward, she worked as a bakery waitress.

Schanzkowska also had a taste for changing identities, as she took a new surname, Shantskovsku. Perhaps she didn't want to be found by her family or someone else. At eighteen, she took a factory job assembling grenades, and she married a young soldier who then died on the front during the Great War. (As Anna Anderson she claimed her Russian soldier husband had died in some kind of brawl.) A 1951 gynecological examination showed Schanzkowska either gave birth at some point or had a late-term abortion.

In 1916 she was involved in a tragic incident. She apparently fainted at work, and a grenade fell from her hands, rolled across the floor, and exploded, killing her supervisor. She received a few wounds, which might have later been blamed on mistreatment at Ipatiev House. This was a decisive event in Schanzkowska's life. She had a severe nervous breakdown soon afterward and was sent to a psychiatric hospital—where, again, she played fast and loose with her identity.

From then on, she was transferred to a series of clinics and hospitals, one after another. Ultimately, she was released and sent home to the care of her mother.

Now, farther than ever from the good life, Schanzkowska worked as a farm laborer at a site adjacent to a camp for Russian prisoners of war. She might have heard a good bit of the Russian tongue there. But in fall 1918, as the war was ending, one of the Russian soldiers attacked and beat her with something like a pitchfork. Again, there were scars and lost teeth, in keeping with what Anna Anderson later demonstrated. Schanzkowska wandered back to Berlin, where she was often heard complaining about terrible headaches in her rooming house.

It's here that the trail goes cold. Franziska Schanzkowska seems to have vanished just as a desperate young woman was pulled from a Berlin canal. It's hard to imagine she would have submitted to months or years of additional hospital life. Perhaps she would finally have succeeded in taking her own life were it not for a magazine article that fell into her hands at the right moment—in much the same way that a book on the same subject fell into her husband's hands many years later.

The woman who took on more new names—first Mrs. Tchaikovsky, then Anna Anderson—and spent thirty-one years in Germany, much of it trying to establish her identity through litigation in the longest German trial on record. There were times when she indeed attained the life of luxury she craved, being visited and entertained by White Russians and the curious. The only problem was the incessant questioning. She expressed little interest in the old Romanov story, or talking about her departed family, or giving proof of her identity. She just wanted enough credibility to live a comfortable life.

In the end, the German court made no judgment on who she was; it wasn't proven or disproven, legally. What mattered was she had failed to meet the burden of proof that she was a Romanov.

Interest in her began to wane. She was now seldom pampered in castles and glamorous homes. As she grew older and even more erratic, her little home, a former army barracks, fell into poor repair and was prowled by sixty cats and a few dogs. Tourists came to peek over the fence. When she was found in a coma one day, she was hospitalized again, and finally accepted Gleb Botkin's invitation to come back to the United States, where she spent her final sixteen years.

It was at this time that she met Jack Manahan, a wealthy history professor.

In the early years, the Russian communities in various countries followed the Anna Anderson matter with great interest and mixed reactions. Olga Tolstoy was one of the believers. She was the granddaughter of Mikhail Rodzianko, the Duma chairman who figured so strongly in the abdication of Nicholas II. Her husband was the grandson of Leo Tolstoy, the great author. And years later, her daughter Masha would marry me.

Olga had an unintended but momentous impact on the Anna Anderson story. Her son, Michael, happened to borrow a friend's copy of Rathlef-Keilmann's book *Anastasia, a Woman's Fate as Mirror of the World Catastrophe*. Olga picked up the volume and found it fascinating and highly credible.

Then, in 1959, with the book in hand, she traveled with her daughter Masha to Bermuda. Masha had been diagnosed with double pneumonia, and fresh sea air was recommended. Olga happened to have a good friend named Svetlana Umrichin in Bermuda, where her husband, Nicholas Umrichin, was involved in the construction of an airport. Olga then loaned the borrowed book to Svetlana, and Svetlana, in turn, handed the book to her old student, Dr. John (Jack) Manahan. He'd been a history professor at the University of Virginia in Charlottesville. Manahan, like so many readers, was spellbound by the story. His great passion in life was genealogy and family trees, and this woman, with her allegedly royal blood, fascinated him. He flew to Germany after meeting Gleb Botkin and learning Anna's address.

By 1968 life in Germany had just about played out for Anna Anderson. Her health wasn't good. Her sixty cats and various dogs had been taken from her and put down. Neighbors were tired of the awful smells and the constant traffic of the curious. Gleb Botkin said there was always a place for her in the United States, and she decided to accept the invitation.

The next thing Olga and her friend Svetlana knew, they were receiving invitations to the wedding of Jack Manahan and the Grand Duchess Anastasia. They were flabbergasted. How had this happened? All by loaning a book? They discussed the proper protocol for greeting the daughter of Nicholas II (should they curtsy? kiss her hand?) but in the end, there was no money for travel, and they simply sent their congratulations.

Jack sent Svetlana a photograph and words of gratitude for leading him to meet his wife. The traveling book had done quite a bit of work.

Anna Anderson-Manahan lived in this curious marriage until 1984, when she passed away; her ashes were buried in the churchyard of Castle Seeon in Germany. At the time, the last traces of her, for the purpose of identification, were missing, just as they were for the Romanovs (as far as the public knew, that is). It seemed her true identity would remain a mystery forever.

Time passed, and people began to forget, other than the occasional TV movie or *Unsolved Mysteries* documentary. Life moved on. Some, like Olga, passed on in the firm belief that Miss Unknown/Anna Tschaikovsky/Anna Anderson-Manahan was truly the last surviving member of her royal family. Others remained adamant she was an impostor.

By 1993 Olga's daughter Masha, whose illness initiated the fateful connection in Bermuda, had grown to adulthood and married me, a sea captain. We shared distinguished Russian genealogies, and I, in particular, was still taken with the idea of finding and identifying the remains of the Romanovs. In 1993 the Russian Expert Commission Abroad (RECA) invited me to participate in a meeting in New York City. The group felt there was unfinished business in the question of the mystery woman, now dead for almost a decade. The science of DNA was opening all kinds of new possibilities. But cremation meant there was no basis to conduct any meaningful test.

I spoke to a former East German police investigator named Willi Korte, who also happened to live in Virginia. I asked Korte, "Why not check all the local hospitals in Charlottesville? There could be X-rays or something else we could use."

Korte did some investigation and found that indeed the woman had been at the Martha Jefferson Hospital in 1979 for a colon operation. More important, it was common procedure for the hospital to save samples of tissue. This was amazing news. Now there was the possibility that something could finally be done.

I worked through channels other than RECA afterward, focusing more on search and scientific proof. But I attended the meeting that set forth the process of answering the question of Anastasia.

After some time, the hospital admitted that a viable tissue sample was available for DNA testing. That's when the battle broke out. Who was in charge here? There were no children, no immediate family members—Anna's husband had followed her in death six years later. Increasing the public interest, it had recently been announced that remains had been located near Yekaterinburg, but that *Anastasia's* remains seemed to be missing. This was the first time there was any reason to give credence to the rumors. The youngest daughter may have survived that basement after all. Now, with DNA identification, the late claimant finally seemed to have a chance for vindication.

At this point, Marina Botkin Schweitzer stepped forward. She was the only daughter of Gleb Botkin, and granddaughter of Dr. Botkin, who had died with the Romanovs—and she and her husband had been friends of Jack and Anastasia Manahan. Through her husband, Richard Schweitzer, she sought standing before the court. Her position was that her grandfather had been a victim of the crime in Yekaterinburg, and his remains were part of this story. For these physical reasons, and also the historic loyalty of the Botkins to the Romanovs, Marina Schweitzer should be able to petition the court for access to the remains for DNA testing.

Things then grew incredibly complicated and frustrating. In a memo, Schweitzer told me what had happened after the suggestion to Korte to check Charlottesville hospitals. It was a careful, orderly memo that he promised to expand upon in the future. His position was only that he and his wife had pure motives. They were requesting rights for the hospital to release the remains for testing—nothing more. The Schweitzers were not seeking any personal gain, control, or possession. They wanted the scientific work cross-checked. And they were willing to pay all costs.

But Virginia law was a little vague on the point of who could have a say in the use of bodily remains. And another party now became involved: the Russian Nobility Association (RNA), in partnership with Anastasia Kailing-Romanov, who claimed to be the long-lost child of Anna Anderson—thus the heir to whatever might belong to Anna. This party was working through a powerful Washington, DC, law firm, plus another firm in the Commonwealth of Virginia.

To the Schweitzers' disappointment, the judge allowed the RNA group to participate. The group promptly sought to block the Schweitzers' requests on grounds of prejudice, suggesting the Schweitzers couldn't be trusted. They further held that the scientist engaged by Marina—Dr. Peter Gill—wasn't up to the task. They wanted to use another scientist, Dr. Mary Claire King at Berkeley.

When Dr. King heard about this, she was upset, and approached Marina, asking if she and Dr. Gill could simply work in tandem. She had the utmost respect for her fellow DNA scientist. Yet after that, she bowed out. There seemed to have been some form of legal pressure. The Schweitzers were concerned at this point that the whole proceeding had gone off the rails and become a mockery.

The concern was that the RNA group was seeking full control of the testing that had already been arranged. But then, as an impasse developed, the German executor of "Anastasia's" wills stepped forward as if from the heavens. The executor affirmed they could meet the requirements of Virginia medical record laws and then honor the Schweitzers' desires. So the Schweitzers withdrew their earlier petition, an action that sidelined the RNA group—which then threatened legal action to keep the hospital from allowing *anyone at all* access to the tissue. It was a scorched-earth maneuver.

But the RNA request was denied. The German executor had just what the judge was looking for, and the hospital was fully satisfied in releasing the tissue samples. Now all the legal warfare died down, the theatrics vanished, and the scientists were free to do their work.

In October 1995 the results were in. The news leaked a few days before the formal announcement. DNA from Anna Anderson-Manahan's colon sample showed no match with the Romanov line. After seventy-five years of questions, she could now be labeled an impostor or, at best, a victim of delusions of grandeur. She was not Anastasia, the grand duchess.

The scientists also analyzed blood donated by Carl Maucher, the great-nephew of Franziska Schanzkowska, the Polish woman who was most likely the true identity of Miss Unknown. She had vanished at the same time the claimant had appeared. Members of her family had positively identified her in Germany.

The DNA result found an undeniable match, suggesting Carl Maucher was a maternal relative of Anna Anderson, the woman in question. In the end, after all the controversy, after all the books and novels and Hollywood films—one of them starring Ingrid Bergman—it all seemed to be no more than a case of a woman in a mental hospital, fresh off a suicide attempt, spotting a magazine story that suggested a possible future.

Yet to many who believed, a great number of questions remained. What about the tantalizing physical matches—the curvature of the thumb, the transverse flat feet, the identical ear? What about those experts who mapped out the face and skull, declaring they were in perfect accord? What about the handwriting samples?

Some of it was a stretch. Some coincidental. And some, apparently, falsified. The greater portion of the comparisons were subjective, such as handwriting and ear comparisons. These are open to observers seeing what they want to see, and there was no shortage of people who wanted to see something that introduced a grace note, a fairy tale ending for a historical act of brutality. Others saw the possibility of attaching themselves to fame or even a claim to the supposed Romanov fortune (which didn't exist).

Some suggested marvels seem too good to be true, yet "evidence" has a way of collecting. People will offer their "proof" that John F. Kennedy Jr. survived his plane crash, or that their late parents visited them at a séance. Our power to believe is deeply entangled with our desire to hope. But in the end, that which seems too good to be true usually is.

In 1997, well after the case was utterly closed, 20th Century Fox released a full-length animated cartoon called *Anastasia*. The producers talked about the incredible detail of the film, using actual dresses, toys, and the spaniel owned by the real Anastasia. They sought to capture her well-known mischievousness. Yet in this version, the claimant who steps forward turns out to be the real thing. Rasputin appears as an actual sorcerer, plotting behind the scenes out of his hatred for the Romanovs. (The real Rasputin was killed in 1916.) For those paying little attention to headlines or true history, the movie studio once again revived the myth, including some of the myths about Rasputin. But not to worry—they got some of the dresses and toys right.

But in the world of truth, the book was finally closed on Franziska Schanzkowska—except for a lingering question. Could she have been a project of the Soviets to create discord in the West? Might that explain some of her knowledge of matters inside the royal household? A few observers had that suspicion, and it wasn't baseless. Operation Trest was a counterintelligence operation of the Soviet Main Intelligence Directorate between 1921 and 1926. The idea was to set up fake anti-Bolshevik groups that would attract and thus identify true activists the Soviets might want to silence. This organization kidnapped and murdered the White Army's Gen. Alexander Kutepov, who had worked with General Rozanov in Moscow. Could they have used a false Anastasia as some kind of magnet for White Russians?

In short, investigator Vladimir Soloviev scoffed at the idea. "I think nobody knew about Anna Anderson in the USSR, and she was of no interest to anyone," he told me. He detected no signs that this disturbed woman was a foreign asset.

The mystery of Anastasia was solved. But as the nineties moved on, there were revelations from Yekaterinburg—and the central mystery was reopened.

PART 2

Peter's Story

10

Americanizing

The United States has always seen itself as a city upon a hill. The phrase goes back to the Sermon on the Mount in the Bible but became associated with the American Experiment as early as John Winthrop's 1630 sermon in Plymouth. President John F. Kennedy quoted the sermon and revived the phrase in 1961, setting forth the ideal that the United States could be a beacon of hope for struggling people across the globe.

During that same year of 1961, my sister, Kathy, and I traveled from Argentina and joined our parents in Sea Cliff, New York. Our parents had made the change from France to Argentina in years past, so they knew what it was like to begin in a new and very different culture. For Kathy and me, this transition was much more profound. We admired how our parents had quickly established themselves in the White Russian community of Sea Cliff, and how they were already adopting American ways.

Sea Cliff was a special destination for those who had fled Russia. It's a small village on the North Shore of Long Island, and it sits upon a 120-foot bluff, looking out to sea. From the late 1800s it had become a place for New Yorkers to spend the summer, or perhaps to settle, with its many beautiful and historic Victorian homes. During the 1920s, just after the Russian Revolution, a few refugee families had gathered in the Upper West Side of New York City. They found work, did well, and in time began to vacation a short drive away in Sea Cliff. They would rent *dachas* (cottages). In 1932 a man named Malitsky had the idea of renting a larger home and opening it to his friends. This was on Prospect Avenue, on the water. It was nicknamed Versailles and became a welcome place for Russians in that era.

Within the next decade, a handful of Russian families moved to Sea Cliff directly, bypassing New York City. Soon there was a petition asking for an Orthodox church for the community—the closest one was out of reach because of wartime gas rationing. Our Lady of Kazan was quickly built with the help of a local architect; an old garage and property belonging to Boris Ryabov was sold into a chapel. The church attracted many more Russian families, and it was enlarged twice before my family arrived. In 1961, when Kathy and I showed up, there were 120 families in the church, and it was a packed house every Sunday. We were part of the Russian Orthodox Church of America, which meant we still reported to the church bureaucracy in Moscow.

There was some controversy over our church asking for total freedom from the church in Moscow. Having anything at all to do with those in the Soviet Union—even *asking* for separation from them—was frowned upon, and some of the families left to join another Orthodox church over on Carpenter Avenue, this one affiliated with the Russian Orthodox Church Outside of Russia. That sector was formed after the 1917 revolution, in defiance of the revolution. Those who now joined this other church believed you should ask nothing at all from anyone in Moscow; you should just turn your back and walk away.

Our Lady of Kazan was smaller after the mass exodus, and there was a bit less unity in the Russian community in Sea Cliff. This reflected the uncomfortable transition of trying to honor Russian heritage in a world where Russia was now connected to communism. All of us may have hated Soviet communism more than other Americans because it had robbed us of our land and our tradition.

My father observed it more from his vantage point as a Frenchman, since he had only married into all these Russian questions. He couldn't see a good reason to leave a church where he was comfortable. "If you put ten beautiful women in front of me, I can tell you who's the prettiest," he said. "But to make this choice? Choosing another church over the one I know—that's something I cannot do." So we remained at Our Lady of Kazan. I became an altar boy in the church, assisting the priest and deacon.

There was no question our new town was a lovely one. My first experience with the United States was the kind of place people go on vacations, and it was dominated by my beloved ocean, so I had no complaints. But it was difficult for two kids who spoke no English. I was quite happy to meet a girl in my fifth-grade class who spoke Spanish, as well as two other boys who knew Russian. One of those was my cousin Nick, so it was also nice to have a sense of family around. And I had other cousins there in Sea Cliff as well.

But I was on my guard, too, being the new kid. We'd lived in a poor community in Argentina, and I'd learned how to fight when someone was looking for trouble. I didn't immediately understand the difference between a poor town in South America and a resort town in New York—I just assumed the kids here were also looking for a rumble. But I was wrong; everything was more relaxed. This was one of my first impressions: in the United States, fewer fistfights.

I made a friend named Bob Marsden, who invited me to his home to watch the NFL championship game in 1961. Of course, football was another difference between the United States and everywhere else. They wore helmets and carried a ball that wasn't round. He taught me how to play this game, then another American-made game—baseball. Kids in America loved these games, and their heroes were the professionals who played them. Everyone here seemed to have a television set for watching the games.

Bob got me into baseball and Little League, and once I even hit a home run. It was a lot easier to learn these games than it was to speak the language. But over the next few years, Kathy and I became fluent in English. It wasn't until I could speak English as well as everyone else that I really felt this was my home, that I belonged here, and that I was as good as anyone else. I began to think of myself as an American as I grew older. It wasn't too difficult considering how many of my friends were also new to this country.

We retained our sense of Russian heritage, in my case particularly because of the stories my grandmother told me. I knew that on my mother's side, Russia was in my blood. It was the same for my friends and relatives. My cousins Vladimir, Gregory, and Nicholas Svetlovsky were born in Canada and France. I had other friends who'd come from Germany and, in one case, Mongolia.

In 1961 I joined Saint George's Pathfinders, which was part of the Russian Youth Scouting organization. The USSR had long since banned that group, as they did anything that didn't overtly promote communism. Nicholas II had created it in 1908, in the wake of Robert Baden-Powell's international scouting movement, and Tsarevich Alexei was the original Russian scout. What was most valuable about the organization for émigrés was that we were taught Russia's history and religion. Other scouting groups don't do that.

It was odd having Russian blood while growing up in a country in which most citizens would have said the country they hated most was Russia. This was the height of the Cold War, and we had to go through the bomb drills along with elementary school children across the nation. We'd kneel facing the hallway wall and keep our heads down between our legs, lest my mother's home country drop bombs on us.

A year after we arrived, the Cuban Missile Crisis occurred, and again there was a terrifying tension between our new home and the Soviet Union. Some people worried about Soviet agents coming to America and infiltrating all kinds of organizations, due to books like J. Edgar Hoover's *Masters of Deceit: The Story of Communism in America and How to Fight It*. The idea was that Red infiltrators could be lurking behind every bush, even though those would be Soviets and not White Russians like us. But I didn't experience much anti-Russian sentiment. My friends would have identified me as the kid who'd moved from Argentina. My last name was Greek. I was mostly able to enjoy life the way most American kids were doing, and I was growing more and more American all the time, particularly after the language barrier was overcome.

But one day, I was walking along with my cousin Nick when a group of kids stepped out in front of us. "Your friend here is a Russian," they told me. "And we're going to give him a beating."

"You'll have to fight us both, then," I told them, stepping forward. It wasn't just about Nick being my cousin. He was my friend, and to me, friends stood up for each other. I think I gave the impression of someone who'd been through his share of fights, so the gang of kids backed down pretty quickly. The odds were no longer so appealing.

I guess if my last name had been Ivanov or Smirnoff, I might have been singled out more often. But what was I, anyway? A Russian? An Argentine? Was I American? Greek? Sometimes I felt like the neighborhood mutt who was a mix of several breeds. Even though the United States was the great melting pot, particularly around New York City, there were so many Americans who were born here and had an identity that was just *American*, period.

I didn't worry much about it. There was too much fun to be had on the streets and along the shore in Sea Cliff. I enjoyed the sense of family in the Russian community, and I was enjoying team sports and school activities in the American community. Slowly I felt the undertow pulling me, as it does all immigrants in time, to the American community. I was blending in.

As a teenager in 1966, I became an American citizen on the same proud day my parents did. We knew we'd found our home, since we had the best of both worlds: Russian friends and relatives, yet also a free country, and a booming economy where my father could build a thriving business from his mastery of carpentry. And my future could be whatever I chose.

That future had begun to take shape very early in my life, as I watched U.S. naval ships sail into our port of Mar del Plata in Argentina. Ships fascinated me the way horses or cars or airplanes have fascinated children in other times and places. Growing up, I never lived away from a coastline. These ships came in over the horizon, left the same way, and suggested exotic worlds and boundless adventures. At the age of six, I would take wood scraps from my father's shop and fashion them into toy boats, setting them down in the muddy, rain-filled tracks of horse carriages. It was crude, but my imagination saw great vessels steaming across the globe.

As I sat and studied the harbor, I knew long before we moved that I wanted to be an American naval officer. And arriving in Sea Cliff, with its lofty, picturesque view of the blue horizon, did nothing to avert my hopes. Onward through my classes at North Shore High School in Glen Head, New York, I held onto my ambition of going to sea with the navy. I got my high school diploma in 1968 and enrolled immediately at the State University of New York Maritime College, located in the Bronx, and graduated in 1972 with a degree in meteorology and oceanography, Third Mate's U.S. Coast Guard license.

I received my commission as ensign, U.S. Navy, and I was ready to see the world. I had many directions to choose from. I worked through my apprenticeship as a young sailor, and at age thirty-two, I stepped on board my first ship as master.

During these years, I was as consumed with my progress in the maritime world as most young men are with their own careers. I thought less often of those stories told by my grandmother—stories of another time and place, of war and revolution, and of a box that held within it the keys to a mystery. But that world, too, was in my blood.

I was still a young ship's mate when I visited for the first time the land that Anna had fled.

11

Leningrad

My first job after graduation was on the research vessel *Robert D. Conrad.* I spent six months in the South Atlantic. I enjoyed my work, and I was comfortable spending so much time on ships. I'd chosen the right career. But I wanted to experience the real merchant marines of that era, moving important cargo across the oceans. I also had my eye on a master's in oceanography.

I talked my way into graduate school at City College of New York. I also worked as assistant dean of students at the Maritime College; I'd graduated from it just two years earlier. At the time, I was engaged, so I had to look toward having a marriage and a seagoing or scientific career. But the relationship didn't work out. Now I could just focus on sailing. I gave myself eight years to get a U.S. Coast Guard unlimited master's license.

It was my colleague Walter Nelson who introduced me to the personnel manager at American Export-Isbrantsen Lines, where I was able to sail as third and then second mate. AEL was the leading shipping company between the U.S. East Coast and the Middle East and Far East regions when I was beginning my career on the sea. I knew I needed a year of sailing as third mate and to pass a three-day exam from the coast guard to get that second mate's license. Beyond that was the goal of chief mate.

Somehow, I found time to have a social life; that can be a challenge when you spend much of your time somewhere beyond the horizon. But I stayed active in the Russian community, and in 1974 my cousin Greg Svetlovsky and I decided to attend the Petroushka Ball at the Plaza Hotel in New York City. For more than fifty years, the ball has been held as an important charitable event for the Russian Children's Welfare Society. It's named after the Russian puppet character.

In the early seventies, the ball was still held under the patronage of Princess Vera of Russia, the last member of the Romanov dynasty to be born in Russia. She was a great-granddaughter of Tsar Nicholas I of Russia and had escaped Russia at the age of twelve.

For Greg and me, this was a wonderful place to socialize with others who shared our heritage. As we gazed across the crowded ballroom, one young lady caught my eye. She was walking across the dance floor. Greg seemed to know just about everyone in that community, so I leaned over and asked, "Who is that one?" gesturing toward the girl.

"Oh, that's Masha Tolstoy."

"Really?" Everyone knew the significance of the name Tolstoy. Very few Russian names were household words in America—apart from Lenin, Stalin, Tchaikovsky, and Leo Tolstoy, author of *War and Peace* and *Anna Karenina*. I was eager to meet her, but our paths didn't cross at the dance. I wondered if I'd ever see this beautiful young lady again.

In December of that year, I signed on as third officer on board an AEL vessel going to Leningrad in the Soviet Union.

We brought massive loads overseas. For this job, our ship, the SS *Exford*, was carrying a truck factory to Leningrad and backloading plywood and vodka on the return trip. This was only the second American vessel to dock in the Soviet Union during the Cold War. I was excited and a little nervous.

The SS *Exford* was a six-hatch break-bulk ship built in 1946, and she would sail for only three more years, being scrapped about the same time as the company itself. I was the only one on board who spoke Russian, but our captain, Peter Kanellos, wanted me to keep that to myself. Let them think we didn't understand what they said to each other in our presence. An old trick but a useful one—or at least, it *would* have been.

Once we'd docked, the Russian dockers came on board to discharge the cargo. We set about unloading a set of large wooden crates, lashed with wire. I stood atop the no. 3 hatch and instructed more than a hundred longshoremen, using both English and sign language, to remove the lashing, coil it up, and stow it all under the winches.

One of them told me, with highly creative expletives, where I could shove the wiring. Naturally, he said it all in his native tongue. He probably figured I'd catch his drift without knowing the precise translation.

I came right back at him in English, dropping F-bombs between the nouns with precision. He glared back in surprise, then barked out another stream of profanity, this time explicating on my manhood. The only lashing going on was a tongue-lashing.

By this time, all the longshoremen were laughing and gathering around to watch, but that manhood challenge was about all I could take. I answered with the most potent invectives I had, based on some really next-level Russian profanity my father had taught me.

The forward part of the ship fell silent but for the creaking of the crane hook as it moved back and forth. Someone shouted in Russian, "Hey, he's one of us!"

And just like that, I was surrounded by local men asking questions. Some of them were curious where I'd learned to speak their language that well. You don't learn those words in a high school language course.

I told them I'd just picked it up while at anchor. Of course, they knew that an American ship in their harbor was extremely rare.

But they didn't particularly care. What really interested them was what I had for them to buy. Anyone who was ever in America had access to things not available in the Soviet Union. We brought chewing gum, umbrellas (the type that pop open), panty hose, blue jeans, and other assorted treasures. It's amazing what wasn't available or accessible behind the Iron Curtain. So I had the chance to do a little bartering. It was also an opportunity to learn who I could trust because some of the longshoremen reported anything sketchy to the KGB or the police.

A ruble was worth $1.40, but American dollars weren't usually available (or legal) to them. We sold them a black-market rate of $1 for every 15 rubles. I was rich in rubles quickly, but what was really worth buying in Soviet Leningrad? I purchased a kilo of black beluga caviar and brought it back home. My father ate it by the spoonful. He said, "I'm the only carpenter in the world who eats caviar for lunch."

I'd heard about Russia all my life from my grandmother, but I didn't view this as the same Russia. This was the Soviet Union, I was an American, and this was our enemy. I wasn't a political person, and I didn't feel any real kinship to this country other than to hate communism. Leningrad was just another port out of many I would visit.

But at night, after I'd gone to sleep, the longshore bosses and port officials would come knocking at my door, whispering. Here in privacy, they wanted to know what was going on in the world—including in their own country. They figured I had access to the truth and they didn't. The government controlled their press, and they knew they were fed lies and propaganda on a daily basis.

One of them asked me to pass on to the people at Voice of America radio that the broadcasts should talk more about what was happening in the Soviet Union. They were starving for honest information. Again, I told myself, *I'm not political, I don't care about all this stuff.* But the earnestness of these people, their hunger for freedom, left a huge impression on me.

This was a significant matter, doing business in the Soviet Union. After Franklin D. Roosevelt, no American president visited the USSR until Richard Nixon in 1972. Détente began in 1969, when Nixon and Kissinger sought to strengthen relations with both the Soviets and the Chinese. But things were still a bit tense on the waterfront. We were confined to the ship at night, which isn't appreciated when you've been out at sea for a while and want to get on dry land, maybe explore the town. Only the captain was given shore privileges, but none of ours took advantage of them.

Soldiers were posted to make sure we didn't slip out. We had a good time gathering up snowballs and pelting them from the decks. All they could do was point their pistols at us. You can't return gunfire from a snowball attack. We blasted them with a good bit of American rock 'n' roll too.

Security was very tight. I couldn't even read the draft of the ship without leaving my seaman's documents at the foot of the gangway. They'd be returned when I went back on board.

Not that these security measures stopped any black-market trading. Wherever there's security, there's an inventive mind to breach it. One of the third mates would stock up with gum, panty hose, or other items at the Port of Baltimore, and we'd sell our contraband on the ship. The longshoremen would then stow their purchases in the garbage dumpster brought onboard by crane. This dumpster was actually the cargo bed of a truck. It discharged, again by crane, right onto the truck itself, conveyed directly over the heads of the soldiers whose job it was to keep this kind of thing from happening. Again, we had to laugh about the gun-toting guards.

Everything went smoothly until the day a platoon of soldiers marched right up the gangway and headed for the captain's office. The leader claimed we were harboring an American spy—a Black man who wore a white uniform, in their words. The only people we had who matched that description were in the steward department.

Captain Kanellos summoned the steward and his men. As soon as they arrived, the soldiers pointed to Jackson, the second cook. "This man is the spy!"

"Why do you think that?" I asked.

"Each day, at the same time, this man goes to the bow of the ship. He puts on headgear with two antennae, and he turns the dial left and right—spying!"

I looked at Jackson. He said, "I ain't no spy, mate. Just listening to my radio."

"Go get it," I ordered him. He did so, we showed the radio to the Soviet officer, and I put on the earphones and turned on the radio. I got mostly static; we were surrounded by metal, which interferes with radio signals.

I called the officer a fool, saying, "You are a *durak*, man! This is an ordinary radio."

The officer glared back; the soldiers looked at each other, and all they could do was leave with their heads down and the full intention of getting revenge on me later. Which they tried.

Reading the draft is an essential task on a cargo ship—something I did every day. Large, white draft marks on the bow and stern show how deep a vessel is in the water. The heavier the cargo, of course, the lower the ship lies, so the mark rises or falls as cargo is loaded or offloaded. From the difference in drafts and a little math, we can measure approximately how many tons of cargo have been discharged.

One day, as I was handing the Soviet guard my documents so I could go read the draft, I spotted a lovely blonde girl checking cargo information. After I'd been looking at nothing but longshoremen and Soviet soldiers, she was particularly easy on the eye.

I introduced myself as third mate on an American ship. She smiled and told me her name was Anna Tikhanova, and I immediately asked her to go out to dinner with me. She agreed, and we made plans to meet at the bus stop outside the port and find a restaurant from there.

I was in a good mood. On the way out, I saw the stevedore manager. Stevedores are like longshoremen, but they manage cargo operations. I asked him how he liked the seat belts I'd bought him for his car; seat belts were yet another luxury in the Soviet Union, apparently. Americans ignored them and took them for granted, while Russians coveted them. Their cars had no seat belts.

The man leaned toward my ear and said, "Please don't speak loudly. We don't want other people listening in." That comment stuck with me. It summarized a whole nation in one sentence. We just weren't as furtive and suspicious as people were used to being over there.

Our dinner that evening was at the Astoria. This was the restaurant at which Hitler had planned to have his celebratory dinner after taking Leningrad—something that never took place. I was enjoying my date. I looked into Anna's eyes and said, "I wish we had candlelight." And just as I said it, all the power in the hotel went out. Waiters brought candles, and I had my wish.

Maybe it wasn't considered so romantic in Leningrad, however, since the power went out regularly in countries behind the Iron Curtain. I also remember feeling under the table for microphones. I guess the stevedore manager had me looking over my shoulder.

But the date went well and was followed by several more. I noticed that Anna seemed to have only one nice dress for these occasions, so I asked my mother to buy three new ones for her. I knew there would be another trip to Leningrad, and on my return, I could make Anna a little gift. I just needed to be discreet about it. The Soviets were serious about not letting their people have anything nice. On the next trip I met Anna outside the port, in our usual spot, and unwrapped the scarf around my neck—it was one of the dresses. She was delighted.

The next day, I brought her the others, this time wrapped around my waist. But the guards had their eyes on me. As I walked down the gangway, the guard stepped up and commanded me to open my coat. He lifted a Tokarev pistol and pointed it at my heart. I looked up at the bridge wing of the ship, where our captain was looking down upon the scene, and said, "I think I'm in trouble."

Immediately I heard a siren, and here came a military car at full speed, racing along the dock. Soldiers with machine guns and plainclothes inspectors hopped out, swarmed around me, and commanded me to sit in the back of the car.

I took mental inventory of my situation. For one thing, there were plenty of illegal rubles in my pocket, and I had no proof of where I'd exchanged my money to acquire them. Worse, though, I carried a piece of paper with the names and phone numbers of people I'd met in Leningrad. If these names were associated with me, the Soviet authorities would have a list of people to harass.

"May I smoke?" I asked in Russian. They nodded, and I removed a pack of Marlboros from my shirt pocket; simultaneously I was pulling out that slip of paper. I slowly balled it up while I lit my cigarette and smoked, then casually threw both items out the window at the same time.

We stopped at the gate. "What is your position on the ship?" asked a plainclothes cop.

"Third officer," I replied in his language.

"You speak Russian?"

"Yes. My grandmother taught me."

He stared at me for a second, then he picked up a nearby phone. After he returned, he gave instructions, and I was rushed to the jail at a fast clip. I was thinking, *That's all, folks. I'll be sent to Siberia, left in a gulag, and nobody will ever hear from me again.* I was the first of my family to set foot back in Russia. After all my grandmother and her family did to escape, after the high price they paid to leave everything behind and get to the West—how sad if I let myself get caught this easily, over a few dresses to impress a girl.

Before we arrived at our destination, the car lurched into a U-turn and screeched to a halt beside an ugly cement block of a building. They hustled me up the steps, surrounding me as if I were Public Enemy No. 1, and now I was inside a depressing rectangular room with peeling yellow paint on the walls. There were oak file drawers and classical piano music playing; I recognized it as Chopin. At one end of the room sat a fat, bald man, regarding me coldly. I was pushed into a chair in front of him.

"Your name," he snapped. And the questions were fired at me, one after the other, with an emphasis on my background and how I came to speak Russian. And, "Why do you smuggle?"

"It was simply a gift for a young woman. To impress her, you know? She owned only one dress."

"Why then do you hide it?"

"I had no bag for carrying it. I wrapped it around my waist for convenience."

"What is this girl's name?"

"Her name is Tania." I hoped I could keep Anna out of trouble.

"And how did you meet?"

"In a restaurant."

"Her last name?"

"She didn't tell me."

"Phone number?"

"She wouldn't give it to me, because she was afraid someone would know she went out with an American man. She said it's against the law."

Fist pounded. "It is not against the law!"

"She believed she might lose her job and her family could be sent to Siberia."

"This does not happen! What is this woman's last name?"

I shrugged. "Tania is all I know."

"To bring her these dresses, you have seen her before. How then would you meet with no phone number?"

"The first time we agreed to meet by the entrance of the Hermitage Museum. I would arrive between March 15 and 20, and at five in the afternoon each day, she should check to see if I was there."

I handled all the questions, having gamed out this calamity in advance. The bald man finally sighed deeply and said, "You will write out a confession to all these things. Then we will decide."

"I'm not as good with the written language." He just glared back at me, but within the hour a translator appeared, and I dictated my confession and signed it. Then I was discharged.

I was driven back to the dock, and the captain was relieved to see me. But that was the last I ever saw of Anna—a nice girl who was lots of fun and who loved to sing to me.

I hoped my adventure had reached an end. As a matter of fact, on the following afternoon, I left the ship's gangway, crossed the train tracks on the dock, and saw the doors slide open to one of the wagons. I was looking at a bevy of machine guns, all pointed my way.

It was the *durak*—the officer I'd humiliated and called a fool after his spying accusation.

"Open your coat!" he shouted triumphantly. This was his moment; he'd planned for it carefully. I was a known smuggler, and this would be his triumph as he exposed my illegal deeds.

I opened my coat, and this time, there was nothing at all there but my shirt and my pants. No way I'd have been taking any risks the day after an arrest.

I laughed. "Vyi pravda durak!" I said. *You are truly stupid.*

I enjoyed his obvious disappointment—he really thought he was about to lower the boom. But I'd learned my lesson. As much fun as it was to have a few extra rubles in my pocket, I wasn't eager to play any games with the KGB. I'd have to find something else to do with my time in Leningrad. I researched family history—on my father's side.

I had discovered the Central Naval Museum was nearby, situated on the Neva River. That might be the very best place to learn more about Eustace Sarandinaki, who was a naval hero in the late 1700s. He was at the Siege of Ochakov in the Russo-Turkish War with the Russian Potemkin and the American John Paul Jones.

The staff of the museum asked me to come back three days later while they sorted through their files, and I ended up with a treasure trove of information on my ancestor.

I identified strongly with Eustace, who had lived out his life on ships. No wonder I'd felt the call of the sea since childhood. It was in my blood. Still, like most young men, I kept an eye out for that special woman who was meant for me—someone with whom I could build a home. I thought about Masha, whom I'd seen at that dance, but a year passed, and then another year, and another.

Finally, in 1977, the two of us came together on a blind date. Her cousin, Liza Bouteneff, invited us to dinner separately. But the moment she walked through the door, I recalled how I'd been struck by the sight of her at the Petroushka Ball in 1974. And it was just like in the movies after all—I knew I was going to make Masha my wife. There was absolutely no more thought of Anna from Leningrad, or any other woman. I set to courting Masha with intense focus. Five dates later, I proposed, and she accepted.

The day of our wedding, we'd seen each other only twelve times. I've never been much for stretching things out. Our wedding feast was held under tents on the grounds of the Tolstoy Foundation Center, and it was clear I was marrying into an extraordinary family. There were four hundred guests from the bride's side, and no more than fifty from mine. I enjoyed our few minutes with Alexandra Lvovna Tolstoy, Masha's godmother. She was Leo's youngest daughter and secretary, who first established the Tolstoy Foundation. She was ninety-three, but we persuaded her to come out and join the festivities.

I thought, "My wife's godmother once took care of Leo Tolstoy's business, when she was a teenager. This elderly lady was the executor of his will." I knew Leo Tolstoy had left a legacy of children as impressive as that of his novels and essays. There were thirteen children, though only eight survived their childhood. Most of them escaped Russia between the 1905 revolts and the Bolshevik Revolution twelve years later, but some would return to their homeland, including Masha's grandfather, who fought in the Russian Civil War.

Of course, with another world war, hard times returned, and again the Tolstoys and others became refugees and expatriates. In 1939, the year Hitler began his invasions, Alexandra Lvovna and her friend Tatiana Schaufuss created the Tolstoy Foundation. The two of them had served together as nurses on the front lines during World War I.

Two years later, thanks to a generous donor, the foundation acquired Reed Farm, a lovely parcel of land not far from New York City. Over time and through Alexandra's leadership, half a million refugees were helped to build new lives in the United States. First for White Russians and then for Soviet defectors, Reed Farm represented the American dream of freedom.

Vladimir, Masha's father, was among those who came through the Tolstoy Foundation Center. He was the son of Michael Lvovich Tolstoy. Vladimir bought some land, built a home, and began a new life with his family, including Masha.

A Russian Orthodox church was established, and old traditions were passed on, but there was also assimilation into the American way of life. Children like Masha and I consolidated lessons from two worlds, one in the West and one in the East. We saw how our parents cherished this new land that offered freedom and security, and where home was truly home, once and for all.

12

Skeletons

My life was falling into the rhythm of routine. I was an experienced seafarer; I'd found someone to love and with whom to build a home. By then I was thoroughly and enthusiastically American, while still proud of my Russian and Greek blood.

Historical events were doing what they do—drifting farther into the dust of history, at least for me. I still cared about my grandmother's story, but I was fully involved with a busy life.

What I didn't know was that two men were in the Soviet Union poking around in the long-settled dirt of those past events. What they would find was destined to change my life and to rewrite the history of the Russian royal line and how it ended.

Dr. Alexander Avdonin was a geologist who'd grown up in Yekaterinburg. Coming from the city that was known at the time as Sverdlovsk, he had a natural interest in what had happened in the mad events of 1918. He'd grown up with the legends of the Romanov disappearances and other stories of Cheka atrocities. Everyone in the area knew the stories, heard about them from the elders and the children of the elders, and speculated on what had really happened. Did any Romanovs survive? Were the bodies burned or buried? Where did these things happen?

Sokolov, of course, had documented his investigation in a well-known if suppressed book, but that volume had been answered by Pavel M. Bykov's *Last Days of the Romanovs* (the Western title was *The Last Days of Tsardom*), which was written in 1926 within the Soviet Union. Sokolov's conclusion, based on what he'd been able to uncover with very limited time and resources, was that the bodies of the Romanovs had been burned to ashes. Bykov disagreed. He claimed the bodies, after burning, had been taken away from the mines and buried in some swampy locale nearby, where no excavations could be expected. Dr. Avdonin asked questions around town carefully, without exactly wanting to be involved in a serious search. It was too dangerous.

In 1976 Geli Ryabov, an investigator and government filmmaker, as well as a thriller novelist, had been poking around in Yekaterinburg and, like so many other people, fell under the spell of the story. The locals directed him to Avdonin as the one who had gathered the most information. Ryabov was working on a documentary about the Russian militia—the nonpolitical police, as opposed to the KGB. He was in a position to request otherwise restricted documents from the Soviet archive, including Sokolov's work. He secured a copy and showed it to Avdonin, who was fascinated to read for the first time what the original investigator had written.

Avdonin, a geologist, was accustomed to digging; as a scientist, he knew how to research with patience over time; and as a local citizen, he knew his way around the area. He and Ryabov created something of a yin/yang fit, Avdonin quiet and cautious, and Ryabov, the artist, more daring and willing to poke at forbidden subjects.

For all his fascination with the Romanov story, Avdonin was terrified of attracting the hostility of the Soviet enforcers. This was a common stance in Sverdlovsk—furtive interest controlled by deep fear. They knew bits and pieces of the actual story, but this was a thread that, if pulled, could cause things to unravel quickly.

Sixty years had passed, but some of the children of 1918 still lived and sometimes offered compelling scraps of information. Gennady Nikolaevich Lissine had been fifteen when he helped Sokolov search the area. Sokolov had instructed Lissine and a few other young people to walk through the woods in line, spread six feet apart, and place anything they found in a bag. They'd come up with buttons and other small items, all from around Ganin's Pit, nowhere else. Thus, Sokolov had restricted his focus to that area. Now, in 1964, Lissine ushered Avdonin to the Four Brothers Mine, where this pit was located. Avdonin looked around but did little else for the time being.

Once Ryabov showed up around town, he began pressing Avdonin to take up the search again. Avdonin, always frightened of the subject, took some convincing, but finally agreed to help the filmmaker—as long as everything was kept under wraps.

The two men began with what they knew and didn't know. Bykov said the remains had been removed from the burning site and buried elsewhere, though he didn't specify the details of "elsewhere." Sokolov hadn't come to that conclusion—there simply wasn't time to gather that much information—but he did say that the truck had gotten stuck, that railroad ties had been taken from the railroad operator at the crossing, and that a makeshift bridge had been laid down for the truck to use.

Yurovsky, who had been in charge of all the Romanov matters, had the bridge built. But for Sokolov, the truck and the railroad ties seemed like an insignificant story detail. He didn't stop to consider the strange length of time the men lingered there with the truck. For him, if buttons and scraps of clothing were found near Ganin's Pit, everything must have been done there. But what if this just meant the clothing was removed there? Indeed, that's what had happened. The clothing was removed and burned at the open pit.

The Yurovsky Note—Yakov Yurovsky's account of the murder and disposal of the Romanov remains—offered the first reference to the burial party crossing the railway to the other side of the pit. Before, searching was done only on the pit side. Avdonin and his wife, Galina, who was assisting, now concluded that the Romanov grave was elsewhere, but not too far from this site, and on the other side.

There was a photo, this one from the government archives, showing Peter Ermakov, Yurovsky's right-hand man, standing beside the bridge. He had scribbled in pencil on the back of the photo, "I am standing on the grave of the tsar." This picture was important evidence that seemingly everyone had missed, but it wasn't used until years later in the search for the two children buried elsewhere.

The closer they drew to the truth, the more terrified Avdonin felt. Ryabov reassured him, "I work for the minister of internal affairs, and I'll protect you." Ryabov explained to the Romanov biographer Robert K. Massie that Internal Affairs had no suspicion of what they were doing. As far as it was concerned, this was a film project about the Soviet militia. They never asked questions, just issued whatever was requested. Therefore, he supplied Ryabov with highly secretive items out of the archive. That was crucial. If it had been known these men were poking around in the Romanov murders and burials, doors would have slammed shut.

Feeling a bit reassured, Avdonin said, "If you'll supply the materials, I'll do the searching." So in 1976 they began their search in earnest, knowing that whatever they found would inform posterity—at least through a small chain of transmission. They couldn't publish their information. Avdonin would simply share it with his children as a legacy to pass down, including the burial site. Ryabov had no children. The idea was that if they found any remains, the Soviets would destroy them just as they were about to demolish Ipatiev House. Soviet leaders were allergic to pre-revolution history. Tourists were coming to see the house where the royal line had reached its end point. In fact, a visit to Ipatiev House and its basement was what had moved Ryabov to his commitment to find the truth.

The two sleuths focused on the question of what had happened during those nearly five hours when the truck was on the spot where it had gotten stuck—and the picture with its surprising inscription about "standing on the grave," when plainly the bridge was shown. Had the bodies been disposed of right there on the spot, during the delay?

During the time of these searches, there was an incredible stroke of good fortune: Ryabov found Yakov Yurovsky's son, a retired admiral, living in Leningrad. It turned out that the son was guilt-stricken by the past activities of his father and wanted to make amends. He supplied his handwritten copy of his father's report, known as the Yurovsky Note, describing the key details of the executions and their burial. This was a secret document no one apart from Soviet insiders had been allowed to see, and it gave the clearest possible firsthand account of the burial events. It was a breakthrough acquisition.

Questions Avdonin had harbored all his life were answered here. Indeed, Yurovsky affirmed, the bodies had been buried at the site of the immobile truck. He described the placement of that site—how far along the road, how close to the rail line, and so on. If the bodies had not been removed or lost to deterioration, they could now be found with a little diligent digging.

The men dressed in geological surveyor uniforms to avoid suspicion and proceeded to the area of the Four Brothers Mine, where Lissine had brought Advonin years earlier. They began their searches at the mine, but still there was too much ground to cover. And when the weather became cold, they'd have to put off all investigation until spring.

They explored Koptiaki Road, named by Yurovsky, and identified four low areas within the range he described, where the truck might have stalled out. But there was no small bridge made of railroad ties. It had never been moved—just ignored, trampled over countless times, and pressed five centimeters into the ground and then covered with soil. The road itself had rejoined nature.

Avdonin studied Yurovsky's descriptions again, looked at the pictures in the attempt to relate them to the current terrain, and decided the site had to be adjacent to a small meadow along the road. He searched there with two friends, an engineer and a fellow geologist. Finally, Kochurov, the other geologist, climbed a tree, looked again, and from this high vantage, could make out an outline that was consistent with a makeshift bridge. The correct site turned out to be twenty-five centimeters from the Old Koptiaki Road.

The men took core soil samples to see if there was any suggestion the earth had been disturbed. The soil was mixed, rather than layered, and at the bottom the consistency was like clay, foul-smelling. Someone had definitely been digging here in the past.

The men got to work and dug down to the planks. Sure enough, the railroad ties were there, sixty-one years after they'd been placed. And directly underneath—human bones. There was no mistaking them. Three black skulls lurked together as if in wait. The men stopped and took in what they'd just discovered. Against all odds, those skulls were precisely where the men had stuck their shovels.

Avdonin told Robert Massie his whole life had pointed toward this moment, though he never expected to find the remains, and in fact never really wanted to. "All of it somehow happened by itself," he told Massie. The moment they lifted that planking to peer underneath, he thought, *Don't let there be anything. I don't want to find it.* He didn't believe he could carry on his shoulders the weight of such a discovery. But then, when he saw the skulls, he knew it had "happened by itself." He was a simple geologist who was helpless against his own fate, like a fate-cursed character from a Russian novel. Nothing to do now but go forward and test these skulls.

The men wrapped them up, then closed the hole they'd made in the earth. It wouldn't do to invite curiosity. As much as possible, they set everything back as they'd found it. Then they went into town, found a priest, and had a prayer service for the souls of the dead whose grave they'd disturbed. They were very conscious of the spiritual significance of disturbing a burial site. And though they trusted the priest, they also attempted to mix the famous Romanov names among others, so the minister wouldn't put two and two together.

Then they divided the skulls among them. Avdonin felt he should keep what was thought to be the tsar's skull (it was actually that of the chambermaid), and Ryabov took the skulls that proved later to belong to the Grand Duchesses Anastasia and Tatiana. Ryabov's plan was to find a scientist or lab that would agree to test the skulls quietly, unofficially. The tests would show whether these were in fact the skulls they seemed to be. But he found no one willing to take on the risk.

In 1980 the two men agreed to give up on testing, and there was no safe or decent course but to rebury the skulls and simply wait. Someday, when perhaps less-intimidating leaders were in control, they could come forward and provide instructions on how to find the site.

But when they re-dug the hole, another skull turned up. This one was later proven to belong to Empress Alexandra. When this happened, it seemed as if the skulls were finding *them*. The first three had been exactly where the shovel broke the earth; this one seemed to appear from nowhere. Even Ryabov felt intense fear. The men were pleased to replant their morbid cargo and go their separate ways.

Ten years passed, and the secret was kept. Somehow, with all the excursions to the woods and the questioning around Sverdlovsk—along with all Ryabov's requests for files and skull tests—no suspicions were aroused at the Kremlin. But the two investigators continued to behave as conspiracists, checking in with each other, watching their words, and, in Avdonin's case, keeping no telltale documents at home. They thought about attempting to communicate with the victim's descendants and wondered about how to keep the information alive in the event of their deaths. But ultimately, they could think of nothing safe outside of silence. So the years dragged on.

In the end, their patience outlasted the Soviet Union. The communist nation began to change during the eighties, weakening under the weight of its own grim personality. Two new terms entered the global geopolitical lexicon: *glasnost* (transparency) and *perestroika* (reform). The first had to do with ending a culture of secrecy and coverups in Moscow. The second was about cleaning up the corruption beneath those coverups. Openness and positive change were of course, ideals more than realistic expectations, but during the time of Mikhail Gorbachev, general secretary of the Communist Party, the world began to see a new Soviet Union—one that might even allow a little *glasnost* in the cold case of Tsar Nicholas II and his family.

Avdonin visited his friend occasionally, and in 1988, as it was clear that communism was in its death throes in Moscow, Ryabov suggested finally coming forward with the news of their find. Avdonin wasn't convinced; he was certain he and his older son would be arrested by the KGB if their discovery was publicized. Ryabov had an article ready to go, and Avdonin felt it was well written but that it was still too soon to release it.

Ryabov felt safe enough to write a letter to Gorbachev to ask for government cooperation on the matter of the Romanov remains, but he received no reply. Naturally, however, the word leaked out that he was claiming to have seen the Romanov remains, and after Ryabov was pursued by editors, the article was published first in *Moscow News* and later, in longer form, in the journal *Rodina*. The headline was "The Soil Revealed the Secret."

Ryabov described the process of finding the graves and the skulls, but he never mentioned his partner. Ryabov's reason was credible: Avdonin had repeatedly expressed his fear of being found out—though in actuality, Avdonin had written a letter to Boris Yeltsin in 1991, asking permission to excavate the remains.

Predictably, there was great excitement and great controversy over Ryabov's claims. Some regarded them as something akin to finding the Loch Ness Monster or Bigfoot. If the burial site hadn't been found by now, there must not be one, and this was all an elaborate hoax, like all the Anastasia stories.

But certain highly placed parties did believe Ryabov, and it was fortuitous that he'd stopped short of pinpointing the site of the dig. Avdonin had warned him that even then, some in the government would quickly destroy the evidence. The Ipatiev House had indeed been torn down. So Avdonin had suggested changing the location description by half a kilometer as a kind of failsafe. And sure enough, when he did just that in a subsequent article—moving the location slightly—a government truck showed up to the false site several days later. There was much digging and carting away of dirt—nothing *but* dirt. Avdonin wasn't paranoid after all.

By 1990 Boris Yeltsin was coming into power, elected chair of the Russian Supreme Soviet. He made it known that he favored an exhumation of the Romanov remains, entrusting the operation to the local authorities. Now, with guarantees in place, the true burial location was revealed, and a group of specialists proceeded to Old Koptiaki Road to dig up any remains. Avdonin, who understood the science of archaeological digs, felt that the exhumation may not have been completely in line with scientific best practices but was still far better than typical criminal exhumations.

Seventy-three years after the hurried burial beside a stalled truck, a far more able team was at the site, bringing up whatever was still left of a group of corpses after being shot, stabbed, beaten, burned, and bathed in acid. Those who watch movies and read books about crime tend to believe the human body is easily erased from existence. The burial party in 1918 discovered the fallacy of that, and in 1991, after all the attempts to disguise the corpses, and all the time that had passed, each of the skeletons was identified.

Archaeologist Ludmila N. Koryakova from Ural State University was the team leader for the exhumation. July 1991 was a rainy month, so a great tent was set up to house the site. Inside it, bright lights helped with visibility for the diggers. Quite a delegation attended the expedition: armed police, detectives with cameras, town officials, forensic experts, and Dr. Avdonin.

The specialists worked with brushes and knives. First, they found the box containing the three skulls that had been reburied a few years earlier by Avdonin and Ryabov. Then, one and a half meters down, other bones began to appear. By the second day, five skeletons had been removed. The bones created an impression of having been unceremoniously thrown into the pit, face-down and body upon body, in haphazard fashion. The 1918 burial party had been at its wits' end, ready to see the last of these corpses. They wanted to finish their grisly work and go home.

The bones were oddly colored, given the acid thrown on them (the broken vials were present), and the most damaged skeleton was the one at the bottom. The acid had trickled to the lowest point and done its hardest work on that set of bones.

By the third day, the work was complete. Bones had been carefully lifted and arranged in an initial attempt to assemble something close to complete skeletons. Remarkably enough, adipose tissue (body fat) had been preserved on one skeleton, and there was calcified brain tissue. No clothing or jewels were found, though there were bits of rope, a few bullets, and acid containers. Everything was in line with Yurovsky's account.

The story of the burial was thus laid out before them, but the brutality of the murders was also more than clear. The fronts of the skulls had all been shattered by rifle butts, and the jaws were all broken. Limbs were fractured in some cases. There was evidence of victims shot while lying down. The forensic specialists pointed to the bullets' angles of entry. Finally, the railroad ties had been placed above them and the truck had driven back and forth over the makeshift bridge, smashing more bones and grinding these bodies into the earth.

Dr. Koryakova had worked with plenty of skeletons in the past, but never any like these. She admitted to being sickened by what she saw.

With the work done and the skeletons more or less assembled, the biggest piece of news was a glaring one. The final count was nine skeletons—four male and five female—meaning that two bodies were unaccounted for. Everyone knew speculation would surge. Did this mean Anastasia escaped execution after all? If so, who else was missing from the group? Everyone hoped that science would fill in most of the blanks and clear up these mysteries once and for all.

All the skeletons were taken to the Yekaterinburg Bureau of Forensic Medicine for examination and identification. Sergei Abramov was tasked with the all-important process of telling the world yes, these were the Romanovs, or no, these were somehow other people. Oddly, this was the very moment when the Russian army was moving into Moscow to make sure Gorbachev left as Yeltsin and the new government consolidated power. It was difficult not to think about the condition of the murders in 1918, as Czech forces moved into Yekaterinburg. History sometimes rhymes.

Abramov worked with the hundreds of bone fragments over about ninety days and under the glaring eye of various government entities. No photography was allowed, for example. There was almost no budget, so DNA comparisons were out of the question. He quickly concluded that a great many of the bones were missing. He sent Avdonin and others back to the site, and the diggers came back with 250 more bones.

Without DNA, a little creativity became necessary. The team assembled all known photographs of the victims and made three-dimensional models of the head shapes of each, superimposing them on the available skulls. It was a strikingly accurate method, as each skull has its own unique shape. Abramov proudly boasted that no one else had ever used this process. After bodies and names were brought together, a mathematician was brought in to calculate the likelihood that this combination of skulls could be any other unknown group of nine people. Based on the charted matching measurements, the likelihood of the group being any other than the 1918 Romanov group was 3 in 100 trillion (vastly more than earth's population over all time). Abramov had produced DNA-level accuracy without using DNA.

Two of the bodies were those of the Ipatiev House cook and the valet, and those were excluded because there were no known photographs of them. These could be identified by process of elimination later. Dr. Botkin's skull, however, was an easy call: he had no upper teeth and had worn dentures.

The most difficult were the three young women, who were about the same size and a bit similar, but again the skull differences made accurate identification possible. Anastasia was linked to the sixth skull. And one daughter was unaccounted for: Maria. She and the tsarevich had not been buried with the others.

So the Anastasia mystery was finally solved. She had not survived. She had not led a romantic life on some other continent. But that question was now replaced with another one. Where were the other two children?

13

The Americans Join In

On Christmas Day 1991 the Soviet Union officially ceased to exist. Now the map had a brand-new look. That mammoth section of the globe that had been the Soviet Union for most of a century was now divided into independent states: Kyrgyzstan, Azerbaijan, Uzbekistan, and nine others with names seemingly unpronounceable in the West. But they were names worth learning—these states were now open for Western business.

The year 1992 would prove to be President George H. W. Bush's last full year in office. His secretary of state, James Baker, spent a great deal of his time overseas, building relationships in the new markets. The largest market of all was Russia itself, the successor state to the USSR. While U.S.-Soviet relations would deteriorate several years later, the early Yeltsin days saw much effort toward cooperation between the two powers. After forty years of Cold War tensions, the idea of positive relations was a hopeful one.

Secretary Baker made a stop at Yekaterinburg on Valentine's Day 1992. The city had reverted to its former name the preceding year. Remarkably, Baker was visiting a once-secret nuclear facility. This showed an openness on the part of the Russians that would have been impossible even a couple of years earlier. The idea of the invitation was to show Baker what Russian science had to offer.

The next day was open for rest or tourism for the American delegation. It offered a chance to explore Yekaterinburg. Bush had a spokesperson named Margaret Tutwiler, and she was the member of the party most energized by this opportunity. She held a deep interest in the Romanov story and intended to visit the site of Ipatiev House, knowing that sadly, the house itself had been knocked down years ago. At least she could pay her respects.

Eduard Rossel, governor of Sverdlovsk Oblast, however, offered Baker and Tutwiler something equally fascinating: an invitation to view the bones that had recently been exhumed. They did so, surprised to find the bones simply laid out on tables. Baker held one of the tsar's bones in his hand and also met Alexander Avdonin. They discussed the years of searching and the amazing moment when those three skulls had peered up from the soil. The two Americans were highly impressed by exhibits showing how the skeletons had been matched with their proper identities through computer-generated superimpositions.

At this point, Governor Rossel stepped up to make a personal appeal to Baker. To the world, including some Russians, the question of identity wasn't yet closed. Could American scientists help to further examine these bones, so that the world would believe the Russian assurances that these were the Romanovs? He understood that American science had more credibility; people still suspected political agendas in any statement made by Russian officials.

Baker saw this as a simple request that would help American-Soviet relations that much more. On a personal level, he was also genuinely interested in the question of the Romanov skeletons. Back at the White House, he made it known that the State Department should do everything in its power to assist Yekaterinburg and the team there. Not only did it help a potential ally for the future, but it was great international publicity for American science. Tutwiler joined in the cause enthusiastically, putting out the word, and soon top scientists from Walter Reed Army Medical Center and the FBI were involved.

These scientists were far ahead of their Russian counterparts in forensic technology. Many of them had experience working with crime evidence of all kinds, as well as identifying bones returned from the Vietnamese War. They were leaders in the emerging possibilities of mitochondrial DNA. This was somewhat of a dream team in the field of identifying human remains.

The team quickly prepared to fly to Yekaterinburg. Then, at the last minute, Moscow sent a message for them to stand down. The Yekaterinburg people had made their own selection: Dr. William Maples, a specialist whose research was done at the University of Florida, in Gainesville, Florida. The state team was surprised and disappointed but also puzzled. For one thing, Maples couldn't offer DNA analysis.

Still, Maples was an expert in his own right who was dealing with two to three hundred cases per year, including those involving serial killer Ted Bundy. He helped refute the long-standing myth that in 1850 U.S. president Zachary Taylor had died of poisoning. He visited Honolulu annually to help identify military remains from Vietnam, as did members of the state team. Maples drew his funds from a generous donor rather than the taxpayers. Score one for the private sector.

It had happened this way. During James Baker's visit to Yekaterinburg, reporters had written about the governor's request for American help. Maples, who was familiar with the story of the tsar and his family, heard about it immediately at a conference. Without realizing that Secretary Baker was also on the case, Maples quickly put together his own team, including forensic pathologist Michael Baden, forensic odontologist Lowell Levine, and hair and fiber expert Cathryn Oakes from the New York State Police.

On university letterhead, he wrote with the offer that his team would travel at its own expense, and also organize a conference to promote the results of the team's work. He later called Alexander Avdonin directly, and an invitation followed shortly for the Florida team to come to Russia.

Maples had done an excellent job of salesmanship, and he'd done it quickly.

One day in 1991, at my home in New York, I heard the name of Nicholas II on a TV news broadcast. Immediately I sat up and listened closely. I heard about these remains being found near Yekaterinburg, and it was exciting—here was a piece of history relevant to my life, and I might even have useful information about it; I had spoken to an eyewitness to Sokolov's physical evidence.

But I was also skeptical. Being on television didn't make something true. There were hoaxes in the news occasionally: the Hitler diaries, that kind of thing. Like many, I tended to distrust news that originated in Russia. But I kept an open mind and made it a point to listen for more information, if the story held up.

The following year, 1992, I was master of the SS *Sea-Land Expedition*, a container ship. Each day, during our coffee time, we'd gather at the officers' saloon and have a wide-ranging discussion. Officers shared about their lives and families, and we had some great talks—our version of a water cooler at the office. Naturally, I told my family story, including my grandmother and the box of evidence, and our connection to the events of 1918 and the Romanovs.

My chief engineer brought me a copy of the *Orlando Sentinel* one day. He had the paper folded to a feature on a man named Dr. William Maples, who was taking a team to Yekaterinburg to test those remains I'd heard about on television. He said, "I figured you'd want to see this one."

The article added a touch more credibility to what I'd heard. It sounded legit, actually. I still remembered what Sokolov, the close friend of my grandparents and great-grandparents, thought—he believed the bodies had been burned to ashes. But he could have been wrong, and I also didn't want my family's role in a historic event to be forgotten. I still had a drive to tell that story; Anna had entrusted it to me, and I felt it was up to me to keep its memory alive by passing it on to future generations.

As soon as I got the chance, I called the Orlando paper, told the reporter the short version of my story, and asked for contact information for the Maples team. I knew that whenever I spoke up, there was the chance I wouldn't be believed. But the reporter listened closely and trusted me with the phone number for Dr. Maples.

I made the call. Margaret Maples, his wife, was handling media for the project, and she answered the phone. I introduced myself and again recited the story I'd told so many times. She too believed my words, and I was thankful.

Would any of these scientists follow up? All I could do was wait.

In late July the Maples team arrived in Yekaterinburg and was given full access to the bones, with permission to test and examine them. The team examined the room, looked at the skeletons lying in wait, and began to set up all their equipment. Then someone pulled out a camera and was quickly told by a guard to put it away. The officials were very hostile to any attempt at photography. They saw images of the bones as their intellectual property.

This was an indication of the struggles between local government, Russian government, and the news media. The local government approached the discovery as a purely local issue and a marketing opportunity. Moscow saw it as a Russian matter; the tsar and his family belonged to *all* Russians, not just the ones who lived in his place of death.

The Americans, for their part, were suspected of coming to do their capitalistic thing and steal the whole story out from under everyone. Their science was welcome, but their imperialism could wait outside. The writers would come and make their money. The TV shows would come and make theirs. Yekaterinburg was determined to protect what it believed was its own.

After having his cameras forbidden, Maples dealt with the situation coolly. He and the team spent a few hours simply looking at the skeletons, studying the most important bones, and finally began pointing to each one and identifying it—this one was Olga, that one was Tatiana, here was the tsar himself, and so on. The reasons for identification were rattled off easily—age, teeth, height; the Russian observers were duly impressed. Then the team put away all its equipment, walked to the front desk, and announced its work was done. They were going to go grab lunch.

Nikolai Nevolin, the morgue director, all but fainted. They couldn't be finished already! Why, a genuine American study should take days . . .

Maples explained that indeed they were done here, unless, of course, photography was allowed. Documentation was a necessity for any credible scientific work, and documentation could only be accomplished through photography. Without the ability to take pictures, visual ID was all they had to offer.

Nevolin sighed. He told them to go to lunch, then return for further discussion. They did that, and when they came back, the policy had miraculously changed. Photography was allowed, unlimited. The Americans had carte blanche.

Maples's team wasn't bluffing with its preliminary identifications. Even with plenty of work still to do, and plenty of bases to cover, they'd seen enough to know these were indeed the Romanov skeletons, and they were almost completely certain which was which. Their experience in bone work made things fairly simple. Height and body proportions have to do with sex and age. A middle-aged woman with fine tooth fillings had to be Empress Alexandra. German dentistry was an excellent form of identification. The short, middle-aged man with bad teeth and a particularly smashed face had to be Nicholas II. And inside it, something rattled around as they handled the skull—the shriveled remainder of the tsar's brain.

Demidova, the maid, and Botkin, the doctor, were unique individuals who were easy to identify. The skeleton identified as Botkin's had no upper teeth. Sokolov had recovered his dentures from the pit decades earlier. The valet and the cook—the latter being the most deteriorated body from the bottom of the stack—could also be picked out.

The three young females were the only challenging ones, and it would be interesting to study them further. Maples felt that Anastasia wasn't in the room, because all three skeletons seemed to be from bodies older than her seventeen years. Based on her last known photographs, she couldn't have had enough of a growth spurt to match one of these skeletons. Dental and height issues also led him to exclude the youngest daughter. The two youngest children, the girl and the boy, were not here.

Dr. Maples and Dr. Abramov had a difference of opinion on this, and a strong one—Abramov believed Maria was the missing daughter. Both agreed young Tsarevich Alexei, who would be quite easy to single out, was not there. Though many had praised Abramov's photo reconstructions, Maples believed them to be crude and inaccurate.

But one thing that couldn't be doubted: this was the group of individuals who were murdered and buried in mid-July 1918. Even without DNA testing at this point, there was simply no credible way they could be some random group of nine Russians in a mass grave that happened to lie beside the Old Koptiaki Road. Other than missing two children—and Yurovsky had suggested why that might be so—this was the right combination of males, females, ages, head shapes, dental details, and other evidence. Acid had coated them. Bullets were present, and consistent with the type used in the executions. And these bones had been found precisely where Yurovsky, the leader of the operation, had described burying them. Nothing at all was inconsistent with the known facts of the Romanov group burial.

The two missing bodies, it was felt, might never be recovered. Yurovsky had written in his report that two bodies were burned, one indeed being the tsarevich, the other being misidentified as Demidova. Perhaps those two had indeed been reduced to ashes. The truth, of course, would be revealed later.

Maples filed his report with the suggestion that DNA testing should be done. He also recommended carefully preserving the remains. (The team wasn't impressed with the conditions of their storage.) He also recommended a thorough search for the firepit described by Yurovsky. With thorough searching using modern technology, that site might still be located. Cremated remains should be given to the appropriate specialists.

As the Maples team published its opinion, these credentials were given: "The American forensic scientists have over one hundred years of forensic experience collectively and have identified hundreds and hundreds of remains of individuals who perished under all types of circumstances. They have been involved in many other high-profile cases such as the Assassination of John F Kennedy, Martin Luther King, Josef Mengele Identification, the Disappeared of Argentina, Mass Graves of Bosnia, many aviation accidents and other Mass Disasters, and many, many other similar cases. They are quite experienced in this type [of] case."

It was difficult to argue with that kind of résumé.

The Yekaterinburg Conference immediately followed the completion of the Maples team's work. It lasted two days and was sponsored by the Sverdlovsk regional government. It was entitled The Last Page of the History of the Imperial Family: The Results of Studies of the Yekaterinburg Tragedy.

This was—at least in format—a scholarly conference in which papers were presented by scientists, and the idea was to offer a comprehensive view of the whole story. But it was also the beginning of what many felt was an intent by the city to profit financially from this tragic event.

Yekaterinburg is a proud city, founded by Peter the Great and named for his wife. At the very time when Russia was becoming more open to Western ideas and commerce, there was a definite aroma of capitalism in the air—discussions of setting up attractions to lure tourists, rather than respecting the remains in the way we usually treat the dead. For the 1992 conference, the city attempted to charge exorbitant fees to reporters simply for attendance. Then there was a proposal of charging $10,000 for media rights to view and photograph the bones. Naturally, reporters made a lot of noise about this treatment, and the ideas fell through. There's a lot of money-making in the West, but there's freedom of the press too. The city was being approached by various promoters, and the lure of a financial bonanza proved irresistible.

In any case, Alexander Avdonin was on hand at the conference to tell the story of how the bones were found. What was once a fearful secret was now a narrative he was asked to relate over and over. I knew that feeling.

There were a number of other speakers with varying degrees of relevancy. A Moscow professor attacked the "rude violations" of the exhumations. There was a presentation on the bullet damage to the skeletons. The finding of hairs, including pubic hairs—remarkably and dangerously delicate—was recounted in another paper.

To American observers, it seemed that Russian scientists had a way of working independently and privately rather than as a team. They would draw their conclusions based only on their one limited angle of perspective, rather than sharing information back and forth and coming to a consensus. It was like the old fable of the blind men and the elephant. One felt the trunk and felt an elephant was like a snake; another felt a leg and theorized that an elephant was like an oak. Western scientists were more accustomed to putting together the observations and coming up with a comprehensive conclusion. Russian scientists were constantly wary of having their information "stolen."

At the conference, Abramov again demonstrated his computerized superimposition of old photographs and existing skulls. His examples never failed to impress. Another speaker's great agenda was the certainty that Demidova's skeleton (as identified by both examinations so far) was actually that of a male. And there were presentations on the advantages of DNA analysis, which had yet to be done and wasn't generally available in Russia. Finally, there were some nonscientific presentations relating to the Romanov family or topics that seemed neither here nor there.

Oddly, the Maples team wasn't front and center among these presentations. There may have been a certain amount of aloofness toward the American team, or it may have been the language barrier. But Maples himself was invited to present his findings at the close of the conference. He took questions from reporters for a portion of his time. But his presence tended to underline some of the local tensions around the Romanov remains. The Yekaterinburg governmental officials had invited the Maples team but hadn't informed, for example, Abramov and his associates, who had noticed that the Americans had the photographic privilege that Russian scientists hadn't been given.

Again, the Russian tendency toward personal evasiveness rather than cooperation caused some degree of questions and rivalry. But Abramov had a point, and James Baker would have agreed: this should have been the perfect occasion for Russian and American scientists to work side by side.

Abramov was surprised when Maples told the conference his firm conclusion that the Romanov daughter Maria was among the skeletons but that Anastasia was still missing. Abramov had great respect for all these specialists, and he could see the thoroughness of their examinations. Yet he had concluded just the opposite about the two girls. Afterward, Abramov advised Maples to be careful about passing this opinion around in America with certainty. His feeling was that in only three days of study, the Maples team, with all its experience and science, was capable of getting this one wrong, and getting it wrong would be detrimental to the team's reputation.

The two continued their conversation one year later, when Maples was in Russia for a U.S. TV documentary on identifying the bones. In comparing notes, they discovered a prominent reason for the discrepancy: they were measuring different bones. The Maples team measured the bones of the forearm, because the femur had been sawed in half, making it impossible to make an accurate measurement based on the femur. Abramov, however, *had* measured that longest and strongest of bones. Both agreed that the femur was a more accurate gauge, but between the two examinations, someone had taken the saw to it—one of a number of ill-advised acts in the treatment of the evidence.

In addition, there was the possibility that the measured forearm bones had come from a different skeleton. The team that removed the bones from the ground didn't always observe the best practice, and besides, all the bones sat on tables where any visitor could pick them up, as James Baker had done, and perhaps replace them incorrectly. Various scientists had examined the bones at different times, and there was plenty of opportunity for confusion. Between using different standards and the possibility of a bone originating from a different set, there was no wonder the conclusions differed, underlining the need for more and better testing—particularly of DNA.

The two men got along well and wanted only to resolve the question. When Abramov asked for a referral to a Western scientist who could provide an independent judgment, Maples suggested Dr. Richard Helmer, a forensic science professor from Bonn, Germany.

Abramov was familiar with his work, was enthusiastic about getting another expert opinion (one that, for a change, an American and a Russian had collaborated to suggest), and invited the man to confer with them. Two months later, Helmer was meeting with Abramov and reviewing the photographic superimposition. He said it was the best system he'd ever seen, and that he agreed with Abramov's conclusion that Anastasia, not Maria, was among the retrieved skeletons.

At the very least, then, the question of the missing daughter was an open one, calling for the need for greater research.

Maples wanted Avdonin—whose local questions and wanderings in the wood had given birth to this whole discovery, and all its ramifications—to have his chance to speak directly to American scientists. So, in February of 1993, he invited Avdonin to appear before the American Academy of Forensic Science, whose conference was held in Boston that year. The AAFS is a prestigious group of the best crime investigation scientists not only in the United States but, despite its name, a number of other nations.

Avdonin offered a review of the murder and burial, underlining the fact that the Bolsheviks' brutality and secrecy had set the stage for the many myths and legends that had arisen about the fate of the Romanovs. "Concealment of the true facts of the death had commenced an epoch of disgusting lies on the state level," he said, and offered as a matter of irony the words of Lenin: "We need the full and true information. Truth should not depend on the people whom it serves."

He offered a few words about his life, his lack of desire to become the one to find those remains, and how it was nonetheless almost inevitable that he would, because he had been a curious young man, a lover of the sciences who grew up near the site of the crime—and because the many secrets of modern Russian history served only to fuel his curiosity and others'. The more we try to hide the truth, the greater will be the efforts of others to discover it. Thus, he was one of a multitude of his countrymen who distrusted the lessons fed to him by the state, and who could only wonder what other secrets were being covered up.

He had relied mostly upon Sokolov's manuscripts, though he had access to just four of the seven volumes. Here he was given the truth of which individuals were killed and where the bodies were taken—to Four Brothers, with its abandoned mineshafts. Sokolov had found the famous upper denture of Dr. Botkin, along with a manicured fingertip, the body of Anastasia's dog, and other miscellanea. But the material evidence Sokolov had collected, said Avdonin, was lost. (I later told Avdonin, of course, about my grandmother's experiences with the box containing some of these items.)

Avdonin recounted his early experiences interviewing those still alive and the children of the events' participants, as well as reading the evidence given by Yurovsky and others.

Then he turned to the question of who ordered the murder. The answer was obvious. Yurovsky had written, "Sixteen July a telegram came from Perm in code, containing the decree to exterminate the Romanovs." The direct line with Moscow wasn't working, thus the command had been relayed through Perm. Lenin and his men would only own up to executing the tsar, because of the tsar's supposed plotting against his captors. But the victims included his wife, all his children, and several attendants, whose only crime was being close to the monarch. This was cold-blooded murder, and Lenin had understood from the beginning that if people knew, the knowledge of it would show the lies and hypocrisy of those who had overthrown the government.

As Dr. Maples and I had become good friends, I'd asked if it were possible to bring Avdonin to New York, where the Russian community could have an opportunity to get to know him. I had yet to meet him myself, so I was pleased when Maples agreed. This was the first time we heard the facts of the case as they were now known. Our information had been based on Sokolov's 1924 report.

Before he came, Avdonin asked me over the phone if I could arrange for him to meet Bishop Basil Rodzianko of the Orthodox Church in America. For forty years, the bishop had been a beloved voice on the radio all over the world, speaking on behalf of Christianity and Orthodoxy, particularly to the Soviet Union, which sought to erase religion from Russian life.

I told Avdonin, "That's an easy one! Bishop Basil is my mother-in-law's brother."

He was delighted to hear that, of course, and went on to ask if he could meet Princess Vera Konstantinovna, the emperor's niece. She was the longtime sponsor of the Petroushka Ball, where I'd first set eyes upon my wife. The princess had escaped Russia through Sweden during the revolution, but her Romanov brothers were murdered on July 18, 1918, the day the tsar's family was being moved between graves. I was able to facilitate this meeting as well. These were people Avdonin had always wanted to meet, and he wanted to make the most of his stateside visit.

There was one other request, and this one I was unhappy to receive. The Russian Expert Commission Abroad, a group of scholars—none of them scientists—asked for a meeting with the geologist. This organization had been assembled quickly after the announcement that the gravesite had been found. Immediately the group's stance was to throw the whole discovery into question and to belittle anyone who advocated for the bones' authenticity. The group's main activity was lobbying the Russian Orthodox Church not to accept the scientific findings. Needless to say, this gathering turned out to be quite an unpleasant one.

The meeting was held in a church library in Nyack, New York, and it was mostly a group attack on Avdonin and an attempt to intimidate him. RECA commissioned its own "experts" and came to the predetermined conclusion that the bones weren't what the Russian government and the American scientists were claiming. In particular, these critics pointed to a supposedly missing scar on the skull assigned to Nicholas II, who had been attacked in Japan as a young man. Much later the scar was indeed located on the skull, precisely where it should have been.

The group continued to attack the work of the government commission as it investigated the murders. Members made a trip to Moscow in 1995 and were invited to study the pertinent documents in the archive there. They did so, then visited Yekaterinburg to view the remains and the site of the exhumations, as well as talk to the experts.

Not surprisingly, the RECA visitors were unconvinced, comparing the bones to fakes manufactured by the American CIA. The burial ground itself was a fake, they said, and the KGB and other nefarious Soviet agencies had falsified all the evidence. None of the current investigators were to be trusted; they should have been cleaned out when communism in Russia collapsed, just as Nazi authorities had been cleaned out at the end of World War II. They believed the whole thing was a way to prop up the new Russian government—building sympathy for the tsar.

The group also pointed to the structure of the investigation and complained that it wasn't the way Americans do things. There should be an independent prosecutor. The chain of evidence and everything else should be approached according to Western standards. Most of these wild complaints and conspiracy theories were directed toward the Russian Orthodox Church, and sadly, the church paid attention. The group also sent out scores of press releases to American media and probably received attention out of proportion to its actual significance as a group.

Our meeting with the RECA went as might be expected, and to our dismay, the meeting with Princess Vera went poorly as well. The princess, who was in her late eighties, was dependent upon a caretaker who for some reason saw Avdonin as a "Soviet" and therefore someone who must be full of lies. Bishop Basil, who attended the meeting, attempted to reason with her gently, but the caretaker was immovable and disruptive, and we had to leave.

The White Russian community in the United States was conditioned to distrust any message that originated in their home country. Even if there was no detectable agenda, the default reaction was to cast doubt on whatever was being said. When a government drives you out of your ancestral nation and strips you of everything you own, resentment and distrust can linger for a long time. No one hated the Soviet system more than the White Russian community, and the fall of communism wasn't quite enough to bridge that chasm.

At the same time, Avdonin had indeed been a Soviet citizen all his life, with his own corresponding tendency to distrust White Russians. When a nation is spread across the world, cultural differences become obstacles in reuniting its people. Science was attempting to speak, but it was being drowned out by loud arguments.

There was one final meeting with Avdonin, and we were relieved when it went well. For whatever reason, a Russian American group in Washington DC was welcoming and receptive to the message.

Overall, Avdonin's American visit hadn't been all that we hoped. He was puzzled by the mixed reception, and particularly appalled at the so-called Russian Expert Commission Abroad. Uncovering bones was one thing; uncovering buried resentments was quite another.

14

Digging Deeper

The village where Boris Yeltsin was born is only a three-to-four-hour drive from Yekaterinburg. By Russian distance standards, that's a hop, a skip, and a jump. The people in that city looked upon him as one of their own, and considered it perfectly natural that, as he became the Russian Federation's president, he would support the exhumation of the Romanov remains. He was a proud native of Sverdlovsk Oblast and the Urals region, and he knew what was good business there.

On the other hand, by 1991 he had a vast and complex nation to worry about. If he'd been a tsar, he would have been called Emperor of All the Russias. So he was expected to do what was right for the nation as a whole. He had ordered the Romanov bodies to be recovered in 1991, but would he take a stand on giving priority to the Ural Federal District in the matter of handling those remains? Or would he stand with the Russian government?

It was difficult to tell at first, because his place in the new establishment was unstable. Old-line communists weren't giving in without a fight. Yeltsin had taken office on July 10, 1991, seven days before Governor Rossel of Sverdlovsk announced the discovery of the bones. A month later, a major coup broke out from within the government, driven by those who opposed *perestroika*. Yeltsin showed up in the midst of the tumult, climbed atop a tank near the White House of Russia, and made an impassioned speech for peace. The sponsors of the coup disappeared, and Yeltsin became a hero, a unifying figure.

But with a total government shakeup and the end of the Soviet system, there were far more urgent problems than who had authority over the bones in Yekaterinburg. So Moscow's inattention during this time allowed the local government to take the initiative and hang on to it. James Baker's invitation to help, and Maples's commission to investigate, both came from Yekaterinburg, but tensions with Moscow became evident as early as the Yekaterinburg Conference that followed the three-day Maples examination. Didn't the Romanov story belong to *all* Russia, even in a sense the world itself, as a key chapter in world history? In Sverdlovsk it wasn't seen this way. These were the *locally* buried bones from a *local* execution at the hands of *local* political activists.

But the center could not hold in such a strained position. The power still resided in the federation, even in the case of a new and chaotic government. In 1993 a government commission from Moscow was established to investigate the Romanov matter. Vladimir Soloviev, from the Office of the Public Prosecutor, would be responsible for investigation and evidence-gathering. The committee would rely almost totally on Soloviev, who was a serious, competent, and honest man.

Since the exhumation of the bones, Soloviev had been involved with this case, assisting the Sverdlovsk deputy investigator. In the beginning, he'd been as skeptical as I was in hearing the news that, after all this time, the remains of the Romanovs had miraculously been located. But as time went on, and Soloviev read Yurovsky's account and looked at the other archival evidence, he'd felt an ever-deeper connection to the case.

Soloviev wasn't involved in Russian politics; he viewed the work through a scientific and criminological lens only. He established that this was a criminal case like any other. As such, he would interview witnesses and search for a perpetrator. If this was a murder, as seemed obvious, who was the murderer or murderers? He understood that those guilty would have seen themselves as carrying out a sentence, that is, performing a legal execution from a lawful government. Was this true? Were they vested with the power to perform executions?

He realized these were questions no one had been courageous enough to ask for many decades, and there were those who didn't want the questions to be asked. He was performing a strange blend of historian and criminal detective and, in some sense, potentially rewriting the verdict of history. And there was no shortage of areas where his Russian countrymen were a little touchy. He also knew his work would intersect with areas where the church would have something to say. In short, Soloviev knew that his work would be complex, sensitive, and probably lengthy.

He was right on all counts. Soloviev would dedicate most of his time to the case for many years to come. He would feel pressure from various directions, but his commitment to the truth remained unshaken. He was determined to discover once and for all whether these were authentically the bones they seemed to be, how and whether these victims were killed, and who was responsible. This would be yet another examination of those bones, but with no time limit or political agenda. He wanted to dig deeper—deep enough that the lingering questions could be answered definitively.

Handing all this material over to the government commission, he could leave it to that group to decide what should be the state's response.

At the outset, Soloviev was aware of Russia's one greatest deficiency when it came to the identification process: it lacked DNA analysis. Why was it behind? At one time, the Soviet Union had been a worldwide leader in science. There had been progress in molecular biology along with other fields. But Stalin had executed his best scientists in 1953, suspecting them of plotting against the government. Genetics in particular was associated with the Nazi "science" of eugenics in the minds of communist leaders. So the United States, Great Britain, and others had pulled ahead in DNA analysis and other biological fields. During the early 1990s, funding for scientific research as a whole nosedived as Russia lurched through its transition.

Russia was forced to look to the West for help with genetic identification. And this time Great Britain would receive the nod.

The story of the Romanov executions and exhumations carries the persistent theme of timing.

The timing of World War I affected the timing of the Russian Revolution, which affected the timing of the abdication of the tsar. The execution of his family and entourage was affected by the timing of Czech troops moving toward Yekaterinburg, and many years later, the timing of revealing their discovery was affected by the timing of the end of Soviet communism—the same Soviet communism behind the crime. History is a set of dominoes, colliding and pushing each other forward until the world looks very different.

But scientific progress has its own timing, and this, too, transformed the story. In 1991 DNA research was blossoming into new possibilities. Dr. Peter Gill, a British scientist, worked with his country's Forensic Science Service and began researching DNA in 1985. Gill was a pioneer in showing the implications of DNA for forensic criminal evidence. He and Dr. Alec Jeffreys of Leicester University wrote a paper demonstrating how DNA could help in crime investigation, and their methods have become accepted everywhere. If the bones' discovery in Yekaterinburg had been revealed in 1979, the science wouldn't have been ready to answer the necessary questions.

By this time, most people have at least a rudimentary understanding of what DNA is. It has become fashionable to arrange for information about our ancestry, and even to find relatives we didn't know, through DNA samples provided to commercial laboratories. And we hear about finding criminals, and sometimes even proving innocence, through DNA analysis.

DNA (deoxyribonucleic acid) is the basic building block of human identity. It carries all the information about our looks, our minds, our weaknesses. These little pieces of information—eye color, for example—are carried in sections called genes, and found in cell arrangements called chromosomes.

In its earliest phase, DNA examination involved a certain level of destruction of evidence. Sampled material needed to be sufficient and "fresh," that is, undegraded—the older a DNA sample, the more it degrades. Gill helped develop a new kind of DNA profile that needed no more than a few cells, thus destroying little evidence. In addition, its sensitivity even to degraded material was far better. It's known today as low template DNA profiling (LT-DNA).

During the summer of 1992, the Russians reached out to Gill. He agreed to work on identification of the bones with Jeffreys and Dr. Erika Hagelberg of Cambridge University, who specialized in genetic analysis of bone remains. Dr. Pavel Ivanov, Moscow's leading molecular scientist, would be the fourth member of the team; Great Britain would host the testing. With a DNA approach, the initial question would be: Is there a family present among these skeletons? DNA identifies patterns that link people genetically as families. That would be the lowest bar to clear—if several of these skeletons were unrelated to one another, they could not be the Romanovs. It was understood, of course, that Dr. Botkin, Demidova, and others were also present.

Then, should there be enough uncontaminated DNA, the scientists could be more precise about these identities. If the living relations of the Romanovs would provide samples of their DNA, a comparison could be made to whatever information was derived from the bones. There could finally be a definite answer, at least scientifically speaking, as to whether this was the Romanov group.

Gill's home was in the village of Aldermaston, a little more than an hour's drive from London. The Forensic Science Service had a laboratory there as part of Great Britain's atomic research facility. There the DNA work was pursued for almost a year.

As always, Russian tensions accompanied this arrangement, originating from the revolution. When the Russian Revolution led to Tsar Nicholas's abdication, the Romanovs looked to England for sanctuary. King George V was a first cousin, and the family relations had been good ones. But after consideration, King George decided not to admit the royal family of Russia into his country.

When the Romanovs were executed, along with other relations within Russia, many White Russians were infuriated with Great Britain and what they saw as a family betrayal. Such feelings don't die quickly but are passed down through generations. The British hoped that this cooperation in identifying the bones of the Romanovs would help heal the remaining anger—if quietly and without much publicity.

The samples taken were tiny, but the surfaces were quite obviously in poor condition for examination—both in terms of age and exposure to the elements for all that time. This was the most difficult DNA examination yet done for forensic purposes, and it wasn't clear how successful the team would be. Given the tiny samples scraped away from the bones, the men used a new method that analyzes and then imitates the ladder-like strands of DNA, synthesizing a much larger sample to work with.

In examining X and Y chromosomes, the team was able to establish the sex of each skeleton. The earlier conclusions were verified: four males and five females. Abramov and Maples, of course, were in disagreement over the identity of one of the females.

The next step was to determine whether there were genetic family relationships in the group. Chromosomes have sections that show pattern repeats between family members. These are called short tandem repeat sequences. The finding was that five of the skeletons (nos. 3, 4, 5, 6, and 7) showed the patterns indicating family.

Not only that, but no. 4 and no. 7 could be identified as the parents of the other three. Conclusion: If this family was in fact the Romanov family, then one daughter and the young son were missing from the grave. According to DNA, the adult skeleton previously identified as Nicholas II was indeed the father of the three children represented. The female parent skeleton, then, would presumably be Empress Alexandra, as predicted.

But what about individual identification? This was where mitochondrial DNA came into the picture. This is a type of DNA transmitted only through mothers. Mothers pass it to daughters in identical form, with no change, unlike the nuclear DNA the team had worked with earlier. Sons inherit this form of DNA but don't pass it to their children. However, a straight line of female descendants will have the exact same mitochondrial DNA.

Again, the scientists took tiny samples and multiplying them for examination. They found that the DNA was perfectly preserved. DNA profiles could now be established for all nine bones that had been sampled. It was time for genealogy: finding samples from living relatives. Prince Philip, the duke of Edinburgh, turned out to be the perfect donor. He was, of course, the husband of Queen Elizabeth II. He descended in the line of Empress Alexandra's older sister. Buckingham Palace was approached with the request, and he graciously provided a blood sample.

The results showed that the skeletons identified as Empress Alexandra and the three daughters were a perfect match with the DNA in the duke's blood sample. At this point there could be no credible dispute: the bodies of the empress and three of her four daughters had been recovered from the ground. This, of course, made it inconceivable that the male parent was anybody other than Nicholas II. Still, science must be totally objective, continuing as far as the path allows, and the tsar's identification was pursued as if the other evidence hadn't been found.

Finding a DNA donor was far more difficult in the case of Nicholas II. Pavel Ivanov felt that the best course was to use DNA from the brother of Nicholas

II. Of course, he wasn't alive, but his corpse was accessible in its tomb at Saint Petersburg. Or was it?

For one thing, exhumation would mean plowing through Italian marble. Replacement would be incredibly expensive. A potential financial donor was found: a Russian cellist named Mstislav Rostropovich. But first Ivanov needed to visit Japan.

That's when Ivanov had his brainstorm. The mention of Japan reminded him of Nicholas II's 1891 visit to that country as tsarevich. A Japanese man had attacked him with a sword, slicing his forehead. The attacker was a policeman assigned to the protection of the heir to the Russian throne. Nicholas's cousin knocked the sword away with his cane during what would have been the second blow, and after a chase, the assassin was captured. But Nicholas was left with a scar for the rest of his life. The scar wasn't readily visible on the skull, though it was found much later, and the critics of the scientific work would cling to that supposed discrepancy for a while.

Ivanov happened to know that the blood had been stopped with a handkerchief, which was still displayed in a Japanese museum in the city where the incident occurred.

Remarkably, money wasn't available for a trip to secure the handkerchief. The Russians claimed no funds, and the British, who were footing all the bills for the research, thought this was an unnecessary addition. Rostropovich finally paid up, and even convinced the emperor of Japan to loan out the cloth.

Unfortunately, the cloth sample didn't prove suitable. It had simply been handled by too many people. Any sample might be contaminated.

At this point, a living relative of Nicholas II was found, but he refused to participate. He believed the bones were a hoax, and he was angry that Ivanov was working in England, which he saw as a slap in the face of Mother Russia. And he had his suspicions that Ivanov was just another KGB agent.

The genealogist went to work one more time and produced two relatives. One was a countess living in Athens and Paris. She was delighted to help. The other was Lord James Carnegie, the third duke of Fife and earl of Macduff—a Scottish farmer. The relationship was a distant one, going back to a German princess married to the king of Denmark. She was the grandmother of Nicholas II. The duke was also happy to help, but at the time, anonymously.

As it turned out, there was a small discrepancy between Nicholas II and the two modern donors. The DNA of all three was very close, but at one position, a letter was different. (DNA uses letters A, C, G, and T in mapping.) How could this be? After further study, in which a few samples matched the two living donors and others didn't, the scientists concluded that Nicholas II actually had *two* forms of mitochondrial DNA. This is known as *heteroplasmy*. It's a mutation that isn't common but crops up perhaps once in three hundred generations. In other words, the chance of it showing up in one specific subject such as this one was a third of 1 percent. Given the novelty of DNA at the time, little was really understood about the causes of heteroplasmy.

It certainly didn't mean the skeleton was not the late tsar. Taken with all the other evidence—a buried family in which the mother and daughters perfectly matched just the living donor they should—there shouldn't have been much consternation. But a worrisome mutation wasn't the slam dunk result the scientists were looking for. A simple, neat match for Nicholas II, like those that had been attained for the female subjects, would have made the story more powerful. Heteroplasmy was obscure and required explanation and, for the impatient and skeptical, gave permission to continue doubting.

The Forensic Science Service held a press conference in July of 1993, one year after the Russian appeal to the British for help. Gill performed the always difficult task of explaining DNA analysis to laypeople—reporters, filmmakers, and the public. Considering all the extensive research and the results, including Nicholas II's genetic abnormality, they projected a 98.5 percent certainty that the skeletons were those of the Romanovs. This was a conservative estimate. Simply based on logic, it was difficult to entertain the idea that these bodies could be anyone else, but scientific standards are strict.

The world received the news that, in all probability, the fate of the Romanovs was now understood—at least for all but two of the family.

The story, of course, never really is completed, and more twists and turns lay ahead—even in the area of DNA research. There would be more, including some with my involvement. Now that I understood that these bones were something more than a hoax, my interest in the case soared. And I wasn't the type to sit on the sidelines.

In the Western world, anyone interested in the story of the final tsar and his family goes to one source: Robert K. Massie's work of history, *Nicholas and Alexandra: An Intimate Account of the Last of the Romanovs and the Fall of Imperial Russia*. The American writer published this book in 1967, inspired by the fact that, like his subjects, he had a son who was a hemophiliac.

The book has stayed in print for more than fifty years, including being added to Random House's prestigious and popular Modern Library series. It was made into a Hollywood film in 1971 that was nominated for Best Picture at the Academy Awards.

When news about the family's execution exploded into headlines across the world in the early nineties, Massie was as interested as anyone. When he did his research for the book in the sixties, the best source he had on the burial of the Romanovs was what Sokolov had published in the twenties. According to that version, the bodies of all members of the family, and those of their attendants, were burned to ashes. There was no reason to doubt the conclusions of the one objective investigation that had occurred, and the Kremlin wasn't about to open its files at that point.

In 1996 Robert Massie's volume *The Romanovs: The Final Chapter* corrected the record and then some. Based on all the new evidence, including Yurovsky's Note and a lot of fresh interviews, he offered a new account of the execution itself and the burial. He told the story of how the bones were discovered, explained the politics surrounding the issue, recounted the various expert examinations and the burial, and also gave a full account of the various Romanov survival claimants. I was honored to serve as his interpreter during many of these interviews.

The sequel made a fine, one-volume combination of all the new stories. The book even touched on the part my grandmother played in helping bring away the box that contained evidence of the killings. But I disagreed with my friend's subtitle, *The Final Chapter*. I knew there would be further chapters to this story. The future is always full of surprises. This volume offers later developments. And who knows what we may yet learn? There will always be more avenues to investigate.

During the nineties and beyond, I ramped up my own efforts to find the bodies of the two children plus those of Nicholas II's brother, Grand Duke Mikhail, and his secretary.

I met Bob Massie through mutual acquaintances of him and Masha, my wife. At a fundraiser Masha was throwing at the Tolstoy Foundation Center, she was talking to one of her cousins, Marina Romanov Beadleston, and mentioned that I'd become much more interested in the Romanov story. Marina told her I needed to get together with Bob Massie, who was writing a sequel to his book *Nicholas and Alexandra*. The two of us had the same focus, so why not get together? Masha invited Bob Massie for lunch. When he heard I knew Avdonin, he was thrilled. That was the first person on his list of must-interviews.

I told him I was interested in making a trip to Russia to see the sites in question for myself. It was natural that we make that trip together, especially since Bob needed an interpreter. Masha and I were able to facilitate some appointments for his trip, as we'd done with Avdonin. Masha set up interviews with the leading scientists in the case, with the investigator Vladimir Soloviev, and with the Avdonins in Yekaterinburg.

Our first trip was to the morgue, and there I saw those stainless-steel tables with bodies lying guarded but in sealable plastic domes. I looked at each of the sad, bare skeletons, caught in their processes of deterioration and returning to dust. These had once been people—members of a celebrated, privileged family; in three cases, young ladies who never got the chance to become wives or mothers. All of them were reduced to bones and dental work, with the occasional bullet hole visible in a skull. They'd been killed brutally and discarded unceremoniously. I wanted to do all in my power to help verify them and give them a proper, Christian burial. Most of all, I wanted to reunite them with two missing family members.

Then came the trip I'd been thoroughly anticipating: the Four Brothers Mine area, then Pig's Meadow. I knew the landscape had evolved, as nature is always in motion. But still, I figured I should be able to get some idea of how things transpired on those two dark nights. As Massie and Avdonin chatted about the events of 1918, I let my eyes roam across the rampant weeds, the stones and the trees, and realized I was within the setting of my grandmother's stories—stories she'd told me many times.

This was the little setting I'd tried so hard to imagine. I was retracing the steps of her friend Sokolov, who'd had such limited time to make sense of hidden activities. Avdonin showed us a round hole in the ground called Ganin's Pit (Ganina Yama in Russian). I knew that Sokolov wasted a month on this spot, trying to pump out the water and its contents. A rotting fence divided the bottom of the pit. Sokolov's people would search one side, then dig up the other.

Sokolov had seen the rubbish thrown into the pit, and his search did find Anastasia's dog's carcass and a human finger, particles of ash and some shreds of clothing. In the area, he found traces of two bonfires and a few corsets and buckles. These he had saved.

As we lingered at the relevant sites, I could envision the drunken mob on that first night, Yurovsky's frustration with their chaos, the carts squeaking under the weight of the bodies, and later, the truck mired in the sludge. It had been anything but a smooth operation. Yet for more than six decades, their purpose had been accomplished; nobody had found the evidence of the crime.

Bob kept a busy schedule, packing in as many interviews as he could, and I served as interpreter. He was glad to have my language skills, and I was glad to be a fly on the wall and hear all these men talk about their work.

Avdonin was a huge fan of the book *Nicholas and Alexandra*. He knew that Bob Massie was an American who thoroughly understood the Romanovs and what they endured. And he wondered if somehow all this digging and identification could help to heal the breach between the Russians in-country and the Russians abroad. "These remains should be the reason for the unification of our people who were split by the revolution," Avdonin said. He spoke eloquently of the worlds of religion, of science, of every chasm between the two Russias, and how people should be able to come together over this discovery and its meaning.

Yet just as the Romanovs were injured in life by slander, he felt it was now happening in death and exhumation: "But again, nothing is working out, the fate of these people continues—various kinds of disinformation exist as well as the distortions of information, and when we say something, we have to think through, very carefully, what we are about to say."

His overview of the whole sad situation was right on target. I enjoyed each day of my trip, but I felt a growing desire to find those two missing children. I called Maples in Florida to recount my adventures in Russia and to begin talking about how to find Tsarevich Alexei and his sister. Avdonin shared our desire, but as usual, there was no funding to be found in Russia. We felt there was at least some chance we could find these bodies, though, of course, new discoveries would only unleash more skepticism and willing disbelief. Many people were totally invested in their refusal to accept the science.

Sadly, though, Dr. Maples developed a cancerous brain tumor, and his health began to deteriorate. He knew his travels were at an end after a long and distinguished career, but he introduced me to anthropologists at the U.S. Army Central Identification Laboratory in Hawaii. He died in 1997 at the age of fifty-nine.

Soon, my career dovetailed perfectly with that lab.

15

Keeping the Dream Alive

I was heartbroken to learn that Dr. Maples couldn't join in our coming search, given his poor health. He encouraged me to continue the quest without him, and I had every intention of doing so. Dr. Maples had been a wonderful ally, but by this time, I was determined to see this endeavor to fruition by writing, by making appeals, by working with new friends and old—anything that might keep the world from losing interest in the Romanov story. To help us move forward, Dr. Maples pointed me to the U.S. Army Central Identification Laboratory at Hickam Air Force Base in Hawaii (CILHI).

This was a group whose mission is to search, recover, and identify remains of those who disappeared in American wars. It was combined with a prisoner-of-war and missing-in-action task force later known as Joint POW/MIA Accounting Command. Then, in 2015, the group was deactivated by the U.S. Department of Defense.

Dr. Maples believed CILHI, as part of the well-funded American military, had the expertise, equipment, and experience to carry out the search we intended. I could imagine that if any group could make the difference in finally locating the missing Romanov children, this would be the one. The question was, how would we gain the agency's interest and commitment? Were they willing to send a team and technology to Russia for a search that could be dismissed as another country's business?

Dr. Maples gave me the phone number for CILHI's senior anthropologist, Dr. Thomas D. Holland. Once we were able to talk over the phone, in early 1996, my hopes were kindled a bit. The group was willing to listen, but I'd have to travel to Hawaii and appear before Col. William H. Jordan, CILHI's director.

My ship at the time was the SS *Sea-Land Discovery*, an American flag container vessel. And around that time, we just happened to receive a route change to the U.S. West Coast—including Hawaii. Now I could drop in on Hickam Air Force Base when I was in the neighborhood, so to speak. On my own dime, a trip to Hawaii just for a meeting would have been very expensive.

As soon as I was able to visit Hickam, I met the lab's top anthropologists, Dr. Thomas Holland, Dr. Thomas Mann, and CILHI's director, Colonel Jordan. I told my own story, offered a background of the Romanov burial search and investigation, and then made my proposal: a joint U.S.-Russian expedition to find and identify the two missing children. Again, a selling point was the opportunity for the two countries to cooperate in a post-Soviet world.

At our meeting on April 4, 1996, I was received warmly. Holland was enthusiastic, even intrigued by the idea of a search for these lost royal children. He was all but ready to make his travel plans. We made a tentative list of team members we'd require: an anthropologist, a medic, a quartermaster corps officer, a senior NCO, and a linguist.

I wanted these scientists and officers to understand this wasn't my *thing*. It wasn't a personal project, nor a case of me reaching for glory or credit of any kind. Bringing closure to the Romanov executions was simply a dream I'd carried inside me from the earliest days of my grandmother's stories. I hated to think of those small skeletons still lying in the cold earth in unmarked graves. No one deserves that—least of all children, even less murdered children.

Now that the rest of their family had been located, that family needed to be reunited in a sanctified burial. People needed to be able to come, pay their respects, and understand the hardest lessons of our history.

I think my personal passion for this work was evident, and I had no problem enlisting CILHI's scientists. Then came my most important appointment, the one with Col. William H. Jordan, the director. He was a large, imposing figure, a soldier in fatigues who had served two tours in Vietnam. He'd spent ten years working on POW/MIA issues, was planning his final identification mission at the time, and would retire soon afterward. He had the no-nonsense demeanor of a drill sergeant, and I wondered if I were about to navigate rougher waters. This was, after all, a Cold War veteran.

As I took my seat, Colonel Jordan said, "What's up?"

"Sir, I appreciate your meeting with me. Our mutual friend Dr. William Maples suggested we talk. You may have heard he's facing some medical problems, sadly enough, and he had to discontinue his work on IDing the remains of the Romanov children."

The colonel nodded, listening attentively.

"I've heard great things about the work of CILHI," I said. "I know of its expertise and experience with the delicate work of identifying remains. And I'm hoping your group will take an interest."

"I understand," he replied. "You just need to know that there's a lot of red tape in something like this. Bottom line, if you want to get something from the army, you have to go higher than me. Matter of fact, best-case scenario would be a request from the State Department. That would open all the doors."

I nodded and showed my appreciation. But of course I'd hoped for a green light, the beginning of concrete plans. I'd waited many years to see this opportunity arise, and I was impatient for action. Red tape was my greatest fear.

"I'll tell you what I *can* do for you," he said. "I can send your request up the chain of command to Gen. James W. Wold at the Defense POW/MIA office. It's in Crystal City, Virginia."

I left that meeting fearing that the fog of bureaucracy was about to roll in. On the plus side, I was confident the colonel was willing to do what he could. I was willing to face down whatever bureaucratic blockades were thrown our way.

I turned now to my contacts on the Russian side. By June 7, 1996, I had in hand an invitation from Vladimir Krysov, vice president of the Sverdlovsk region in Russia. I forwarded it to Colonel Jordan and Dr. Jonnie E. Webb, deputy director of CILHI. The message read: "The Government of the Sverdlovsk region welcome your decision to provide charitable assistance to the Yekaterinburg Obretenye Foundation in their search for the remains of members of the imperial family along with our specialists, who will provide the necessary cooperation in accomplishing these tasks. And in the event these searches are successful, any following identification studies and publications of the results will be done, without a doubt, only with your participation." This established an official invitation from the Sverdlovsk government and a promise that the Americans would receive full cooperation and no interference.

I also asked Avdonin to make a request of his own. He could speak with the authority and appeal of the very man who had begun this quest, who had been steadfast for twenty years, and who now needed expertise that was available nowhere else.

In late August he wrote his own letter to Colonel Jordan. He reviewed the basic situation and the need to either find these last two sets of remains or demonstrate once and for all that they could not be found. He knew that a period of nearly eighty years was a long time for human remains to lie in the soil, unprotected—this would be a great challenge. He mentioned his friendship with me and the positive relationship I enjoyed with the Russian foundation. He underlined the financial situation: a nonprofit organization in an economically struggling nation. Moscow could not or would not help, and this created the need for charitable assistance.

Dr. Avdonin referred to the boost James Baker had provided as secretary of state. It was a strong reference. Though a Democratic administration was now in office in Washington DC, Baker was highly esteemed by both parties, and his name was a powerful reference in a situation in which the U.S. State Department would make the call. He further described the help Dr. William Maples and his team had provided; Dr. Maples, of course, was well known in CILHI circles.

Dr. Avdonin made his appeal for American assistance. "It would be an act of great generosity on your part," he concluded. Full accommodations would be provided and local specialists would be available as resources. And he closed with some practical information: the summer months would be the logical time frame for a search, and the area to cover would make three square kilometers, most of it woody with quite a few ditches.

These communications kept the subject in the air. But I wasn't through. I thought about the fact that I was searching for the remains of those missing in action—people who were killed on foreign soil. That gave me the idea to contact my friends Peter and Marina Afanasenko. This couple worked at the State Department as interpreters, and they knew many of the people who could help us in an overseas mission of identification.

I called Peter and updated him on what I was up to, and he suggested I write a proposal letter to Ambassador James Collins at the Bureau of CIS Affairs,

U.S. State Department. My letter was dated October 23, 1996, with an attached proposal sheet. I spoke of the lifelong dream of those of us from Russia to have closure on the fate of the tsar and his family. I asked for his willingness to review the proposal and advise us whether a search for the final sets of remains would be feasible.

The weather was growing colder as late November arrived. America had just reelected its president three weeks earlier, when I received my reply from Thomas Lynch, director of the Office of Russian Affairs at the Department of State, on behalf of the ambassador. He assured me the U.S. government had been following the discovery of the Romanov remains. He wrote, "Because this is a matter with important international resonance, the State Department would support the participation of specialists from Hickam Air Force Base in the latest search proposed by the Sverdlovsk Oblast. We hope that their expertise contributes to your success." I felt deeply encouraged and optimistic for the coming year of 1997. This would be the year Boris Yeltsin would sign the Russia-Chechnya peace treaty; as always with Russia, we had to hope the conditions would remain stable enough for us to get something done. One way or another, I felt we'd make a breakthrough either soon or never.

Holland wrote to me in a letter dated January 21, 1997. He simply offered the update that CILHI's directors were in the process of making their decision whether to participate in our search—and this would happen within days. It was agonizing to consider that we might lose our chance to work with the best-equipped technicians in the world at locating and identifying remains. At this point, author Robert K. Massie spoke up. As the Romanov biographer, perhaps his was the voice that could tilt the decision in the right direction. A writer always knows the best way to state a case. He wrote:

> Dear Dr. Holland: Please forgive me for breaking in on you suddenly, but I spent all of yesterday with Peter Sarandinaki and Alexander Avdonin, before Avdonin returned last night to Moscow. You know who Peter is. Avdonin, as you probably know, is the geologist from Yekaterinburg in the Urals, who originally discovered the site of the buried remains of nine members of the Russian Imperial Family.

I am an American author who, in 1967, published *Nicholas and Alexandra*, the first serious account of the life of Tsar Nicholas II and his family. In 1995, I published *The Romanovs: The Final Chapter*, which is an account of the discovery of the bones and the multi-national effort to authenticate them using forensic anthropology and DNA technology. I am enclosing copies of two papers from *Nature Genetics* which report this DNA research.

It is, as you also know, Peter's keen hope—and Avdonin's and mine—that you and your colleagues will be able to go to the Urals and search for and find two missing children, the Tsarevich Alexis and one of his four sisters. I am faxing this letter and these materials because Peter tells me that today you will be presenting this project to the senior U.S. Army officer who will be making this decision.

I believe it is important for this officer to know that this proposed effort will not be breaking new ground in this particular field of Russian-American joint effort. Twice before, American government agencies have been asked and have agreed to participate in this effort to identify these remains. In the first instance, in 1992 during a visit to Yekaterinburg, Secretary of State James A. Baker III agreed to put together an American government team to go to the Urals. In 1995, a Russian-American team worked together for three months at the Armed Forces Institute of Pathology in Rockville, Maryland and provided conclusive proof that these were the Romanovs.

Should the senior officer desire me to do so, I would be happy to speak to him at his convenience and provide any details I can.

The bad news arrived on January 27. Col. James H. Colvin Jr., Quartermaster Corps, Commander, U.S. Army, CILHI, wrote that he'd reviewed our proposal and had to decline it. CILHI's resources were already committed for the remainder of the calendar year. Improved relations with China and North Korea, along with improvements in technology, were providing lots of new opportunities in those fields. He further affirmed that the group's primary responsibility was the recovery of the remains of American soldiers from past conflicts. But if the mission schedule changed, he promised to reconsider.

At this point, through my grave disappointment, I wrote a congressman—Rep. Benjamin A. Gilman of New York's Twentieth District. He was the chairman of the Committee on International Relations. I shared with him not only the existing correspondence but also what I'd been told off the record: the U.S. Army indeed had the resources to fulfill their commitments with North Korea and China and also our Russian project. What was needed was a small nudge of the political variety.

Representative Gilman got involved. The deputy assistant secretary of defense (POW/Missing Personnel Affairs) replied to his inquiry on my behalf. The answer was still no, and the primary reason given was the priority of our missing and unaccounted-for servicemen from our various conflicts.

By this time, it was May, and the congressman wrote to let me know there was no better news. Our letters crossed in the mail. I was writing to let him know I could be as resolute as the entire U.S. Army. I knew the Hickam team wasn't going to help us, but I'd moved ahead to seek out other options. I'd located two teams of American forensic anthropologists and specialists who were far more eager to travel to Yekaterinburg and get to work.

There were forensic specialists who came from Dr. Maples's University of Florida labs, and a Colorado State University group from NecroSearch International, under Dr. Diane L. France, who specialized in remains identification. We simply needed a final decision from CILHI and the U.S. military, and we'd be ready to go, except for one more thing. I personally had to raise the funding for these high-level science teams to do this work.

I may have been as resolute as the U.S. Army, but I wasn't nearly as well funded.

1. Anna Rozanova-Naryshkina, author's grandmother, in her later years. Sarandinaki family archives.

2. ABOVE: Lt. Gen. Sergei N. Rozanov (*second from right*) and his staff officers, Penza, 1912. Sarandinaki family archives.

3. RIGHT: Judge Procurator Nikolai Sokolov. Russian State Archives (GARF).

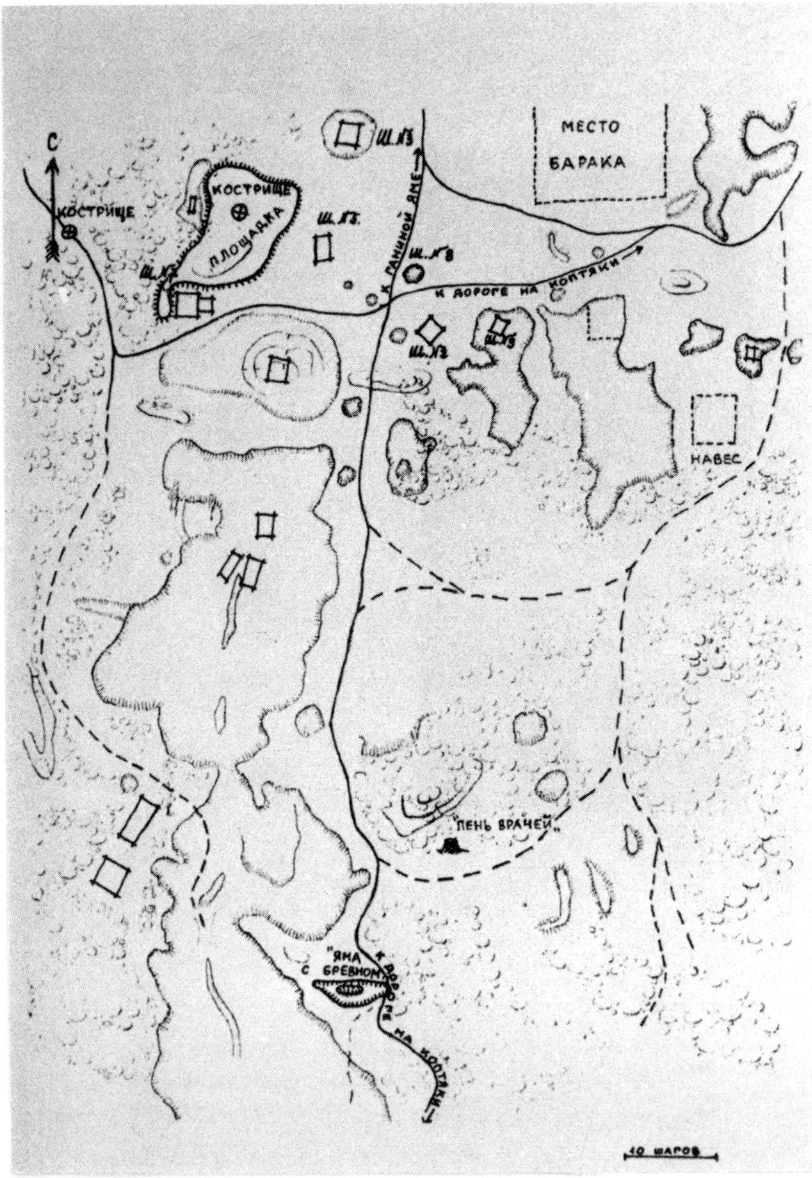

4. Map of the Four Brothers Mine area showing the location of the bonfires (marked with *x*) found by Nikolai Sokolov, 1919. Map by Lt. Gen. Mikhail K. Diterikhs, from his book *The Murder of the Imperial Family and Members of the House of Romanov in the Urals* (Vladivostok, 1922).

5. ABOVE: The open mine at Four Brothers. The pile of stones on the left side of the platform was left for us to investigate. Photo by investigator Nikolai Sokolov. MS Russ 35, Houghton Library, Harvard University.

6. OPPOSITE TOP: Animal bones found at the open mine at Four Brothers. Courtesy of Dr. Sergey Nikitin, Bureau of Forensic Medical Examination of the Moscow Department of Health.

7. OPPOSITE BOTTOM: Bullets found in the gravel pile left by Sokolov. The author found the first bullet. Courtesy of Dr. Sergey Nikitin, Bureau of Forensic Medical Examination of the Moscow Department of Health.

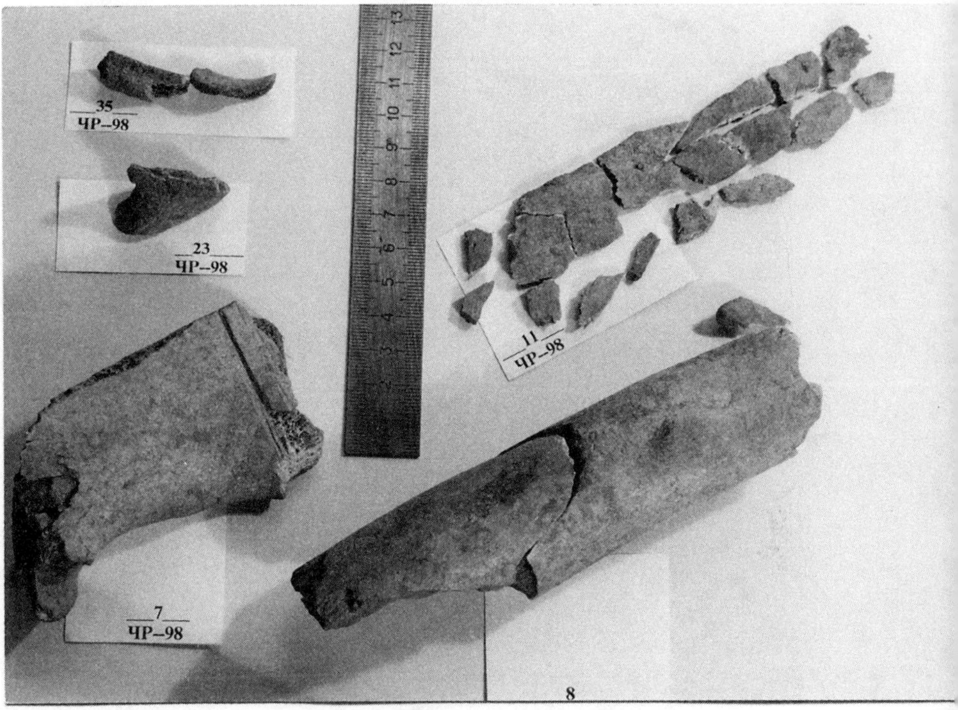
35
ЧР--98
23
ЧР--98
11
ЧР--98
7
ЧР--98
8

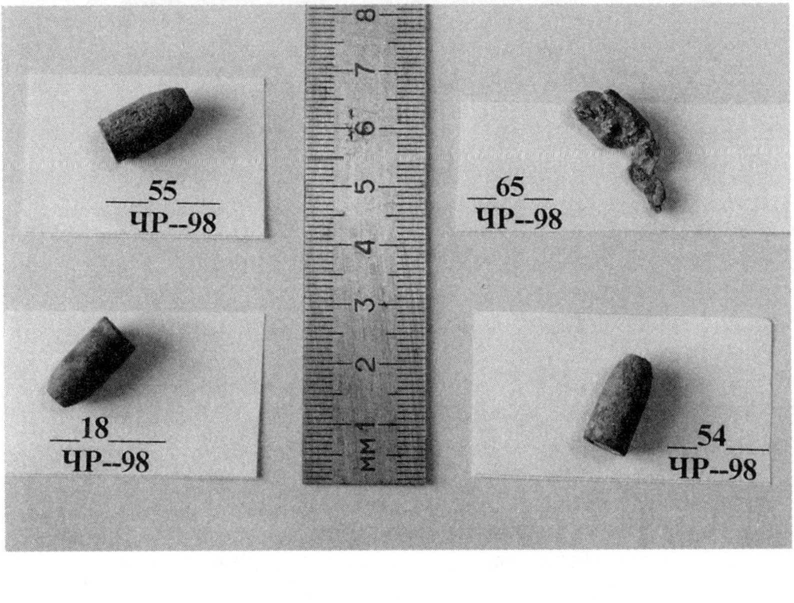
55
ЧР--98
65
ЧР--98
18
ЧР--98
54
ЧР--98

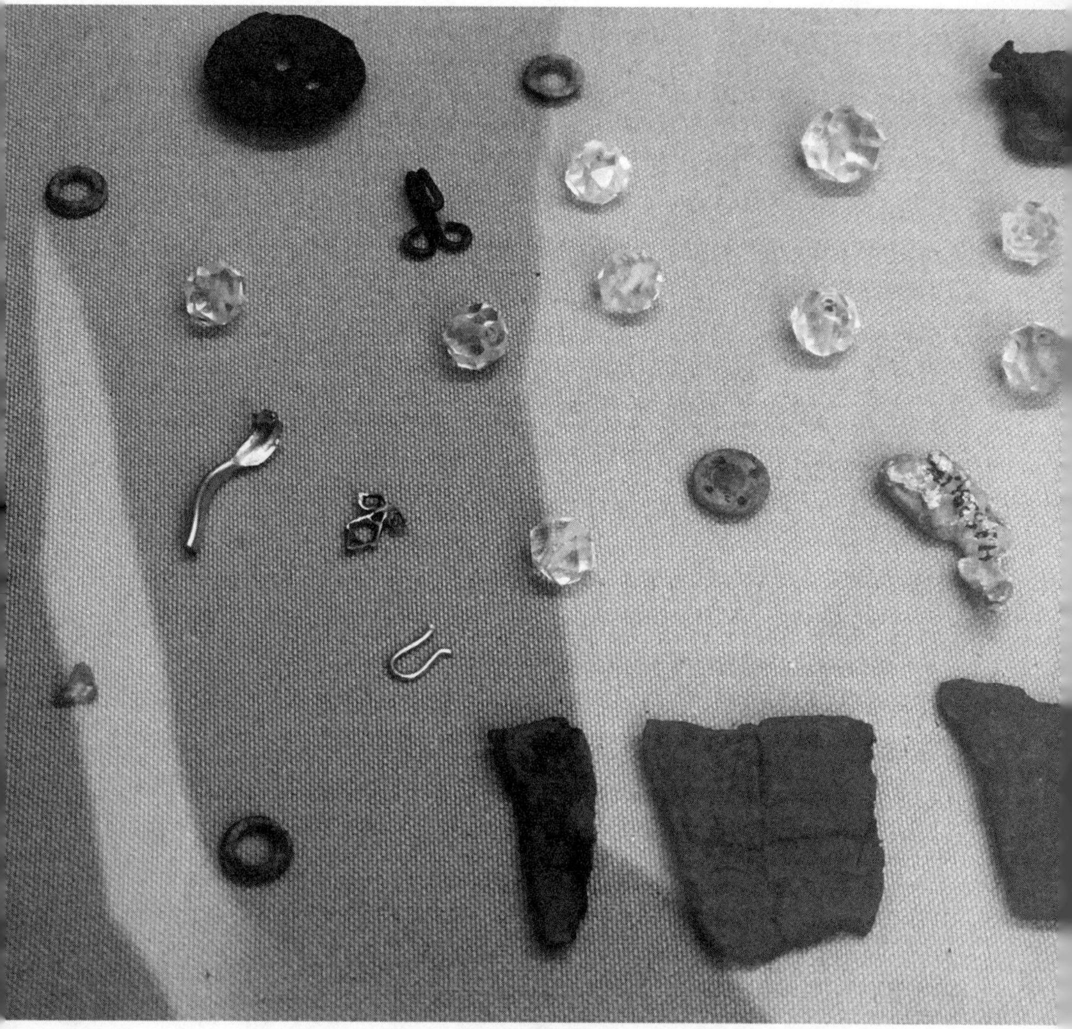

8. Items belonging to the imperial family found at Four Brothers during our 1998 and 1999 searches. Author photo.

9. TOP: Peter Ermakov, second-in-command of the execution squad that murdered the imperial family in Yekaterinburg. Caption on the back of the photo reads, "I am standing on the grave of the tsar." Russian State Archives (GARF).

10. BOTTOM: Military governor of the Amur region Lt. Gen. Sergei Rozanov and his daughter Anna in Vladivostok, 1919. Sarandinaki family archives.

11. Lt. Gen. Sergei Rozanov after being evacuated from Vladivostok, January 1920. Sarandinaki family archives.

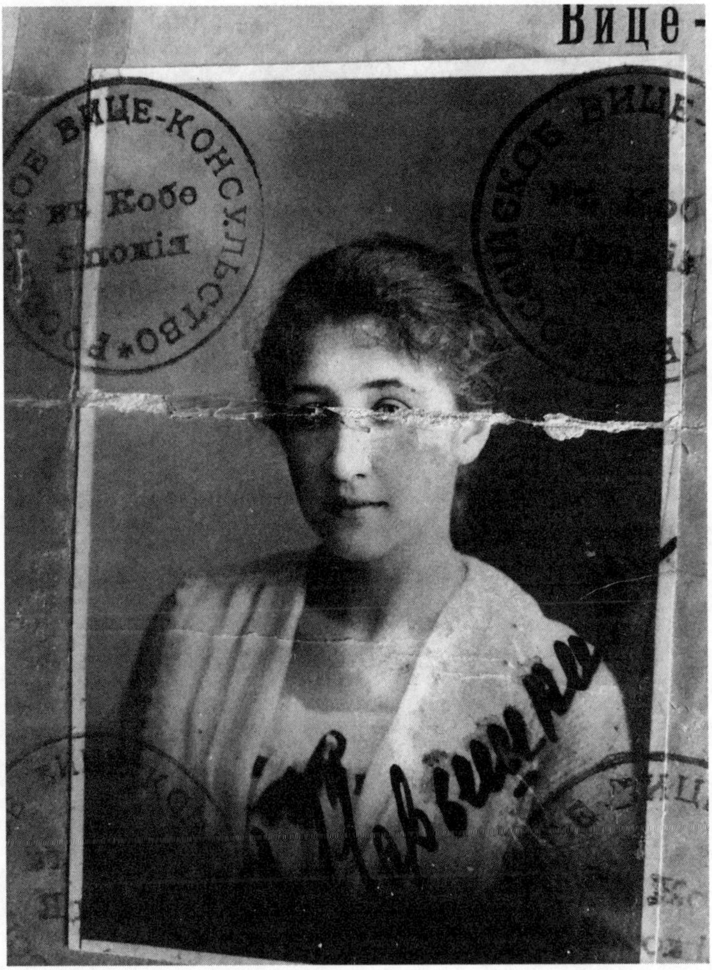

12. Anna Rozanova-Naryshkina, January 1920, after evacuation from Vladivostok. Sarandinaki family archives.

13. TOP: Famed Sokolov Box in which Judge Procurator Nikolai Sokolov carried the main proof of the Romanovs' murder. Author photo.

14. BOTTOM: Dr. Alexander Avdonin and wife Galina Pavlovna found the remains of the Romanovs with filmmaker Geli Ryabov in 1978. Author photo, 2004.

15. The imperial family grave on the Koptiaki Road in 2004 and 1918. Author photo.

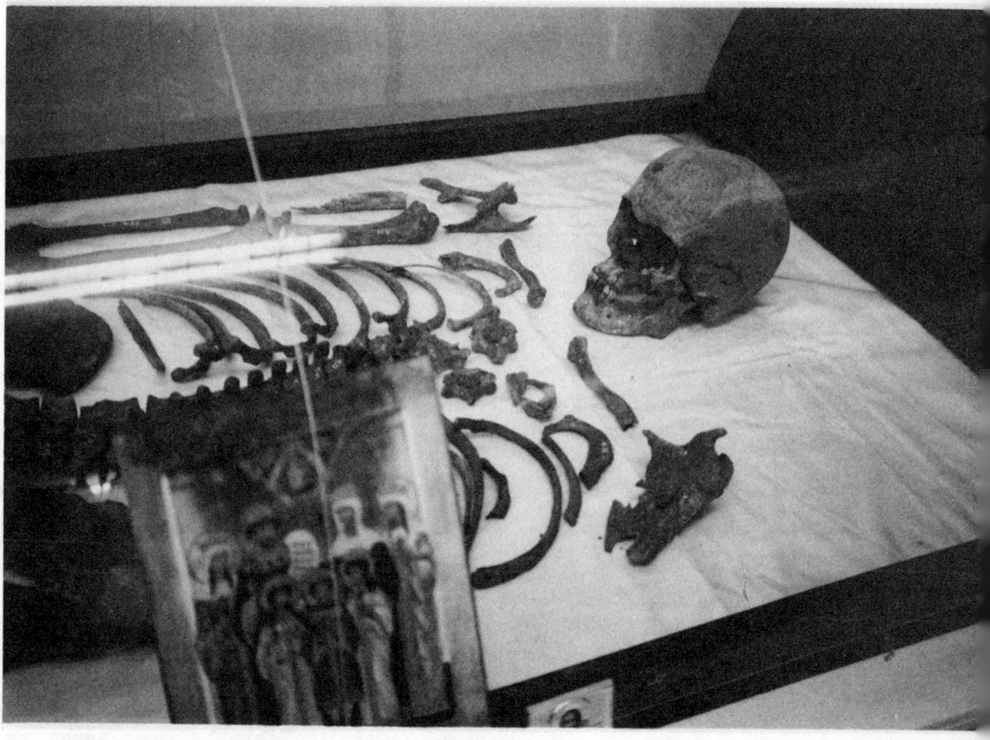

16. Remains of Tsar Nicholas II, kept at the Yekaterinburg Bureau of Forensic Medicine, 1994. Author photo.

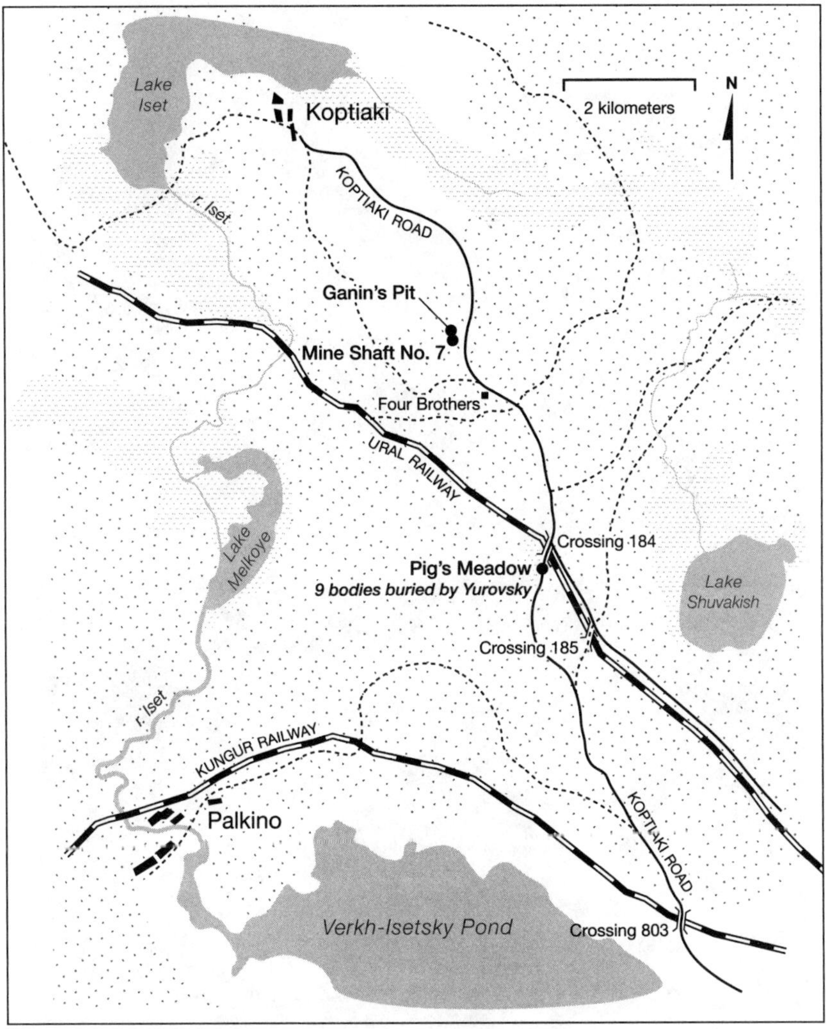

17. Map of the Koptiaki Road. Created by Alexander Trubetzkoy.

18. TOP: Search for the remains of Tsarevich Alexei and his sister Grand Duchess Maria, 2004. Author photo.

19. BOTTOM: Remains of Tsarevich Alexei and his sister Grand Duchess Maria, found at Pig's Meadow just seventy meters from the main grave of the Romanovs. Courtesy of A. M. Kruchinin.

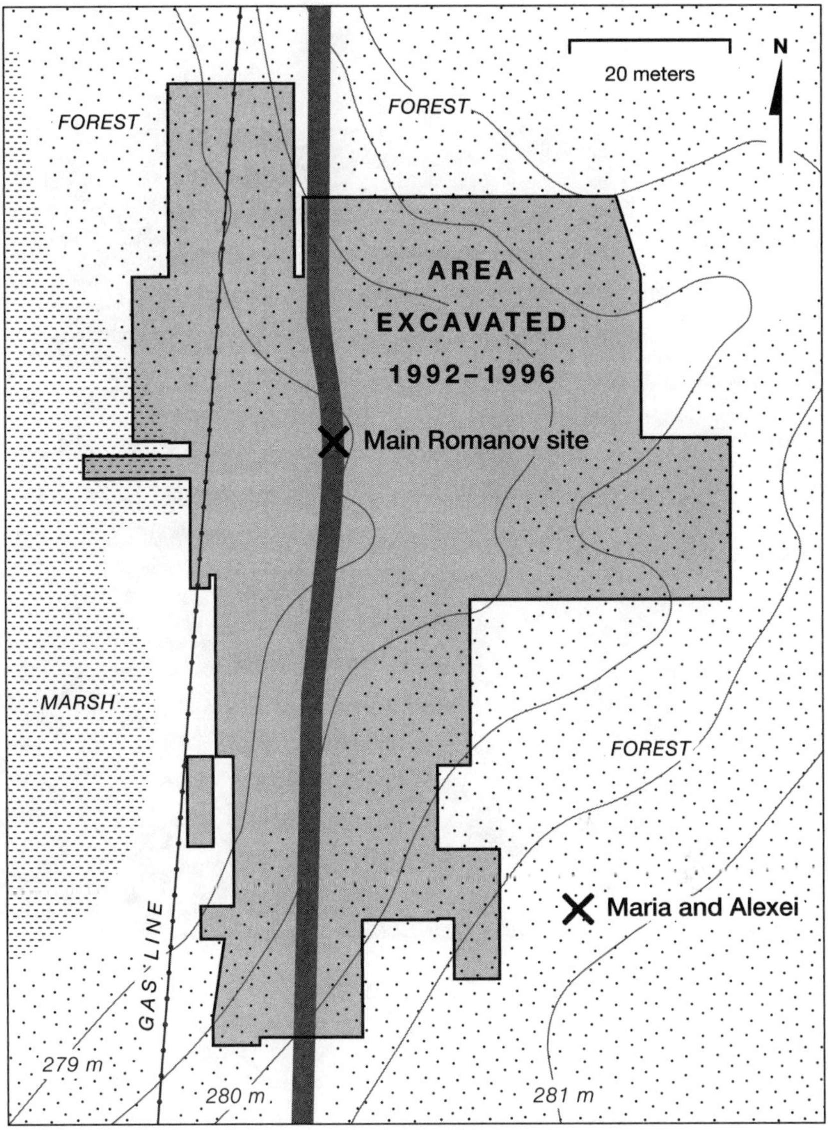

20. Map of Pig's Meadow showing the search area and where the graves of the Romanovs were found. Created by Alexander Trubetzkoy.

21. (*Left to right*) Dr. Michael Coble and Dr. Anthony Falsetti with Col. Vladimir Soloviev, head of the investigation for the identification of the Romanov remains, 2008. Author photo.

22. Author (*second from right*) with Russian team that found the remains of Tsarevich Alexei and Grand Duchess Maria. Author photo.

23. Icon of the Russian imperial family and relics. Author photo.

24. The Holy Trinity—the oldest trees in our search area for the remains of Mikhail Romanov and his secretary, Nikolai Johnson, near Perm. One of the killers carved the trunk of the oldest tree with the initials GDMR (Grand Duke Mikhail Romanov), marking the area where the murders were committed. Author photo.

25. The Fabergé locket that belonged to Empress Alexandra, purchased at auction by Nikolai Bachmakov. Hair found inside was subject to DNA studies by the FBI DNA Laboratory, Quantico, Virginia. Courtesy of Nikolai Bachmakov and the Russian History Museum, Jordanville, New York.

26. Hair found in the Fabergé locket by Nikolai Bachmakov. Courtesy of Nikolai Bachmakov and the Russian History Museum, Jordanville, New York.

27. Frame and photo of Louise of Hesse-Kassel, queen of Denmark, maternal grandmother of Tsar Nicholas II. Hair found in the frame was subject to DNA studies by the FBI DNA Laboratory, Quantico, Virginia. Courtesy of Nikolai Bachmakov and the Russian History Museum, Jordanville, New York.

16

NecroSearch Joins the Hunt

I had known from the start that plan A—to work with the full resources of the U.S. Army's CILHI team—had a good chance of failing to launch. It's no easy task for a single individual to mobilize such a large, government-bound unit. But I had to try. Once CILHI's final denial came in, I had plan B ready to execute.

I wrote Dr. Avdonin on April 2, 1997. I explained to him that politics had once again gotten in the way, this time from the American and North Korean sides. Relations between those two were improving enough that missing American pilots could now be sought. The Hickam team wanted to place their focus there—at least that was the narrative we'd been given.

But now I introduced the two teams with whom I'd also been in communication, from Florida and Colorado to Dr. Avdonin. Together, their experience, equipment, and eagerness made for an excellent secondary strategy. I was also excited to add team members from the animal kingdom: bloodhounds who'd been trained to find remains and graves with remarkable accuracy.

The Colorado part of the team represented a unit called NecroSearch, made up of volunteers using their skills to assist in locating human remains. I'd traveled to Denver to meet with them—again, on my way to my ship, *Sea-Land Discovery*. I'd presented the project to them, and the NecroSearch members had voted to sign on. Their eagerness, mobility, and can-do spirit had encouraged me more than I could express. As a matter of fact, they wanted to send twenty specialists. Dr. France and Dr. Falsetti actually came with strong recommendations from Dr. Thomas Holland of CILHI; he was confident we'd be more than pleased with their work.

What I needed now from Dr. Avdonin was his proposal to accept the combined team for the search for the missing children. Then I could begin raising funds. Allowing for Russian weather, we could come in September 1997 or May 1998, based on how quickly we could get the financial resources in place.

I needed to raise $100,000. I couldn't fund twenty scientists, but at least I could raise the finances to get a small team to Yekaterinburg for preliminary planning. Dr. France, Dr. Falsetti, geologist Jim Reed, and I made that trip in February 1998. Once again, I would be translating between the groups.

I tried to rest on the lengthy flight, but it wasn't a quiet journey. One of the passengers grew ill, and someone asked for a doctor. I turned to Dr. France and Dr. Falsetti. "I know your backgrounds are in anthropology," I said, "but could you help? Maybe you took some required medical courses?"

"We only get them once they're dead," they replied, somewhat deadpan.

So I raised my hand. As a ship captain, I had a bit of emergency medical training. Soon I was checking out the passenger, and it was evident to me it was something serious. The plane landed in Reykjavik, we unloaded the sick passenger, and once again we took flight.

This happened to be the very season when 20th Century Fox released its fact-free feature-length animation *Anastasia*. There it was, playing in downtown Helsinki. Dr. France and Reed posed for a snapshot in front of the theater poster. They hoped to identify the missing daughter soon, but it wasn't going to happen on the silver screen.

Meanwhile, the Russian government wanted nothing more than for the controversy over identification to go away. There was a large public ceremony of interment planned at the Church of Saint Peter and Saint Paul in Saint Petersburg for the eightieth anniversary, in July of this very year, but the Russian Orthodox Church still wasn't ready to accept the DNA results. The "expert commission," which I'd encountered in America, was applying as much pressure as possible to sustain the controversy and cling to mythology rather than what science was telling us.

We finally arrived at Yekaterinburg, and Dr. Avdonin was there to meet us. He took us to Pig's Meadow—covered at the time by a blanket of snow—and then to the morgue, where the scientists would finally get their first glimpse of the bones at the Yekaterinburg Bureau of Forensic Medicine.

We walked the four flights of steps to reach our destination, and Dr. Nikolai Nevolin was there to greet us. As the morgue director, he'd seen his life change as this collection of bones had come under his care. It was under the shocked eye of Dr. Nevolin that the first American group had come here, studied the bones for a few minutes, and offered its basic findings. While he kept watch over these damaged skeletons, it was the guard at the entrance, a quietly imposing soldier with a loaded AK-47, who communicated the value of this room's contents.

As we entered the room, our group fell silent. Just being in the presence of these remains has that effect. Anthropologists, such as those on our team, tend not to treat bones with a cold scientific approach—they realize these were once living souls, laughing and loving, dreaming and dreading. And these were the remains of royalty—important personages in the pageant of history.

Dr. France is often shown in photographs regarding a skull, much like Shakespeare's Hamlet. But instead of "To be or not to be?" her question is "Was or was not?" She must peel away time's obscuring shadow and determine whose face was once worn by this structure of bones and skull. Now, in Yekaterinburg, she lifted to her nose one of the bones of Dr. Botkin and sniffed it. This was something Dr. Nevolin hadn't seen. With these Americans, one never knew what to expect.

Dr. France told the non-anthropologists she'd noticed a bit of adipocere on the bone. This substance, often known as corpse wax, can be found on bones in the process of decomposing, though not often in bones this old. If there was an odor, it could be presented to the trained bloodhounds and offer a significant boost in the search for the two missing bodies—if the bones still in the ground also had this substance. The Russians present were impressed.

I found this interesting as well, but I was more eager to ask Dr. France's opinion of those remains now identified by the Russians as Anastasia. Of the skeletons before us, these were the true "bones of contention." Dr. Maples had firmly believed these were actually Maria's bones, and that Anastasia was still out there somewhere with her younger brother.

The other item for which I wanted a second opinion was the question of beheading. These old myths lingered, insisting that the heads had been removed and taken to Moscow for display. There was, of course, no reliable historical tradition suggesting that—only urban legends. So Dr. France examined the neckbones of each family member. She agreed with Dr. Nevolin that none of these victims had been beheaded. They'd endured terrible treatment to be sure, but not only were the heads accounted for, there were no severed neck bones. The heads had never been detached from their respective necks.

But the verdict on Anastasia was a more troubling call. Dr. France and Dr. Falsetti understood the underlying tensions on this subject. Over time, Anastasia had become the most famous of the children because of the all the stories about her supposed survival. Her name and character had entered the realm of mythology. The popular children's movie playing at that very moment made it all too apparent.

But the real issue was that Russian scientists had agreed on a finding, and American scientists had quickly disputed it. The identity of those bones was now entangled in a question of national rivalries.

The two present American scientists leaned toward Dr. Maples's finding—this skeleton seemed to be a female between her late teens and early twenties. Anastasia had been only seventeen years and one month; her sister, Maria, nineteen. This skeleton was a good fit for the latter, but not for the former. Those were the facts, no matter how inconvenient. This was discussed quietly, though Dr. Avdonin and his wife could hear the drift of things and began to whisper nervously to each other.

Once we'd left and were on our own, Dr. France and Dr. Falsetti stated the case to us: "Those are Maria's bones in there. Anastasia is still missing."

The matter of greatest importance, of course, was not the collection of bones and remains in that room; it was the ones yet to be located. Therefore, our hopes were that this difference of opinion could be smoothed over. We needed to worry about how to search, and how to consolidate our efforts. This wasn't primarily about identification of the previous finds.

Our meeting with the Russian scientists was set for February 8. I was really looking forward to practical discussions. We were invited to a luncheon, and afterward our team would meet with Dr. Avdonin and members of the Obretenye Foundation, his charitable group for overseeing all the activities relating to the Romanov discoveries. We were beginning to call our own group SEARCH, an acronym for Scientific Expedition to Account for the Romanov Children. Dr.

Avdonin initiated a document of protocol to serve as an agreement between SEARCH and the Obretenye Foundation. He defined the task, its target locations, and the equipment and resources to be used. But then we came to the roadblock: Dr. Avdonin's wording named the individuals we'd seek: Tsarevich Alexei and Grand Duchess Maria.

I was translating between the parties. When she heard those names, Dr. France said, "We cannot sign that. Please change the protocol to state that we are searching for the remains of one of the daughters."

I turned to the Russians and translated, gently making the case that our two American scientists felt strongly that Anastasia, not Maria, was the missing daughter. I gave a little of the reasoning, relating to the age indicated by the bones—a bit too well developed for the youngest daughter.

The next two hours were difficult, to put it mildly. As the Russian group saw it, the Americans had once again walked into the mortuary and made a quick determination at variance with the work of local scientists, who had studied the evidence longer and who took great pride in the processes they'd used. For them it was an insult to the Russian men and women who had done so much study. And how could a quick American glance at these bones be classified as science?

While the Russians were badgering Dr. France, Jim Reed typed the word PRAVDA in a huge font on his laptop screen and showed it to her. It's the Russian word for *truth*. In such ways the Americans supported each other and held a united front toward remaining calm during the storm.

The Russians were quite angry and insulting, but we did our best to retain our composure and let the storm die down of its own accord. The document simply wasn't going to be signed in its present wording.

Inside, I was feeling despair. We'd worked so hard to come to this moment. I'd been to Hawaii, to Colorado, to other places. I'd written countless letters. I'd navigated around obstacles as a good sea captain avoids stormy waters. And now things were falling apart over—once again—Anastasia. In life, she had a reputation for being a somewhat impish troublemaker. In death, she was selling movie tickets and stirring international disputes.

Dr. France and Dr. Falsetti weren't offering an unorthodox opinion. Their identification of Maria matched the findings of Dr. William Maples, a forensic anthropologist; Dr. Michael Baden, a forensic pathologist; and Dr. Lowell

Levine, a forensic odontologist and director of the New York State Police Crime Laboratory in Albany, New York, who had traveled to Yekaterinburg in 1992 at the request of the Russian government to help the Russian scientists determine which bones belonged to whom.

In a sense, the clock was ticking, because the grand burial of the Romanovs had been scheduled for July—less than six months from now. The last thing the Russians wanted was a fresh controversy, particularly concerning the whereabouts of the notorious youngest daughter. If a scientific disagreement became widely known, the burial would have to be called off, and that would be an embarrassment to the nation. That wasn't an acceptable solution. In the end, the Russians agreed to a document specifying only that the two missing children (whoever they might be) would be sought. And amid an air of uncertainty, the meeting broke up.

The next day, Jim Reed, our geologist, wrote a lengthy note offering his reflections on the day. "This project is going to push us to the limits of our patience and our tolerance," he said. He was both astounded and discouraged by the cultural differences. It had been difficult to hear the knowledge, professionalism, and integrity of his fellow scientists challenged. Yet later in the day, there had been a mood swing, and the American team had been praised and celebrated. It had been odd and disconcerting to see the emotions go back and forth. The Americans were grateful for the antacids they'd brought along, he wryly observed.

Reed recognized a "closed, secretive, and suspicious society" that jealously held onto every shred of information, yet also a group of men and women who wanted desperately to work with well-equipped, well-informed people of science. Their political and scientific orientations were in conflict.

Perhaps it was a microcosm of Russia itself—struggling to emerge from a culture of oppression and shadows, eager to join the international dialogue, but still trying to overcome generations of dysfunction and self-doubt.

Reed was perceptive in his observation that the coming burial of the Romanovs was immensely profound for the population at large. For them, it was a ceremony that would symbolically lay to rest eighty years of repressed guilt. The death of the imperial family was one of history's most reviled crimes, and the country was desperate to put it behind them as it began its post-Soviet epoch. For such a goal, could they swallow their pride and submit to foreign assistance?

The American team would draft a letter of detailed protocol. It would establish in advance the ground rules that would govern the cooperation between the two countries, and thereby avoid further misunderstandings.

En route back to the States, we discussed the turbulent meeting and the future of our project. My request was that the scientists hold off on press conferences and announcements, as excited as they might be about the bones they'd seen and held, and the work still in front of us. I said, "Our case isn't closed. There's no reason for any statements. We can always verify our findings and tell our stories when those final remains are found."

The two bone specialists agreed this was the best course. They would keep silent about the case for two years, until 2000, when they presented their findings before the Academy of Forensic Science in Reno, Nevada. They explained why they believed Maria to be the skeleton in question, and the Russian scientist who'd identified it as Anastasia was there to present his side of the argument.

In late February of 1998, I wrote my friend Dr. Avdonin, thanking him for his hospitality and the work he'd done to organize the meeting. I expressed my eagerness to learn what the Russian group had done in the weeks following. I also approached the subject of how the American group had been treated by some of the Russians.

I was concerned not about bygones but about future conditions of cooperation. Disagreements were always to be expected, but disrespect must always be avoided as a matter of professionalism. It was important that when the team returned in May, as we then hoped would happen, we would have every assurance that the unfortunate events not be repeated. It was everyone's desire to function as a single team.

"Sasha," I said, "you and I, as friends, can perhaps get angry at each other yet forgive and forget. But outside members of the team must be treated with absolute courtesy. I trust and pray that we may all work together in the spirit of friendship."

I offered the same advice I'd given to our American scientists: we should hold off on announcements and pronouncements on the matter of the body in dispute, agreeing that the matter was still under investigation.

I mailed the letter and then did the only thing I could: I watched and waited. As I feared, the American team received no invitation for a return trip. Dr. Avdonin's explanation was that the burial event was approaching in July, and that's where everyone's focus was. There simply wasn't time to prepare for an American search project.

And with that, I couldn't help but feel that our great moment of opportunity was being buried as well. The unpleasant demonstration had created an awkwardness the Russians, even with their desire to find the last two bodies, couldn't get beyond.

Even so, I returned to the Four Brothers Mine area in September—not with anthropologists, not with scientists of any kind, but by myself.

17

Back to Four Brothers

In July 1998 the family of Nicholas II, along with four helpers, was laid to rest in the Catherine Chapel at St. Petersburg's Peter and Paul Cathedral. It was a momentous, dignified ceremony that the Russians hoped would provide salve for an old national wound. Now, at least, the emperor, empress, and their children would lie in the presence of Peter the Great, Catherine the Great, and other luminaries of Russian history. Interestingly, a footman, a maid, a doctor, and a cook would enjoy the same ceremonial interment.

It was the eightieth anniversary of an execution that occurred in a dark basement room, in secret, and at the hands of a group of thugs. As unspeakably brutal as the killings were, the initial burials were just as unthinkably inhuman. Now, a high church ceremony was meant to rectify all this—without exactly confirming it.

The Romanov descendants were present, as were Boris Yeltsin and other national dignitaries. Absent, however, was Patriarch Alexis II of the Russian Orthodox Church. Surely this was an odd omission, particularly in cathedral settings. The Moscow patriarchate was holding fast to its refusal to affirm the remains as those of the imperial family. They cited "doubts" that must be considered. The church was anxious about disagreements within its own walls as well as with the Orthodox Church Abroad.

The voices proclaiming this to be a hoax, that these were not the Romanovs, and even that the genuine corpses had been beheaded, were a small minority. But as tends to be the case, the angriest voices were the loudest, creating the most disruption. The church, always reluctant to give offense to any faction, sided with the "doubt" position, even though the overwhelming verdict of science left no such thing.

For most objective people, the last tsar of Russia and his family were finally buried with honor and before at least some officials of the church. To that extent, the troubling business of their death was at an end. But there was still the business of two missing children, and Dr. Avdonin and associates remained intent on seeing these questions answered as well.

Three months later, in September, they would conduct a search of their own, without Western scientists and their high-tech equipment. I was the only American present—someone at least fluent in their language, there to help and observe, and not to challenge Russian conclusions. I was a sea captain, not a man of science.

My friendship with Dr. Avdonin earned me an invitation to be present for this new search, but from my perspective, I would be present as a witness for the Russian Orthodox Church Abroad, as well as for the White Russians. Those who had been driven from the country because of these very events—revolution and civil war—needed representation in the final denouement out of the tragedies. I would be able to report back to my fellow churchmen and the Russian expatriate community.

I was disheartened to be coming without the brilliant scientists who were willing and ready to do this work. But this search had been a personal ambition of mine for years now. The important thing was to find those children, and if a search was to take place, I wanted to be part of it.

I was much better oriented to my surroundings this time, as I arrived at the Four Brothers Mine site, Ganina Yama. I'd been here before, and I understood the scenery around me in relation to the Old Koptiaki Road. But the key search area, two hundred meters square, had been marked off, then divided into two-meter sections, with numbered stakes. Also, the forest had been cleared of brush and was ready for our search. I was impressed by the preparation, and remembered again that this was a subject of even more tremendous importance regionally than nationally. Sverdlovsk Oblast supported this work, foreseeing a future of lucrative tourism connected to the Romanovs. An impressive monastery would stand here in the future.

But for now, nothing was changed other than the clearing of foliage and the staked search areas. Electromagnetic and seismic profiling studies were being conducted to find anomaly spots. These, it was hoped, would detect regions where the earth had been disturbed. A team of scientists, archaeology students, and volunteers were on hand to take part in a search that caught the public's imagination. There were none of the bloodhounds NecroSearch might have supplied, but there were plenty of eager humans.

The Koptiaki Road had been unpaved even in 1918, and it was in worse condition now, as nature was in the process of burying the tracks of human transport. The village of Koptiaki itself is far to the north, and the road was never more than a cart path. Years of disuse had all but undone it. I followed its path each day for a thirty-minute walk to the site. There was plenty of mud of the type that had bedeviled the burying party so long ago.

But Alexander Avdonin was better at planning than Yurovsky had been. The right people were present to do the job this time. No drunken villagers were enlisted this time. The right equipment had been gathered, and anomalies had indeed been discovered. We dug down to see if the soil at different depths had been disturbed. If it had, perhaps we would find remains a bit deeper on that spot.

There was so much ground to sift. The idea of a search in the woods sounds fairly simple. But finding the often-tiny remains of something that occurred eight decades ago becomes a matter of working through all the dirt in an area, thimble by thimble, pinch by pinch, to find anything out of place, anything to suggest the activity of people. The vast array of stakes underlined how much work lay before us.

During a break in the hard work, I walked over to explore the mound of stones where I'd sat four years earlier while visiting with Bob Massie. I began to think about why these stones had been gathered into a pile, and then I was working my way through sifting rocks rather than dirt. Sure enough, I saw something that didn't belong: a 7.62 mm bullet from a Nagant pistol. This, of course, was the very type of pistol the Bolsheviks had used to murder the Romanovs. It sent a little shock of adrenaline through me: *Something is here. We're on the right track. More to come.*

Dr. Sergey Nikitin, the Russian forensic expert, studied the old photo of investigator Sokolov in this same area in 1919. It was hard to gather much information when new generations of trees had transformed the landscape. But Nikitin noticed a gravel pile in the photograph that he felt matched this pile of stones. He made comparisons and measured angles, and it became evident that this was the same pile Sokolov had excavated in 1919. How odd to be standing on the very site where my great-grandfather's good friend had done the most important work of his life.

Sokolov had found the open mine, the best candidate of all the mines and pits. He knew this might well be where bodies had been discarded. He had pumped in water to lift out whatever had been thrown in there, and this pile of rocks, upon which I sat, had come from the bottom of the hole. But he had missed or ignored a few small items, as if leaving something for us to find for ourselves. More likely, it was the news of the communists closing in quickly. So here we were to pick up where he and his helpers left off.

We had metal plates with holes, used for sifting and small garden shovels. We sat on low stools, our backs aching and our eyes straining as we leaned forward and peered at our sections of soil and stone.

I handed the bullet to Dr. Avdonin, and he handed me a shot of vodka in celebration. Dr. Avdonin, of course, knew what it was like to find remnants of the tragedy in the ground. But now I, too, felt I had personally connected to the story. My grandmother had seen that box and its contents. She'd been part of the story. Now I felt that I was too. My grandmother had sailed with Sokolov. I had walked in his footsteps and was continuing his search. For all the years of waiting, it may have just been a single bullet, but it was a good omen.

The next day, of course, we dug with increased eagerness and found absolutely nothing. By the third day, I was back to simply feeling uncomfortable on my stool. There was a pile of stone and gravel everyone had overlooked in the past. Neither Dr. Avdonin nor Dr. Nikitin had noticed it when the excavations began. Then Dr. Nikitin found a ring-block from a corset ring. The Romanov daughters' corsets, of course, were now famous for having jewelry sewn in, blocking the bullets. Here was a little piece of metal from one of those corsets that still lay near the surface—a small miracle.

After that, everyone was interested in the little mound of gravel. It was a major find, "Sokolov's pile," as it came to be known, because here were items dredged up from the open pit that Sokolov had drained. When I began to sift through the pile, a bullet caught my eye. I was excited to pick it up and show it to everyone. We were finally making some finds.

Then something else caught my eye, and I found myself holding a multi-faceted white topaz stone. I felt a great deal of emotion as I looked at it and wiped away the dust. This stone must have once glimmered in candle-lit crystal chandeliers from the necklace of one of the grand duchesses. It was royal jewelry, consigned to the ashes.

This was among the jewels that had made the women partially bulletproof—only to lead to the bludgeoning that showed in the shattered skulls. I thought of all these things as I turned over the white topaz in my hand. Nine kilos of stones had been found on the bodies of these family members, but not all had been found. Some had been trampled into the soil; others, like this one, had been swept into the open mine. Sokolov had found fourteen such stones; I had added a fifteenth. The total finding for topaz was twenty-three stones.

The sky grew darker, and rain began to fall, then snow. Dr. Avdonin decided the best course was to move the entire gravel pile to a safer location, closer to shelter, where we could sort through it without nature's interference. We carefully transferred all of it to a large number of bags and moved back to the Geological Institute in Yekaterinburg. In the parking lot, Dr. Nikitin and I found pallets, plywood, and a lengthy hose for cleaning what we were examining. We used some of these materials to set up a worktable outdoors in the light.

Now, as the days moved by, we analyzed bag by bag, looking for any specimen from the world of humans rather than rocks and dirt. It could be dull and monotonous, spending so many hours peering at plain Russian soil. But I preferred our new arrangement to the small stools.

We did make a few finds. It was evident the killers had ripped the clothing from their victims and tossed the garments into the open mineshaft. We knew this had been done with no delicacy, because we'd find the snaps from a blouse still connected. They had ripped the garments directly from the bodies. The clothing was blackened from burning, of course. What we were so busy doing was exactly what the murderers had wanted to avoid—detection, examination of evidence. If they'd known a way to erase every molecule of proof these bodies had ever been in this location, they'd have used it. But these little buttons and shreds of cloth bore testimony to the brutality of the past.

During his earlier investigation, Sokolov had found the lifeless carcass of Anastasia's beloved dog Jimmy in the bottom of this mine shaft, submerged in water, beneath a false wooden floor. This showed attempts at concealment, but the demands of time had limited their effectiveness.

We couldn't be sure all the evidence was contained in this heap of gravel, of course. We spent more time in the woods, looking for likely spots for killers to dispose of charred bones. Nothing stood out—the woods were the woods, and there were no signs of digging, at least none that were visible after eighty years. We did locate the spot where the killers had dug a large hole by the side of the road for burying the burned remains, but that hole apparently hadn't actually been used. It was just another sign of the haphazard process of a mass murder and disorganized burial. Still, it was good to confirm the killers' report stating they'd dug a hole by the Old Koptiaki Road at Four Brothers.

It was cold and miserable work, but our eagerness for discovery urged us on. One late afternoon, after a long, tedious day of work, Nikitin and I were walking back to the Avdonin home from the Geological Center. Our path took us past Yekaterinburg's Red Square, where the communists were having a rally. Even at this late date, some of them hadn't lost their Red zeal. Loudspeakers were blaring the message, the crowd was lively, and we made our way through, covered in mud and dirt, with exhaustion written all over us.

I was wearing Dr. Avdonin's work coat and hat, so I had a pronounced Russian peasant flair. The speaker caught a glimpse of us, pointed us out, and told everyone, "Here are real workers!" He began to praise us as true party members. I began to mumble about grabbing the microphone and explaining we were here to investigate communist murders.

"Don't do that," said Nikitin. "They'll beat us with clubs!"

We laughed about it later over vodka. We didn't want to be the next ones buried in those woods.

Our team was winding down our work now. We'd been through the gravel, and we'd located a few items—gold from a bracelet, pants buttons. We'd spent a bit more time studying the locale, along with the rock pile that contained so many fascinating little items. The two children had not been found, but still I could return to New York excited and proud to have built on the initial investigation of our old family friend Nikolai Sokolov. Best of all, the Russians were already talking about another search in 1999.

The second search indeed took place in June of 1999. I was eager to discover how we would expand on the work we did the previous autumn. The team consisted of Dr. Alexander Avdonin, Dr. Sergey Nikitin, and Kremlin archaeologist Dr. Tatiana Panova. Once again, volunteers joined us to assist with the work.

Gen. Mikhail Diterikhs of the White Army had been present with Sokolov and had created the key map of the burial area. He was also one of the initiators of the misguided accusations that the Romanov killings were ritual murders organized by the Jews. Despite this ugly blaze of antisemitism, his map was a key piece of contemporary evidence, made by an eyewitness to the first investigation, when the evidence was fresh. Our area of focus this time was the bonfires. We used the map to try and pinpoint the location of the second of these. The center of the open mine was our epicenter, and from there we measured distance and bearings to locate the most likely area for digging.

Two bonfires were well known, but there seemed to have been a third bonfire. Dr. Avdonin had read that Sokolov had found traces of such, but again lacked time to search for it. My grandmother, who had spent a great deal of time talking to Sokolov, said that the investigator had arrived at the open mine, noticed that the platform next to it was covered with a fresh bed of clay, then detected the sites of two bonfires. I mentioned this to Dr. Avdonin.

Eleven years later, in 2010, senior investigator Soloviev would write,

> Sokolov, having conducted excavations at Ganin's Pit [Ganina Yama], was able to establish and prove that the Bolsheviks brought the bodies of members of the Imperial Family and persons from the entourage to this area (where a severed finger, human skin, and the dentures of Dr. E. S. Botkin were found). At the same time, the investigation materials and witness testimonies did not give him any objective evidence that the corpses were burnt. The remains of the bonfires were small, and the half-burnt items of clothing and shoes also did not confirm a scenario with large bonfires, in which 11 corpses could have been destroyed.

We also have the account of a witness from February 8, 1919. Lt. Alexander Andreyevich Sheremetyevsky, who was in charge of surveying Ganin's Pit during the first investigation. He wrote that he was with the group pumping out the mine and providing our gravel pit.

"Near this mine, about three fathoms from it, there were ashes from a burnt-out fire," he wrote, "and ten fathoms from the mine were traces of another fire. The fires were apparently small, since each ash took up no more than [a foot and a half square]. The ashes of these fires were sifted before I arrived, and I cannot say for sure what was found there." Nikitin and I located that second bonfire site, but it had been thoroughly excavated and now contained nothing but coal. We determined this was likely the fire where the clothing was burned.

But then we discovered that the third bonfire site had also been located. As we'd been at work, Dr. Avdonin and Dr. Panova had been digging around the platform near the open mineshaft. At a depth of about twenty centimeters, there was evidence of burning. And this time the indications pointed to a larger fire—a site four by three meters.

Initially, we were excited to find about fifty bone fragments, but these were later identified as animal remains. Sokolov had found similar bones, in the same places and in the same layers of earth. Apparently, these were the remains of the burial party's meal.

What we knew from archival research was that Yurovsky's mob had attempted to burn four of the corpses: Nicholas II and his son, Alexei, along with one of the daughters—possibly Maria—and in error, Demidova, the maid, who these men had misidentified as the Empress Alexandra. But the bodies had been lying in freezing water in the bottom of the mineshaft, and they would do no more than sizzle—one more frustration for the burial party; one more indication of poor planning. By July 19 the corpses were already unrecognizable from the abuse they'd been given with rifle butts and bayonets, then the natural effects of death. Given the summer heat, they were bloated. Finding the new bonfire site had been another positive step in our investigation.

Sokolov, having examined the site to the extent that time allowed, assumed that there were no more remains, other than ashes left to rise and fly away in the breeze or vanish into dust. He found a few animal bones, too, but the only human element that turned up was a ring finger, possibly belonging to the empress. It had been chopped off by the communists then tossed into the mine shaft. To these killers, jewelry had value, but royal humanity none at all.

Later I corresponded with Vladimir Soloviev, who was later appointed to investigate the case. In 2010 he wrote to me describing his observation that Sokolov made two important conclusions about the fate of the Romanovs that would take hold in the public's collective knowledge of the crime. The first was that the whole party—family and entourage—had been murdered at Ipatiev House. He found the physical evidence, attained testimony, and even performed scientific research that left no doubt there had been no survivors from that basement room. This was important in restraining the rampant mythology of survivors, of the family's having been transported elsewhere, and other misconceptions.

The other conclusion, of course, was that the bodies had all been burned and destroyed, and questions had been raised from the beginning about this assumption. But the most important achievement of Sokolov's work was the discovery of the makeshift bridge of railroad sleepers. He found these, but he missed their meaning.

The logical link wouldn't have been particularly obvious: since the burial party was under time constraints now compounded by transportation issues, the men would have lost patience and buried the bodies wherever they happened to be, which was this unlikely spot, where the truck had been mired. Sokolov would have attempted to think like furtive men, hiding their evidence, but he failed to think like *impatient* men, desperate to walk away.

Soloviev also pointed out that, while Sokolov believed he hadn't examined the entire area, he actually had, and even beyond. He had checked in a number of abandoned mines and pits. Continuous excavations were conducted in Ganin's Pit and other places that seemed like good candidates for burial. Water was pumped and ground was sifted with sieves. There were days when the search had involved up to a thousand people. So it's incorrect to dismiss Sokolov's investigation as cursory or superficial; it was concentrated and thorough, finding important evidence but failing to take hold of the one idea that would have unlocked the mystery.

As I once again left for home, I was satisfied. We'd continued Sokolov's work, but we'd also repeated his failure to find bodies. On the other hand, we'd located that second bonfire, described by Sokolov and Diterikhs, and we'd resolved the question of the animal bones found near the open pit. A bullet, items of clothing, the melted neck of a wine bottle, and even a topaz stone had been found, along with other miscellanea. Finding the third fire's location, apparently a larger fire than anyone realized, was important as well.

All the soil was replaced just as we found it, the grass was rolled back, and we could only hope to find the two missing bodies elsewhere. I could bring home a positive report to the White Russian community and to our Orthodox Church Abroad.

In the two decades that have followed, the Russian Orthodox Church itself has now taken over the search area. It's not possible to quietly walk through a site largely as it looked and felt in 1918. A monastery stands there now—a lovely and stylish one—made up of seven churches. It's sanctified as a holy site, proclaimed by the church. An evil wilderness has been redeemed in the name of God.

It's comforting to know we searched the area as thoroughly as possible before the bulldozers arrived, however. The Yurovsky papers specified the location of the main grave on the Koptiaki Road at Pig's Meadow—the one discovered by Avdonin. It stated less precisely that the two other bodies were buried separately but nearby. So, we knew they were probably still out there; we simply had to eliminate Four Brothers as a possibility first. Now we would turn our attention to Pig's Meadow.

Meanwhile, I enjoyed the nonpartisan cooperation between the Russians and one American while I could. In just a few months, there would be a conference in Reno, Nevada, and the battle of international sciences over the unidentified daughter would resume.

18

Reno—Point/Counterpoint

During the second search, in September of 1998, I was sitting in Dr. Avdonin's kitchen one evening, talking with Dr. Sergey Nikitin and Valentin Gribenyuk, a geologist. We were, as always, tired from the day's labors. I wished my friends from the American forensic science community could be here. But I knew that the one area of disagreement created too much awkwardness. It was a matter of scientific pride for either hemisphere. As Kipling said, "East is east, and west is west, and never the twain shall meet." Different methods had brought different conclusions. I wished the two sides could agree and work together.

I looked at my friend Dr. Avdonin, who had a lifelong fascination with the fate of the imperial family, and asked, "Who was it that decided you had Anastasia among those remains? I realize it's a strong consensus here, but there must have been someone who was first to arrive at that conclusion, based on their expertise."

Dr. Avdonin was mildly surprised by my question—not so much because I raised the subject but because the answer was simple. "It was Nikitin," he said, gesturing toward our friend. "Didn't you know?"

"No, I did not. Nor does anyone in the West. And to this day, I have three American forensic anthropologists who disagree with Dr. Nikitin's findings. They plan to present their own conclusions before the American Academy of Forensic Science in Reno, Nevada, in 2000."

Dr. Avdonin nodded, thinking about that, then replied, "Then Nikitin must go to Reno, Nevada, as well, and present his paper." Dr. Nikitin nodded and signaled his willingness to do just that.

After that painful moment of conflict seven months earlier, I had urged both sides to refrain from announcements and presentations about the identities of these remains, which would have simply given the world media a controversy to play up. I hoped we'd find the final two children, and perhaps finally come to an agreement. But the Reno conference was now scheduled, and the American findings were going to become public.

As always, I was serving as intermediary between the two groups. I'd spoken with William Goza of the University of Florida Foundation about the inflexibility of the Russian position, and the idea of bringing the originator of that view to the United States for a debate. He'd told me the academy would be excited about a point/counterpoint scenario. At the time, though, I hadn't realized my friend Dr. Nikitin was the very scientist I was describing, the one who would give that counterpoint.

"If Dr. Nikitin would agree to come and present his case, I'll sponsor his trip," I said. It was important to me that, regardless of who was right, both sides should have the opportunity to present their work and their perspectives.

Dr. Nikitin got his presentation ready, and by the time the year 2000 was upon us (thankfully with none of the dreaded complications of the Y2K computer phenomenon), he was ready to present his paper, state his case, and show his reconstruction of the skull he claimed belonged to Anastasia. His chosen title was in the form of a proposition: "Grand Duchess Anastasia was buried in St. Petersburg on 17 July 1998." It was a compelling angle, highlighting the fact that a young lady was entombed with the family, and there was disagreement about her identity. Dr. Nikitin, proud and certain in his conclusions, was stating his case boldly.

Dr. Nikitin's presentation reviewed the 1918 execution, the disjointed burial, and then the discovery of the bodies. He described the original work done by the Russians to identify the skeletons and confirm they were indeed those of the Romanovs and attendants. He described what Dr. Maples and then the second team had determined about the remains and stated his polite disagreement. Then he went on to detail his work to match skulls and skeletons to members of the Romanov party.

Much of that work, of course, utilized photography, computers, and clay sculpture. What was most laudable about the Russian work was its creativity and thoroughness. The Yekaterinburg scientists had no access to DNA sampling. They lacked much of the latest forensic technology that was available in the West. What they did have was information, a library of family photographs, and experience in examining human bones.

Heights of the girls was obviously an important clue. There were a great many photos documenting the parents and children throughout their lives. Dr. Nikitin used these pictures in relation to one another, drawing conclusions about bodily measurements. For example, there was a photograph of the daughters taken in May of 1917. Maria stood beside a soldier who held a rifle. It was an S. Mosin infantry rifle, common in the Russian army, whose precise length was known to be 173.2 centimeters. Dr. Nikitin compared Maria and found her to have a height of 170 centimeters.

From there, he could take that value, as if solving for *x* in an equation, and compare Maria to the heights of two sisters, Tatiana and Anastasia. In one photo they were standing together. Anastasia, he decided, was ten centimeters shorter than her two sisters, who were identical in height.

As for the bones, he was able to measure them—the tibia, for example—with greater precision, having them present in the morgue. Taking the photographic estimates together with the bones and their known relation to height and age, and factoring in typical growth during their final year, he concluded that the remains in the morgue were those of Anastasia and either Tatiana or Maria.

He considered a remaining possibility that Tatiana and Maria were the two skeletons represented. The numbers he had would have permitted this conclusion if the leg differential was fifty-two millimeters. Tatiana's waist indeed seemed higher than Maria's in one picture. But this theory broke down because skeleton no. 5 was inconsistent with Tatiana's having longer legs, which would be true if her waist were higher.

Dr. Nikitin's firm conclusion, at this point, was that skeleton no. 5 was Tatiana and no. 6 either Anastasia or Maria. These two skeletons would become the source of disagreement between scientists from two different cultures.

The skulls were just as important. In 1994 Dr. Nikitin attempted to work from their measurements, reconstruct in new portraits their faces, and assign identifications on that basis. He believed the reconstruction from skull no. 5 resembled Tatiana, while skull no. 6 looked like Anastasia.

Skull 1—matched the maid, Demidova.
Skull 2—matched Dr. Botkin.
Skull 3—matched Olga.
Skull 4—matched Emperor Nicholas II.
Skull 5—matched Tatiana.
Skull 6—matched Anastasia.
Skull 7—matched Empress Alexandra Fyodorovna.
Skull 9—matched the valet, Trupp.
Skull 8—matched the cook, Kharitonov (listed last, because this skull was almost completely destroyed).

Photographs were used to add hair.

This wasn't a simple process. A great deal of thought and careful observation of the photographs went into Dr. Nikitin's work. He used what he called "methods of Russian specialists of anthropological reconstruction." Eight of the skulls were reconstructed, one was too damaged by acid, and two were not yet found. Dr. Nikitin used Adobe Photoshop to superimpose photographs over images of the skulls shown in the correct proportion and at the given angles. He used as key reference points the outer corners of the eyes, the spot directly beneath the nose, the lip line, and the upper contours of the head, marking each.

On skull no. 6, he concluded the points of the corners of the eyes did not coincide with reconstructions taken from the skulls. Points beneath the nose checked out; the height of the parietal bone (upper back of the head) did not. However, with Anastasia's reconstruction, it was a different story. All indicated points coincided, including most of the upper contour of the head. To the minds of Dr. Nikitin and the other Russian scientists, there could be no doubt about the identity of skull no. 6: this was Anastasia.

Dr. Nikitin presented his findings with great confidence and the persuasiveness of visual aids—especially the beautiful clay figures he had created. In Reno, however, those in the room knew that photographic reconstruction wasn't accepted in American courtrooms. For them, it didn't represent the most impressive forensic science.

Dr. France set out to determine just how valuable a tool for human identification Dr. Nikitin's method could be. She sent identical plastic skulls to various reconstruction experts in the United States, and to Dr. Nikitin himself. How much variation would be seen in the results? Would they all lead to consistent replicas of the same face?

Dr. Nikitin had been a guest in my home in New Jersey since early January 2000, just before the Reno conference. He rose to Dr. France's challenge, spending three days creating his reconstruction. He showed me his work and asked, "Who do you think this might be?"

I looked at it and quickly replied, "I think it's Diane France."

Of course, it was. He had quickly recognized the scan by the teeth and the structure of the skull. We carefully shipped his work to Dr. France's house, and as soon as she opened the box, her dog began wagging its tail happily. Dr. France laughed as she told the story, saying the dog had recognized her.

Dr. France also said, "We did indeed find out there's a tremendous variation in the results of facial reconstruction on a known individual (me) and that's as far as we're willing to go." She'd made her point. "Tremendous variation" would allow for skull no. 6 to be one sister or another. As with most strategies, there's a margin for error present in the skull reconstruction technique.

Photography is certainly acceptable evidence in American courts, but with clear caveats. Dr. Nikitin compared heights in photographs of the daughters standing together. Can this be done accurately? Most of us pose fairly casually for such pictures, as opposed to standing exactly straight as we do when our height is being measured. What if one or more daughters was slouching even slightly? What if the ground is perfectly level? How about shoes?

Slight variations could cause inaccuracy. The same is true when a height is partially determined from the length of a gun in the same picture. This can a fairly accurate gauge when the rifle's length is known so precisely, as in this case. But again, a girl's height may not be accurately shown in a picture. It's also true that girls in their teenage years are still growing. How many inches of height were added in Anastasia's final months?

In Reno, the audience listened with careful attention and responded warmly and appreciatively. There was standing room only in the presentation hall. But Dr. France, Dr. Falsetti, and Dr. Maples were too strong in their reputations to be overcome, at least on American soil. They, too, made a presentation, though Dr. Maples had passed away in February of 1997; his findings continued to be important.

This group firmly believed the fifth body to be Maria rather than Tatiana, and the sixth to be Tatiana rather than Anastasia. This meant that the remains of Anastasia were still missing, along with her brother, Alexei. While Dr. Nikitin used degree of wear on the teeth for his identifications, Dr. Maples came to his own conclusions based on dental development rather than wear, along with the pattern of epiphyseal union throughout the bodies. This refers to the fact that bones grow from the inside out, and the bones in a body grow consistently with the maturation of that body. Body no. 5 seemed to be developmentally younger than no. 6, thus no. 5 could not be the twenty-one-year-old female with no. 6 as the seventeen-year-old.

Dr. France offered three primary directions for the conclusions the Maples team had formed: dental age determination; skeletal age determination; and stature reconstruction. As a contrast in the two approaches, Dr. France offered a slide that compared stature reconstruction of the two teams. Nikitin computed two girls' heights relative to the length of a specific rifle. No. 5 measured 170 centimeters; no. 6, 160 centimeters. Moreover, these were based on a 1917 photograph. The American group had computed the girls' heights based on femur length at the time of death, and calculated the results to 170.68 centimeters and 164.76 centimeters, respectively.

The presentation by the Americans was relatively straightforward because it was based on conventional methods of forensic science. The Americans differed only in two sets of remains, but felt their methods, which were proven and acceptable in courtrooms, were ultimately superior to the ingenious but limited methods the Russians had used.

Nobody "won" the debate, because both sides presented opinions. The question would remain about the identity of one daughter buried with her family, and another still out there somewhere, waiting with her brother for discovery.

Before my friend Dr. Nikitin flew back home, we agreed that our searches for the missing children weren't over. Perhaps when we found these two, we'd also have the answer to which daughter was which. We were committed to continue our efforts until the Romanov family was reunited, and the church gave its full blessing. Both of these seemed more elusive goals than ever.

19

Searching Pig's Meadow

Goals and aspirations endure, but time is relentless. It never stops to wait upon us. Somehow four years passed after the Reno event without my making another search in Russia. I was in my fifties now, and increasingly conscious of the fact that I wouldn't always be able to travel across the globe, roam through the woods, and retain the sharp eyesight needed to detect the minuscule clues to the presence of buried bodies that had by then been in the ground for longer than an average human lifespan.

It was July 2004 before I could arrange for another search in the vicinity of Yekaterinburg. In talking to Dr. Nikitin, I was strongly advocating that we focus this time on Pig's Meadow, where Dr. Avdonin first found the primary graves of the Russian imperial family and their helpers. I had convinced Dr. Avdonin to target the Four Brothers Mine area first because General Diterikhs's map showed bonfires there and because we knew Yakov Yurovsky's report stated that nine sets of remains were buried in the main grave. Nearby, Yurovsky reported, a bonfire had been built to burn the two smallest bodies, and the men had moved the fire to the side and dug a hole to bury and conceal what was left of the bones. Having done that, they moved the coals and the fire back over where the bodies were buried. The fire would remove any trace of digging.

Therefore, it made sense to begin our search there at the open pit at Four Brothers, where bonfires had been marked on the map. At the same time, I read Yurovsky's words with just a bit of skepticism, even knowing the Avdonins had found the remains because of his report. So when we found the bonfires, as per the general's map, we tried digging beneath. The soil there, however, had not been disturbed. The positive development had been in locating the third and larger fire for the first time. This was important, the same spot where the Bolsheviks had attempted to burn four bodies.

We also knew that Sokolov had walked through many square meters of forest, and he'd done it with large numbers of searchers. They'd found nothing. Sokolov had procured the wood used to build a makeshift bridge along the Koptiaki Road to protect the truck from becoming stuck in the mud. But he'd never considered the possibility that any bodies might have been buried during the long and frustrating wait, beside the truck. His search was limited to the mine area. Ours was not.

Dr. Nikitin organized the latest search, finding the funding this time within Russia. We kept our search party much simpler than the vast number Sokolov had used. Our team consisted of Nikitin, Moscow medical examiner; Col. Vladimir Konstantinov, one of Russia's foremost ground-penetrating radar (GPR) specialists; and me. We did have a group of Tajikistanis who worked twelve hours per day digging and preparing the ground for GPR.

One challenge most people don't realize is the change of landscape over time. We all know that trees come and go, but ground level changes as well. Tree canopy drops leaves, nuts, and various nutrients to the forest floor. As part of the natural life cycle, all of this decomposes and becomes a growing level of soil, which isn't just "dirt"—it's composed of mineral particles, organic materials, air, water, and living organisms. If Yurovsky noted a specific depth for the burial of the bodies, we would expect to find them a bit deeper after almost a century. Nikitin arranged for heavy equipment to bring the Koptiaki Road down to its 1918 level.

What he didn't manage to do was apply for a work permit. He had forgotten that detail. So here I was, having traveled across the globe once again, and we had no paperwork to perform our search. But I'd learned never to underestimate Dr. Nikitin's creativity. He simply created a sign and hung it from a tree. It read "MIGR." In Russian letters, it stood for International Reconstruction Initiative Group. We were reconstructing Pig's Meadow to its 1919 image, just as Dr. Nikitin had reconstructed eight faces. These official-sounding words went a long way toward avoiding red tape. We did attract a few onlookers who were curious to see what was going on in the meadow. Some simply stood and watched, while a few asked who gave us permission to do any land moving. We were on Yekaterinburg Regional Government land. Dr. Nikitin would simply point to the sign, as if it answered all questions.

Our closest brush with disaster came when a police car pulled up to check us out. I was worried, then I saw that the officer was friends with Konstantinov, our radar specialist, who apparently was friends with most of the local police. So they chatted a few moments before the policeman left us to our work.

Once the ground was cleared and prepared, Konstantinov hooked up his ground-penetrating radar and began working the land, searching for anomalies. GPR uses electromagnetic radiation, and it surveys the subsurface of the ground to investigate the consistency of the soil and rock. It can pick up underground utilities such as concrete, asphalt, metals, pipes, cables, masonry, or perhaps buried objects and creates a radargram presenting this information. This technology enables nonintrusive searches—instead of digging up acres of land, we can "peer" beneath the surface using radiation.

Others who had lacked this kind of instrument had come before us with shovels, disturbing the search site, and that made our work more difficult. We had to revisit every pit dug by archaeologist Beniamin V. Alexeyev and his group, which had created anomalies that slowed us down. Our goal was to search the northern section of Pig's Meadow systematically. Dr. Avdonin had kept thorough records of which areas had been searched, and no one had looked in the northern section. Therefore, that's where Dr. Nikitin wanted to focus.

I looked over the great tract of land that made up our search area. We had a lot of ground to cover, but we decided it made the most sense to begin on that part of our section that had the closest proximity to the main grave. We began our digging and sifting—tedious work with the possibility of yielding the find of a lifetime—and settled into the toil of the search.

Our land was not strictly a meadow. Birch trees had grown throughout the site. These, too, presented a problem, because we lacked the means to search under them without actually cutting them down and pulling out the roots. It was possible a tree had grown directly over the burial site we were looking for, but if so, we wouldn't find it. We had no desire to get into the lumberjack business. Also, our GPR expert told us that special equipment existed that would enable us to check beneath trees without disturbing them. So we agreed that, if we found nothing this time and made plans to return for another search, we'd have access to that technology.

Though our work was here in the Pig's Meadow, the general area where the truck had gotten stuck, I was interested in seeing what the Four Brothers open mine area looked like these days. It was only four kilometers away, but I knew I could no longer stand in the forest and imagine what it had been like at the time of the burials. The mine area had been reconstructed, too, but not to its old face. The Russian Orthodox Church had taken over the land now and built its monastery with seven churches. In doing this, the church had fully invested in Sokolov's conclusion that all the remains of the imperial family and servants had been burned on the site—even though we knew beyond any shadow of a doubt that nine sets of remains had been recovered elsewhere. Four Brothers was now hallowed ground, and there could be no searching in that area even if we'd wanted to do so.

I found the time to visit another church, the Church on the Blood in Honor of All Saints Resplendent in the Russian Land. This one was built directly on the site where Ipatiev House once stood. It, too, is Russian Orthodox. The Russians hadn't wanted that house to stand as a monument to execution and brutality, so they'd replaced it with a church in honor of the victims.

There I met Bishop Vikenty (now Metropolitan Vikenty). I walked up to him to introduce myself. I explained to him that my wife's uncle was Bishop Basil Rodzianko, who is a beloved figure in Russian Orthodox circles through his BBC broadcasts. Once I uttered that name, of course, Bishop Vikenty became much more enthusiastic in our conversation. I had a point of reference for him now.

At the moment, he was in the company of an interior decorator, and they were discussing the gold candleholders to be positioned over the imperial family's large icons in the church. He also told me of their plans to place relics from each family member behind their respective icons.

I said, "That's interesting. And where will you get these relics? Saint Petersburg?" I was referring to where the nine had been re-interred.

"Oh, no," he said, shaking his head. "We don't believe in those remains!"

My face must have shown my deep surprise at his comment. I well knew the stance the church was taking officially, but it was still hard to understand that, even in a private conversation like this, a bishop would discard all the science that had gone into identifying those remains.

"Well, you may be interested in the purpose of my visit, Bishop Vikenty," I said. "I'm here working with some Russian friends to search for the remains that are still missing—Grand Duchess Maria and Tsarevich Alexei."

He nodded politely. I imagine he would have been more comfortable discussing Bishop Rodzianko, or perhaps various styles of golden candleholder. It was a difficult thing for me to comprehend: all the world had followed the recovery of the remains from the Old Koptiaki Road. These remains had corresponded perfectly with members of the royal family and their attendants. Dental work (dentures in one case) had matched. Evidence of beatings and bullets had been consistent. Russian and American scientists alike affirmed that there was absolutely no doubt that these were not just nine random strangers buried together beside a road—these were the victims of one of the most famous political executions in history. And yet still, the church disputed these things as if it were simply a matter of superficial opinion rather than cold logic.

Investigator Soloviev paid us a visit at the work site. He'd now been involved with the case for more than ten years, and he was interested in our work. At one point, we walked about seventy meters toward the southeastern section of Pig's Meadow. For some reason I stopped in my tracks, turned, and snapped a photograph of the men searching the northern part of the field. At that moment, with camera in hand, I was standing over the grave of the two children—I just had no way of knowing it. The burial site of the brother and sister was just a bit farther from the main grave than we'd guessed when deciding where to begin our search.

For that reason, I had to return to the United States once again with the feeling of having worked tirelessly without reaching our goal. I always enjoyed seeing my Russian friends. I liked being among those historic acres, giving my best energy to solve a mystery. But how many more searches could I make? How long before others would remain responsive to my requests for help, for equipment, for permission to search? For now, I knew that Dr. Nikitin was just as committed as I was. There were still people who couldn't and wouldn't rest until all the bodies were recovered and the final questions answered. I just hoped that would occur in my lifetime.

20

Finding the Children

I'd been so close. A matter of inches away.

Looking back, I wondered what caused me to stop at that particular moment and turn to take a picture of our team. I can't say some extrasensory message was coming through to my subconscious; it was probably just a coincidence.

But for whatever reason, I paused directly over the graves we had spent years seeking, and I turned and snapped my photo. If Dr. Nikitin and I had dropped shovels into the ground on the spot, the long search would have been over. Instead, that moment would be for others to experience. For me, it was enough to know those two children were finally recovered and could be buried with the dignity and honor they deserved.

After the 2004 search, I found that life became more complicated in terms of traveling between Russia and America, raising funds, and all the other activities required to pursue this dream of mine. It had now been decades since the main grave had been found. Yet the other two corpses still defied every pursuit. It seemed possible they'd never be found. Was I just setting myself up for further disappointment, while throwing dollars and time after an impossible dream?

I didn't think so. My heart was still in the search. Those two bodies were somewhere, and most likely in the proximity of Pig's Meadow. While I knew that Yurovsky could and did get things wrong, it seemed pretty clear from his statements, and the statements of other operatives, that these two bodies had not been transported away from the site. The idea was to get the job done quickly and be done with it.

But the older we get, the more complicated our time grows. The less freedom and flexibility we have. I found it more difficult to pull together plans for group searches.

In 2006 my ship, the SS *Horizon Crusader*, was laid up for a year. It also turned out there were no other captain positions open in our fleet. I made the decision to stop going to sea and to work in a shipping office, planning cargo stows and scheduling ships. It's an ordinary and logical career transition for a veteran sea captain approaching his late fifties. I'd be sitting at a desk more often, but I still had to curtail my Russian search goals.

I still had my website. I could keep in touch with Dr. Nikitin and my other friends, making future plans. I had started a nonprofit foundation, SEARCH. I could give speeches, show slides, and make sure new generations were interested in this story that was approaching its ninetieth birthday. Otherwise, life went on.

Then, on August 11, 2007, Dr. Sergey Nikitin let me know that there might—just might—be an end to our search. He explained that a Yekaterinburg-based military history club called Mountain Shield, under the leadership of Andrey E. Grigoriev, had found what they felt were the remains of the two missing Romanov children. Their dig had been in the southern section of Pig's Meadow. Immediately my mind retreated to our previous search, three years earlier, and I wondered how often I'd walked past the buried remains of the children.

Dr. Nikitin had no doubts about the find. He wrote,

> On 29 July, the remains of Alexei and Maria were found. Not many bone fragments. Aside from the bones, there were other findings: a few teeth (age 13), bullets (Nagant, Browning), ceramic shards. The people of Yekaterinburg found them; I was there to make examinations 8–10 August with Soloviev. Soloviev will return next week; he has another murder case in the Sverdlovsk Region. Information was not released to the Press yet. A few people only know about this.
>
> Look at the photo where they were found.
>
> Your friend, Sergey.
>
> Peter, I am happy.

I was, too. I'd love to have been there at the moment when something first peeked through the dirt: a ceramic shard? A bone fragment? A spent bullet? I'd have been excited to be with Dr. Nikitin and Soloviev, inspecting the finds. But this wasn't about me. It was about the children, and it looked as if they'd been found. Now I would be glued to my email and my Internet news, hungry for more developments.

I thought again about my grandmother. She, too, would have been pleased.

This search, I learned, had used equipment and reconnaissance methods not previously employed. S. O. Plotnikov and L. G. Vokhmyakov had been the first to find items of significance. They'd discovered, in their bore pit, coals, bone remains, nails, and fragments from a ceramic vessel. At this point, the search party halted and discussed what should be done next. Knowing they'd found the right area, they found it prudent to reorganize their efforts and invite some specialists. Scientists representing various specialties were brought in, including Dr. Avdonin. An area of one hundred square meters was now laid out, surrounding the bore pit that had yielded the items.

Now the search used strict archaeological methods, using draining trenches. This brought up a layer of coal, indicating a bonfire. A bit more careful digging determined this to be a t-shaped burial area. As the coal layer was removed, two overlying, slightly oval pits were detected in the subsoil and perpendicular to each other. The northernmost of the two had scorched bone remains, a few nails, and small pieces of a ceramic container. The southern one had similar contents. Many of the artifacts were quite small and discovered only through rinsing in the drainage pit.

Everything was carefully separated and sent for further study. Soloviev, the senior criminal procurator of the Russian Federation, was to examine bones and bullets in his forensic lab. The initial diagnosis was that these were human bones—and, most tantalizing of all, these bones belonged to a young man between the ages of ten and thirteen years and a young woman between eighteen and twenty-three years old.

The young man could be Alexei, who was a month short of fourteen at his death. The young woman could be Maria, nineteen, or possibly Anastasia, seventeen. Maria, whom the Russians had expected the bones to match, seemed the more likely match.

While the bones always accounted for the headline story, the secondary items were also important. The ceramic shards were identical to those found years earlier, at the main burial site, and there was evidence they belonged to vessels that contained sulfuric acid. The iron and nails seemed to have supported the wood crates in which the acid was transported. Sokolov had developed evidence of acid purchases in Yekaterinburg at the time of the murders, and the skulls from the previous site showed evidence of acid damage—particularly the bottom skull, where gravity had brought the worst effects, rendering that skull virtually unexaminable.

Leonid Vokhmyakov, from the Mountain Shield group, was one of the discoverers of the two sets of remains. His passion was military history, and he'd also become involved in politics in 1989, protesting against communism during the transition time. He had helped to gather ten thousand local signatures to return his city of Sverdlovsk to its original name of Yekaterinburg. He was passionate about Russian history and tradition, even traveling to various locations to participate in reenactments of battles from the past. Combining this with his training in mining and metallurgy, he become involved in archaeological searches for soldier remains. He'd also become a devout follower of Orthodox Christianity.

During the 1970s, he'd read Pavel Bykov's *The Last Days of the Romanovs*, a forbidden book in the USSR. It was written in 1927 by one of the men who'd taken part in the execution of the imperial family. What Vokhmyakov actually read was a bootleg copy, a collection of photographs of the pages. He'd been haunted by the words, "Their corpses rotted in the swamp near the village of Koptyaki."

With all these things coming together in his mind, Vokhmyakov had begun participating in trips to Pig's Meadow on summer weekends, searching for the final two Romanovs with his friend Sergei Plotnikov, a homebuilder. It was in the small hollow, surrounded by silver birches, that Plotnikov heard a crunch as his prodder struck something tough. He and Vokhmyakov began digging about ten meters apart. Vokhmyakov came across something hard, lifted his find high for all to see, and said, "The search is over!" In his hand was the back of Tsarevich Alexei's skull.

Andrei Grigoriev, a member of the search party, expressed a doubt: "Maybe it's the bones of an animal."

"I know human anatomy," said Vokhmyakov. "This is from a human skull." He then produced two more bones, including a second portion of the skull and a part of a young lady's pelvis.

The search began in earnest soon after, but Vokhmyakov was surprised by how quickly it was completed. There were about seventy grams of bones. Throughout the days of work, monastery nuns worked along with the searchers, sorting through and rinsing soil, smiling as they quietly sang hymns. Now, at the end, they stood with wet faces beneath an awning and enjoyed the rain. It made quite an impression on Vokhmyakov, who nonetheless felt the skies were weeping for the dead who'd been found.

When Plotnikov had called Vokhmyakov to invite him on this search, the latter had firmly set into his mind the idea that no bodies would be located without his presence. He had to be there, and it had to happen soon, before the rains started.

One year later, he "came to God," as he put it, through the influence of his wife, Serafima, and the nuns he'd come to respect. Serafima had recited prayers at the cross of the tsar's tomb until he found the site. However, he was quick to give credit to all the searchers who had come before him. In the success of the search, he felt that God's will had been done.

Now, I believed, there could finally be closure. All the victims had been found. The family could be reunited in burial. The most important questions would have their answers.

I wrote to Dr. Anthony Falsetti, who by then had replaced Dr. William Maples as the director of the C. A. Pound Human Identification Laboratory in Gainesville, Florida. We spoke more informally by phone, and I asked him what he thought about seeking a major Western DNA lab to get involved in the identification process. He agreed it was a great idea, and, as I knew, he worked with the Armed Forces DNA Identification Lab (AFDIL). Of course I'd had some experience trying to enlist them on our search several years earlier. Dr. Falsetti agreed to approach AFDIL, and he stated that he wanted to examine the remains personally.

From there, I called Dr. Nikitin in Russia, and we talked about the find and speculated on what would happen now. "Do we know who will do the DNA work?" I asked.

"There are no plans so far," he said. I told him about AFDIL, and he promised to speak to investigator Soloviev, who would have to work such things out with Dr. Nikolai Ivanovich Nevolin, the director of the Sverdlovsk Bureau of Forensic Medicine, where the remains were. So the communications process began.

Falsetti wrote me in early September to inform me that once again, the U.S. Army was rather noncommittal. If AFDIL had committed its resources earlier, I'm certain those two bodies would have been found that much earlier. But now, in 2007, there was a bit of a tentative yes, but chain-of-command approval was still required.

Dr. Falsetti wrote Dr. Nevolin and offered the assistance of his lab and team with the new findings, and on September 11, 2007, Dr. Nevolin sent a formal invitation. He mentioned the disputes that had discolored the Russian and American cooperation years earlier but affirmed that in science, there should be both honest disagreements and good communication. Dr. Falsetti was invited for the dates of October 20–28, 2007. At that time, they could also discuss the participation of AFDIL.

Then I heard from Dr. Louis Finelli, director of AFDIL, who told me that before any final agreement, he needed a letter of invitation from Dr. Nikolai Nevolin that he could pass up the chain of command. He received it soon afterward. He also clarified that he wouldn't be involved in the work; it would be Dr. Mike Coble, chief of research, who led the analysis for AFDIL.

All of this is a simplified version of the correspondence I oversaw during those months. There were different groups of scientists involved, two different nations, one military establishment, and plenty of bureaucracy. But I was excited enough that the remains had finally been discovered that I didn't mind this heavy traffic in the U.S. mail and my email box. In each case, I replied immediately. If things were going to slow down, it wouldn't be on my account. I began working full time on the goal of ensuring American involvement in the DNA and anthropological examination of the remains. I was dedicated to keeping the wheel greased and making sure nothing slowed down this process.

I also recruited a helper: my friend Alexei Zakharin, Russian American senior scoutmaster and retired U.S. Army colonel.

Dr. Nevolin asked me over the phone for an important favor. He wanted me to approach Dr. Finelli about accepting two Russian scientists who would accompany the bone samples to the AFDIL lab in Maryland. There they would be trained to participate in the DNA analysis that would take place. I thought it was a good idea. Dr. Finelli told me, "Normally a lab like ours would only accept doctorate-level scientists for this kind of work. But in this case, I think an exception could be made."

Dr. Nevolin was elated. Russian scientists could be trained in America in this exploding science of DNA.

In late October Dr. Finelli wrote a letter asking some key questions that would allow AFDIL to move forward in its plans to analyze the remains. Part of this, he explained, related to the number of individuals around the world who were poised to be skeptical about any findings in the case. So AFDIL was covering all the bases. The questions:

1. Has the site of the findings been closed?
2. Has there been any other DNA testing?
3. Will the visiting Yekaterinburg scientists be able to stay for the duration of the testing? (It could take months.)

There were rules for the Russian scientists. They could observe only; this was a requirement of the lab's scientific accreditation. Preferably, only one observer could be allowed in the lab at a time, but there could be accommodation if Dr. Nevolin preferred.

4. What genetic tests have been or will be conducted?
5. To whom will the final report be sent?
6. AFDIL requested the opportunity to review any publication of results in advance, and to be included in the author list.

There was one other invitation approved: my own. Dr. Nevolin wanted me to attend the DNA sessions as a witness and a liaison between the two countries. I also helped to arrange for an additional lab to work with AFDIL but independently, to confirm or challenge the results. This is good science—when two or more labs agree on the results, they have much stronger authority. All Anna Anderson's claims to be a Romanov daughter were shut down when different DNA labs confirmed who she was and was not.

The Russians agreed that a parallel testing was a good idea. A total of three labs would examine and analyze the remains of the two Romanov children, because the Russians had already invited Dr. Evgeny Rogaev from the University of Massachusetts and Moscow Vavilovsky Institute to do the work.

It would work this way: Each lab would do its own work, without discussing or comparing their processes. Then they would send their results to Dr. Peter Gill in the United Kingdom for final confirmation. Fourteen years earlier, Dr. Gill had conducted DNA tests on the remains from the larger burial site.

The Americans were pleased because it was good science. The Russians were pleased because one of their own labs could be involved in the testing. And I was pleased that my idea had led to an independent lab.

For once in a controversial story, everyone was pleased. And that pleased me further.

21

DNA Tells All

Col. Vladimir Soloviev, Russia's senior investigator on this case, asked me to coordinate the DNA validation process for the 2007 discovery. I had almost no understanding of genetic science, but I did understand the two international groups most interested and involved in the Romanov remains. I'd been a kind of cultural liaison for years now, I spoke both languages, and many of the key players knew me, so I agreed to help.

With Tony Falsetti's assistance, we brought the U.S. Armed Forces DNA Identification Laboratory and the University of Innsbruck Institute of Legal Medicine Laboratory together to study the remains found in 2007. In November of that year, we traveled with Dr. Michael Coble to Yekaterinburg to meet the Russian team and plan the work ahead. The Russians invited Dr. Evgeny Rogaev of the University of Massachusetts and the Moscow Vavilovsky Institute DNA Laboratory, to represent the third independent DNA laboratory. AFDIL and Innsbruck trained Russian experts from the Yekaterinburg Bureau of Forensic Medicine in the latest forensic DNA techniques, thus they became the fourth lab to join the team.

Dr. Florabel G. Mullick, director of the Armed Forces Institute of Pathology, sent a letter of invitation on January 28, 2008, inviting Russia to send its two scientists to America for training. They were Natalya Anatolievna Bandurenko and Tamara Nikolaevna Tsitovic.

These two were invited to "conduct collaborative research studies with AFDIL's scientists." It was also stipulated that "Ms. Bandurenko and Ms. Tsitovic will transport the remains to be studied and will travel from Yekaterinburg, Russia, to our facilities in Rockville, Maryland."

AFDIL carefully organized the visitors' stay in Rockville. But the Russians failed to follow the script. They flew not to Maryland but to Massachusetts, to the Boston lab of Dr. Rogaev, the Russian scientist whose lab would be participating. It was highly unusual in such an international operation for one side to depart from protocol and go its own way without communicating its intention.

Colonel Soloviev explained to me that the Russians had only the one lab, which they couldn't afford to lose, and he needed to bolster it. The Americans felt this wasn't the arrangement that had been agreed upon.

The Russians were in Boston with Dr. Rogaev for one month, observing and assisting with the research. Dr. Coble, from AFDIL, visited Dr. Rogaev in Massachusetts to talk about the project and to meet Bandurenko and Tsitovic. During the visit, Dr. Rogaev asked Dr. Coble to sign a contract stipulating that the U.S. Army's lab would work under Rogaev, and all AFDIL results would first go to Rogaev. Dr. Coble quickly denied that request. The arrangement that had been politely affirmed by both parties in the beginning allowed no such thing. It seemed as if politics or at least national pride was becoming an obstacle to the work that needed to be done. One nation needn't be submit to another; both should submit to science, which has no politics and favors no groups of people.

Dr. Coble called me on the phone and explained his predicament. He asked me to contact Dr. Nevolin and let him know that AFDIL couldn't sign the kind of contract Dr. Rogaev was offering. It was a deal-breaker, and AFDIL was prepared to step away from the project rather than make such an agreement. Here I was in the middle again, trying to fend off a miniature Cold War.

I called Soloviev and Dr. Nevolin and reminded them that the original agreement, and most prudent course scientifically, was for labs to work independently of each other. Dr. Nevolin wrote an official letter in an attempt to clarify things, as instructed by the Soloviev. He said, "I am officially inviting you to conduct your own all-inclusive molecular-genetic investigation of all samples of the bone fragments for the purpose of establishing identity of Alexis and Maria on the basis of scientific evidence, independent of all other investigators, together with you, working on the solution of the same question." All results should be presented to the Russians and kept completely confidential otherwise.

This didn't seem to answer all the questions that had been raised. On February

28, 2008, I wrote Dr. Nevolin and asked if I could take Bandurenko and Tsitovic to the U.S. lab in Maryland, and I also asked him to clarify the complete independence of each laboratory, as opposed to a hierarchy with one laboratory controlling the conclusions. He wrote me back, agreeing about Bandurenko and Tsitovic and being clearer that the labs would work independently.

Dr. Coble wrote Soloviev and once again stressed the need for independence. He agreed to confidentiality, with the exception of discussing the process with *National Geographic* and Bellwether Media, which were filming a documentary and understood the need for secrecy. Finally, Dr. Coble wrote, "AFDIL reserves the right to then participate in any scientific presentation or publication relevant to our participation in this case. It is our hope that all scientific parties for the genetic analysis in this case can concur on a fair and equitable agreement on the scientific publication."

As always, and as an old sea captain, I could only hope for fair weather and smooth sailing as we moved closer to our destination.

On March 21 I brought the Russian scientists to AFDIL. Tamara Tsitovic carried a small box that held the DNA bone samples. I was surprised by how little there was. I'd learned through our dealings with Dr. Peter Gill that DNA testing could be done with smaller samples now; maybe I was worrying over nothing.

But the U.S. Army DNA laboratory had the same reaction. Dr. Coble was indignant over how little source material had been provided. Of the five samples received, only one was suitable for research, and that one was just half the size normally expected. One sample was little more than powder—not a dense particle of bone. Two of the samples were parts of the skull—thin, black, and burned. These hadn't been requested. One could possibly be examined, but it was too thin to clean properly.

So here was another roadblock. It was difficult not to speculate on what kind of situation the Russian lab was trying to create. Was this an effort to control the results and predetermine the message that went out to the public? The Russians seemed much more concerned with the confidentiality issue than the Americans. They'd failed to gain authority over the project, and now they had provided an inadequate sample that would limit any results at all from the American lab. Needless to say, the American scientists were having second thoughts about participation in such a nonscientific atmosphere. For me, after years of working to make these things happen, it was heartbreaking.

I wrote to Vladimir Soloviev, whom I knew to be a thorough forensic investigator, and described what we were facing. On behalf of Dr. Coble and others, I requested all the samples from both graves, and asked that Tamara Tsitovic be sent back to Yekaterinburg to procure them. I called Dr. Nevolin with a similar message. I described the situation and said, "The Americans are ready to step away. What do you want to do?" If the Russians wanted AFDIL's involvement, they needed not only to agree to reasonable rules but to play by those rules as well. No more last-minute surprises could be tolerated.

Nevolin immediately said, "Peter, you come to us. I'll give you everything we have."

I considered his invitation. We'd suggested sending Tsitovic, but it sent the right message for Dr. Nevolin to request me as the go-between. It was the role I'd played from the first, but it also signaled a willingness to do exactly what Dr. Nevolin assured us he would do. I would not leave without the complete set of remains I knew were needed.

Dr. Coble and I flew to Yekaterinburg, where Dr. Coble was allowed to select the best bones for extracting DNA. I helped hold the bones still as small pieces were sawed off as samples. The samples were specially packed in plastic sheets. Mission accomplished—so far. Dr. Coble planned to fly back separately, and we decided I'd carry the samples with me, fly home, then drive them to Washington DC.

As I packed the case into my knapsack, I couldn't help but think of my grandmother again. Sometimes history gives off an echo. She had traveled by ship with a box of similar samples beneath her bunk, long before DNA was ever imagined. Now, I would carry these bits of bone across the sea as well, just at a much higher altitude. Neither of us ever met the imperial family, yet in a way, we had quite an odd acquaintance with their remains. All we ever wanted, of course, was to see those remains honored, blessed, and buried with the dignity they deserved.

The knapsack was a matter of refusing to put Romanov remains through luggage check. Such a thought was unimaginable—a royal family becoming so much lost luggage. These remains would never leave my presence.

But in foreign travel, we always seem to end up needing some item we don't have. We had no documentation from Dr. Nevolin or his assistant, Dr. Vladimir S. Gromov. They simply gave us no paperwork. This meant I had no proof of the identity of these contents in my knapsack, and once I went through security in Yekaterinburg, I wasn't allowed to proceed.

I contacted Vladimir Soloviev, explained my plight, and asked him to meet me at Moscow's Sheremetev Airport. Dr. Nevolin received word as well. He personally called Customs at Yekaterinburg airport. He was well known there, and they agreed to wave me through with the samples. Yekaterinburg had quite a stake in the Romanov story, so this was a shrewd move on Dr. Nevolin's part. My knapsack moved through Customs with no X-ray, just a wink and a smile. But I still had to get through Moscow.

Investigator Soloviev met me there, reassured me, and escorted me as far as he could go without traveling abroad himself. As I feared, I was singled out for an inspection check. I opened the knapsack and showed them what was inside: the remains of two royal children.

"What is this?"

"These are the Romanov relics. I'm transporting them for DNA studies."

The inspector wrinkled his brow; something like this didn't come up every day, even in Moscow. "Show me your documentation," he said.

My mouth went dry. "Sir, I'm afraid there is none. I wasn't given any, but Customs should have received a call about this matter. They should know I'm coming, and all documentation should be with them."

He only regarded me seriously—an irritation disrupting his day. I asked if I could use the phone, and I called Inspector Soloviev, realizing he may not have arrived home yet, and he may not have even headed home. Hadn't he made arrangements for this situation? If he couldn't be reached, and if no one had a record of a conversation with him, then my knapsack would be confiscated. Who knows what would have happened then? The remains might have sat in the ground for nearly ninety years, only to see the light of day and then disappear again. In Moscow, anything was possible.

I thought of my old days on the SS *Exford*, being arrested for "smuggling." I smiled thinly in recalling it; that was nothing compared to this scenario.

We waited a few minutes, and then Soloviev appeared in a doorway, like a disgruntled guardian angel. He was already in midargument with the head of Customs, and I saw he was a formidable opponent in a dispute, with his razor-sharp evidential mind. It all led to Soloviev's taking my knapsack and my release to fly home, still a free man—free but with a lighter knapsack.

"Grandmother," I thought, "the box has a way of disappearing, doesn't it?"

I wrote to Dr. Coble, who had decided to spend an extra day in Moscow—never imagining the misadventures about to occur: "Michael, I got the remains to Moscow, but that's as far as I could go. Customs wouldn't allow those remains to go over the border. Soloviev took them and is sending them right back to Yekaterinburg."

To save the day, Dr. Coble received the remains again—this time with full documentation, every *i* dotted, every *t* crossed. He wrote of his success moving through Customs. The only issue was that he had to place the samples in his luggage, since he'd have to go through another security screening before getting on the plane. Then we could worry about what might go wrong in New York City . . .

But I met him at Kennedy Airport, where nothing went wrong. And I drove Dr. Coble and the relics all the way to Washington DC. By this time, nothing in the world was going to get between us and those remains getting a full and accurate DNA analysis.

The games were over, but who won? *Science*, I hoped.

The Romanov children, if these were their remains, were now in the hands of science.

In June of 2008 the AFDIL and University of Innsbruck Institute of Legal Medicine labs completed their analysis and submitted it to Dr. Peter Gill for review. His finding was that the two labs' results matched 100 percent. He said, "There is overwhelming evidence to support the contention that the remains found in the second grave are those of Alexei and one of the Romanov princesses." Mitochondrial DNA, it should be noted, identifies family relationships, but not individual identities. Thus the Maria/Anastasia question couldn't be addressed—at least by this particular science.

Dr. Rogaev had data that tripled the result. His results were published in February of 2009. Ultimately all four labs agreed on their findings:

The remains presented DNA evidence of two individuals.
One of the individuals was female, with a biological or developmental age of fifteen to nineteen years old.
The other was likely male, and in the range of twelve to fifteen years old.
Racial/ancestral type couldn't be determined from limited samples.
Three silver amalgam fillings from the crowns of two molars suggest an aristocratic status for that person.
The burial site itself was most likely older than sixty years, based on cultural clues from material found with the bones.

Since mitochondrial tests are based on maternal relationship, the results confirmed that both bodies were children of the tsarina. Prince Philip, duke of Edinburgh, had provided DNA for reference years earlier, so it was a ready-made comparison.

Autosomal STR is more of a paternity test, and its language tends to work this way: these remains are 4.3 trillion times more likely to be related to the tsar and tsarina than two random individuals. And the remains of the three daughters from the main burial site also provided matches.

The remains associated with Alexei were also submitted to Y-STR testing (short tandem repeat on the Y chromosome). There was a match with the tsar's STR profile as well as the closest living relative, Prince Andrew Romanov, who was a cousin of the tsar. These findings were also confirmed by a direct match of the tsar's blood, taken from a shirt he wore on a trip to Japan in 1891, when he bled after an attack by a would-be assassin. Again, the match was perfect.

Those conversant in DNA science agreed that these were very strong figures in terms of providing positive identification.

If these remains had been found, say, in the 1960s, and DNA wasn't used, the case for identifying them with the royal family would still have been overwhelming. This was the right number of individuals buried in two sites, seventy meters apart, precisely where the executioner and overseer of the burial documented for the corpses. Other methods of forensic analysis, including dental evidence, pointed to the truth. Dr. Botkin's dentures and a child's silver fillings, in a time when only the richest families had access to these, offered clues. Buttons and topaz stones and the presence of acid told their tale. And the grisly tale told by skulls savagely shattered in the facial area couldn't be dismissed.

The Romanovs and their devoted attendants were now all present and accounted for.

In December of 2008 Michael Coble traveled to Yekaterinburg with the results from the U.S. Army's and University of Innsbruck's labs. He sat across the table from the Russian scientists who had their own results—but from blood samples taken from a shirt that had been recovered from Nicholas II on a trip to Japan, when he was attacked by a would-be assassin armed with a saber. He survived the attack, but his bloody shirt was then placed in a museum. For DNA results, the shirt could not be cut, but a sample was recovered with clean water and a Q-tip. Again, this was a remarkable achievement that couldn't have been imagined a few years earlier.

Coble had no samples from the two newer sets of remains. So he sat on one side of the table, Bandurenko and Tsitovic at the other, and it was like playing poker, except they were showing their cards with DNA results. A certain number of markers had to match perfectly.

They did. It was a demonstration of the integrity of independent DNA analysis. Different labs worked on their own without comparison and, out of trillions of possibilities, produced identical results in chromosome markers and other measurements.

By December 5 I had arrived, and we held our press conference and made the announcement. All the scientists spoke. And at the very end, I was called up to offer a few remarks as someone who had been involved for so long in this pursuit of finding and identifying the remains of the Romanovs. As I was speaking, a representative of the church spread the news that the patriarch, the head of our church, has passed away. For everyone, it was a shock. For those of in the Russian Orthodox Church or the Church Abroad, it was one of those moments that will be etched in memory—as, for example, when a Roman Catholic pope dies or a world leader passes away.

But particularly for those of us involved in the Romanov story and the quest for recognition by the church, it was shattering. Even as we did the scientific work all these years, we were also doing the political work, so to speak, to involve the church and gain its affirmation. Why is this important? The Romanovs were recognized as saints and martyrs, "passion bearers," the lowest level of Orthodox sainthood.

I announced to the gathering, "May he rest in peace," and there was an air of solemnity in the room. I was thinking of the future. We'd have to start all over again with new leadership. I said to myself, "Well, that's that. There goes the whole case." It should be noted that even with the previous patriarch, we had lacked the church's support. Anything found along the Old Koptiaki Road was denied acceptance. But at least we had worked with that hierarchy. Now there would be a new hierarchy, and we were back to square one.

Sure enough, when Kirill, the new patriarch, was installed, his comment was that not all of the questions had been answered. The Russian Expert Commission Abroad, the group whose purpose for existence was skepticism over any scientific resolution of the Romanov question, had presented a list of their "questions" about our findings. Investigator Soloviev had thoroughly answered each and every one of them, not that this changed any minds.

The new patriarch also suggested he couldn't offer acceptance because the church hadn't been involved in all areas of testing as a witness. I'd tried to be present at searches and scientific discussions as a witness myself, but of course I lacked any official church credential.

The church continued to press the point that it had been denied participation in the investigation—that somehow the scientists had kept church representatives away. But this simply wasn't true. No one from the patriarchate had ever asked to be included in the work, though we informed them all along the way of what we were doing. No one from the Russian Orthodox Church showed any particular interest. I sent all the DNA reports to Vsevolod Chaplin, the church's representative for the Romanov case, but heard nothing back.

Ultimately it seemed as if political pressure from dissenters made the difference. It was a terrible shame that the people of God, devoted to truth and justice, could not take what we felt was the right stand. Even so, we were proud to have settled the question in terms of objective evidence.

As for me, after a number of years, my work in Yekaterinburg was done. I decided to start the search for the remains of Grand Duke Mikhail Alexandrovich Romanov and his secretary, Nikolai Johnson. He was the forgotten victim in the Romanov story, and it was time for the light of justice to shine his way.

Dr. Michael Coble contributed a 2011 article for *Investigative Genetics* that showed he understood the big picture. The Romanov murders with the rise of communism, he said, changed the course of history—but the identifying of the Romanov remains was just as historic for DNA science. It defined the rise of forensic autosomal STR and mitochondrial DNA testing for remains in poor condition.

Autosomal short tandem repeat markers are part of DNA profiling. A panel of these markers create a unique genetic profile that establishes or compares kinships. Today, through websites like Ancestry.com, consumers send in their own DNA samples to find distant cousins they never knew they had. But they're also used to link persons of interest to crime scenes or identify bodily remains, as was done with the Romanovs. Mitochondrial DNA concerns the markers we inherit from our mothers, making these identifications possible.

I'm not a scientist, and these aren't terms I throw around very often. Listening to scientists discuss their work often makes my head hurt. But I understood what Dr. Coble was saying in that article. World history and scientific progress converged in the death, burial, and bodily recovery of the Romanov family. History, in my judgment, was changed for the worse. But forensic science was changed for the better with this fascinating and compelling case.

These bodies had been abused, burned with fire, and left utterly exposed to the elements in shallow earth, in a climate of often extreme weather. Still, DNA science overcame all these challenges and spoke to the world. It said, "These were the Romanovs. Don't believe any other conclusion. Three labs worked independently and examined this evidence. Three labs came to complete, consistent agreement. The last tsar, his family and attendants once were lost, but now they're found. They were the objects of lies and legends, but now the truth is known. The uncertainties can now be pushed aside."

22

The "Experts" Object

In all the years we dealt with the Romanov remains, and worked to get them acknowledged by the world, perhaps our greatest heartache was the lack of acceptance from the Russian Orthodox Church.

Perhaps there were many complex reasons the church was hesitant to look on the vast collection of evidence objectively and come to the same conclusion most of the world had. But an obvious reason was the volume of angry protests raised by a group of skeptics. The most prominent of these called itself the Russian Expert Commission Abroad but is sometimes referred to as the Foreign Expert Commission (FEC).

I've already described my first unhappy exposure to this group on the occasion of Dr. Avdonin's trip to the United States in 1993. The organization was first formed in 1989 by men who were more than skeptical—they somehow saw the finding of the Romanov remains as an affront to all they believed, something to be fought off energetically and viciously.

What was behind this attitude? Those of us in the White Russian community can understand it up to a point. We're people who had come through life with a healthy distrust of anything connected with Soviet communism. Our parents and grandparents suffered because of the revolution. Many lost their land, possessions, and family members. My grandmother and my great-grandparents loved their homeland the way anyone loves their country of birth. All of that was taken away and followed with two generations of what, to us, was an evil government. The Soviets hunted down our families, seized our land, and tried to wipe out our churches.

So there has been a natural reflex among us to distrust all things that came out of Moscow. If Russian leaders made a statement, it was propaganda; it lacked integrity because the government lacked integrity. And when a man named Geli Ryabov, who for many years had worked in Moscow, announced he'd found the bones of the Romanovs, it was natural to be cautious. That was certainly my reaction. It was 1989, the USSR was in an uproar, and suddenly here came someone from the Soviet government to tell the world he'd found the Romanovs—which was already, to us, like solving the Kennedy assassination or suggesting Elvis was still alive. It seemed unlikely, particularly after generations of hoaxes and false leads. And we knew nothing of Ryabov or Avdonin, or why they'd be making such claims.

In time, however, we listened, and we kept open minds. We considered the likelihood of finding this many bodies buried together in the area where the corpses were said to have been taken. We heard they matched the profiles; they showed evidence of violence, and secondary cultural items seemed to validate the age of the bones. I can remember my mind shifting from slightly skeptical to hopeful, and later to solidly convinced.

But not all my friends followed the story the way I did, and few became involved. Many or most in my circle were caught up in the present, in their own lives and problems. This footnote from the dusty history books didn't have much to do with what was important to them. It would be nice if the Romanov remains were finally located, they thought, but they simply didn't take the time to learn much about the evidence. Others, particularly those who were more militantly anti-Soviet, had their minds set from the very beginning to knock down this latest "scam," as they saw it. They'd heard it all before—a new Anastasia or a survivor who was Tsarevich Alexei. There were legends about Romanov gold somewhere in the vaults of London banks. A few dreamed Russia would resume its monarchy, now that communism had failed. But those who were naturally skeptical were not about to be taken in.

From the legions of Doubting Thomases sprang the Russian Expert Commission Abroad, who did more than disbelieve. They worked tirelessly to spread their disbelief. The RECA was dedicated to the endeavor of puncturing any bubble of hope that these Russian remains were authentic. Peter Koltypin, an engineer from Connecticut who had run for Congress, and Prince Alexis

Scherbatow, a university professor and leader of the Russian Nobility Association in America, were the primary leaders.

The RECA believed that nothing that came out of that excavation beside the Old Koptiaki Road was legitimate. It was all an elaborate hoax concocted by the KGB, which was still, they insisted, a force to be watched. Koltypin and Scherbatow, the most of vocal of the group, believed that Sokolov had solved the crime many years ago, and we should leave it at that. The bodies had been decapitated and the heads carried off to the communist leaders for inspection; the rest had been burned. Avdonin and Ryabov were simply KGB puppets out to deceive the masses.

Dr. Avdonin had already encountered the two doubters in Russia. They lurked in a crowd he was addressing and began asking loaded questions. Dr. Avdonin sparred with them and found out it was a useless exercise. He told them Russian scientists would examine the remains. They responded, who would believe whatever these "scientists" said? Dr. Avdonin replied that Americans, too, would join the investigation. They felt that was part of the conspiracy as well. And when he basically told them, "Okay, you know so much—*you* appoint the trustworthy scientists," they simply retreated to the line that whatever happened, Dr. Avdonin and his cronies still couldn't be trusted. No matter who analyzed it, the materials were fake, and anyone who examined them and said otherwise would be lying.

"So, there's no way to prove anything to you?" asked Dr. Avdonin.

Interestingly, they said they would believe DNA but that this was a moot point, for everyone knew that Russians lacked DNA expertise.

The RECA not only cast doubt on the remains. The newly found Yurovsky papers were not to be trusted, either. This had to be a forgery, they said, because it didn't affirm that the head of Nicholas II had been carried to Moscow. And if the skull in evidence *did* turn out to be the authentic head of the last tsar, that only proved someone had dug up the site and planted it there, so it would be found by the searchers.

This group began from a foundation of misinformation, in other words, and built a shaky house on it. The jury had made the decision before the evidence was in. If the evidence didn't fit, throw it out.

It would be easy to view this group as another Flat Earth Society, an organization of disgruntled resisters to science and progress. But the organization's influence was disproportionate to its size, due to an aggressive PR strategy that stayed busy telling everyone in the media, government, or some position of influence exactly where they stood, so that news accounts of progress in the Romanov remains story were always accompanied by mentions of "some skeptics" discounting whatever breakthrough had been made.

As one of many examples, an article in *Smithsonian* described the DNA results but also carried a lengthy section explaining how "not everyone is convinced." The usual naysayers had gotten their message out, and editors felt it made for a good, balanced story, even if these objections had been thoroughly countered. It's good practice to cover both sides of controversies—if they're true controversies. This group's mission, however, was to manufacture controversy. Though the investigation was conducted by the finest anthropologists, lab technicians, and forensic detectives in the world, one or two dissenting voices could make the story appear to be a "maybe, maybe not" proposition. The group's mailing list was expansive. Its responses were sent to hundreds in the media, in government, and in European and Russian aristocracy. Most prominently, its aimed at the Russian Orthodox Church and those who had influence in it.

Russia's government commission on dealing with the Romanov remains, to its credit, attempted to work positively with the RECA, inviting them to come to Yekaterinburg and Moscow, inspect the remains as well as government documents, visit all the sites of the historic events, and engage in dialogue about their concerns.

In 1995 RECA members made that trip. Having seen documents and remains, a spokesman for RECA said there was no reason to be impressed. Everything was fake, and the CIA is skilled at creating duplicates that couldn't be distinguished from the real thing. As a matter of fact, the spokesman said his reason for traveling to Russia was for the opportunity to amplify his disgust at all the fakery being presented by those involved with the investigation. These committee members said that, at the end of World War II, Germany was totally purged of Nazi elements. But at the end of the Soviet era, there was no such purge; all the old elements of the KGB were still in place, and who could expect them to grow a conscience overnight? Surely, they were up to their old tricks.

But why? What would be the reason for this elaborate conspiracy theory, including planting fake skulls in the ground and falsifying old documents, even including American scientists in the ruse? RECA believed that with the fall of communism, it was all about deceiving the West into trusting the "new" Russia, which of course, in the eyes of this group, was not new at all. It would be good public relations for Russians, too. Here was the new, improved Russian government, already finding the bodies that were sought for so many years. It would show the country in an admirable light and perhaps attract foreign aid and business the country desperately needed. And who else but KGB propagandist Geli Ryabov would plant the skull of Nicholas? He worked in Moscow and would be the obvious point man.

RECA still admitted to its respect for DNA evidence, even after the results pointed clearly and unambiguously toward the Romanovs. Koltypin and Scherbatow commented that they had no quibbles with the DNA evidence. They were certain it was accurate—but it identified no individuals, just family line. That wouldn't be hard to do. Lots of Romanovs died in the revolution or some other time. Those bodies could have been gathered and planted in time to be "discovered."

So said the self-appointed "experts." For RECA, dissent was less a matter of honest skepticism than outright hostility, and it quickly became evident that no member of the group was open to changing his mind.

At some point, Vladimir Soloviev had enough of all this. When it came to evidence, reasoning, and conclusions, he was a serious man. He would happily have entertained serious and substantive questions, but the antics of RECA did nothing but make his job more difficult. These people were undermining a serious criminal investigation. They were obstructing justice. Soloviev's job was to clear the air, and their job was to kick up dust.

In his report, he identified twenty-six objections and challenges in terms of how the investigation was conducted, as presented by RECA. And he answered each one. Here are a few of the major ones.

1. The investigation applied "imperfect" Russian laws, rather than those based on the American system.

The investigation had no evidentiary value, RECA said, because, for example, Pavel Ivanov had worked on the samples in both the United States and the United Kingdom. "Chain of evidence" was violated—this was a charge that cropped up over and over. There was no "independent prosecutor." RECA was not involved in the study, which failed to meet Western standards.

In response, Soloviev noted that biological samples had been removed in accordance with Russian procedure in criminal law. Continuous video was taken, and photographs made, when the items were taken from the ground. Everything was packed carefully and sealed in the presence of witnesses. Documentation was compiled.

All teeth, bone fragments, and other remains were photographed, catalogued, and assigned numbers, and all work was recorded in a special journal.

In transporting remains to the United States and the United Kingdom, the same careful procedures were followed. There was no opportunity for anyone to tamper with the evidence without it being recorded on film.

As for using Russian legal standards, this was inevitable and natural, and Ivanov's participation had violated no laws.

2. Although it is known that Empress Alexandra Fyodorovna and her daughters were carriers of hemophilia, no studies in this regard were conducted.

From 1992 to 1998, there was no scientific method for detecting such from poorly preserved bone fragments. But in 2007, when the remains of Tsarevich Alexei and Grand Duchess Maria were discovered, hemophilia testing was conducted on all eleven sets of remains. It turned out that the tsarevich and two of the women—Anastasia and the empress—were carriers of hemophilia.

3. The remains of nine individuals were found in the grave, but only five received genetic testing.

From 1992 to 1998, comparative genetic tests were conducted on the emperor, empress, the tsarevich, and Grand Duchesses Olga, Tatiana, and Anastasia. This was because testing was carried out only with relatives along the female line (mitochondrial DNA).

Between 2007 and 2008, genetic analysis of both sex lines was used to study the traits of all eleven individuals. For each of them, complete mitochondrial

DNA data (including Y chromosome for the male line) was taken. This offered the ability to differentiate individuals. The genetic data of Dr. Botkin, Demidova, and Kharitonov demonstrated genotypes similar to their close relatives. Trupp's genotype was found, but there were no living relatives available for comparison.

4. During the investigation, no assessment was made regarding the damage to Nicholas II's skull caused during his trip to Japan in 1891.

At first, RECA harped on the fact that supposedly, there was no mark on the skull where the future tsar had received a fairly deep injury on his 1891 trip to Japan. Didn't this rule out the remains from being those of the tsar?

Soloviev reported that he had allowed no genetic testing of the skull during the first testing sequences, from 1992 to 1998. He was afraid to shatter the skull; larger samples were required at that time. But later, the issue was resolved. Original medical files from 1891 were produced, documenting Nicholas II's head wound when it was examined and treated just after the incident. The doctors said a bone fragment as thick as a sheet of paper was removed from the wound. This kind of injury wouldn't damage the integrity of the outer, bony layer of the skull. There would have been scraping, but the sulfuric acid poured in during the burial would have leached it away.

5. There's been no conclusive genetic analysis on Nicholas II's blood sample taken in 1992 in Japan.

A Japanese geneticist named Nagai studied the old bloody handkerchief and maintained that the DNA in it did not match what Gill and the others found. This was another rallying point for the skeptics, the chance that definitive evidence could turn up unexpected and utterly spoil the hoax.

It's a misstatement by the media that geneticist Tatsuo Nagai conducted a genetic test on the handkerchief, according to Soloviev. He did not. In 1992 Russian geneticist P. L. Ivanov traveled to Japan, got access to the preserved cloth, and analyzed the sample in Peter Gill's English laboratory. The finding was that the museum piece had been taken out of its museum case and handled countless times, by many hands, and thus thoroughly contaminated. No single genotype could be taken from it.

While the handkerchief proved useless for study, the shirt worn by Nicholas II on that day was a much better subject, and provided DNA consistent with the remains. So as it turned out, the unexpected evidence of the shirt turned up, completely unsuspected, and spoiled not the "hoax" but the accusation of one.

6. Ryabov, Avdonin, and E. S. Radzinsky could have abused the classified files on the Romanovs.

Soloviev held that the activities of these three men were studied in response to the accusations that Ryabov in particular was a secret KGB officer engaging in a propaganda mission of deception. Supposedly Ryabov had created a fake burial place or perhaps added the tsar's skull to what was there.

But none of these rumors panned out. It turns out that in 1990, when Ryabov wrote his blockbuster article about finding the remains, the USSR's State Security Committee was caught flat-footed. The two searchers, Avdonin and Ryabov, were then secretly monitored. Moscow spied on their correspondence—not the kind of response one would suspect to people who were government assets.

The circumstances by which Ryabov accessed the secret files are highly credible. He was a well-known documentary filmmaker working on a project about the police, and he was given permission to get what he needed. As for Radzinsky, the playwright, he never saw any files until they were declassified. As much as RECA may have wished it, there was nothing nefarious about any of these men.

7. There was no study of the Yurovsky Note. Its content offers a sharp contrast with memoirs and accounts of other participants in the execution and burial, and it also shows important differences from the findings of Sokolov.

RECA understood that the evidence for an Old Koptiaki Road burial, as well as failed burnings, came from the Yurovsky Note, which was found, of course, by that busy "KGB agent" Ryabov. Before this convenient memorandum, it was the consensus of many that Sokolov had it right when he said the bodies had all been burned. Right on cue, around the same time the nine corpses were discovered, a note from Yurovsky, the head of the burial party, materialized, telling precisely where those bodies could be dug up. From RECA's perspective, this was beyond suspicious.

Soloviev, however, contradicted the assertion that Sokolov's writings differed from the Yurovsky Note. In the great bulk of the testimonies from those present, in fact, it was agreed that all members of the imperial family were shot, and that the bodies were buried in the Porosenkov Log region (the field of the final burial site). Sokolov's conclusion as to the burning was a hypothesis based on the fact that he had found no bodies and believed burning was the disposal method the killers would have used (as, in fact, they had tried to do).

Moreover, Soloviev's investigation performed handwriting analysis on the Yurovsky Note. It carefully examined the writing materials, to see if they were genuinely from that era. Second and third copies were typed. Yurovsky himself made a revision in one of the copies, and the handwriting matched other papers with his signature.

Soloviev traced the history of the Yurovsky Note and its filing, how it was used, and whether it was ever employed as a form of propaganda—meaning it would be a misleading attempt to cover up such items as beheadings. There was no trace of such usage. The document was made to inform the Bolshevik leaders, was always kept classified, and finally emerged from a copy kept by Yurovsky's son.

8. Russia's archives and document repositories weren't thoroughly examined. Soloviev was not allowed access to the most secret levels.

This is an appeal to the great mystery of what might still lie in the secret KGB files, if one uses his or her imagination—in other words, more speculation than evidence. Isn't it just possible there's some manuscript or item of evidence in there somewhere that utterly turns the investigation upside-down?

Soloviev listed his "expert group," appointed to research all the available channels, including the chief of the state archives in Moscow and many other officials and the locations they searched, which was comprehensive, thorough, and even international. It's true there were some top-level files Soloviev and his team could not review, but it's difficult to imagine that anything in them would overturn the full, detailed, and consistent picture of the killings and burial that ultimately came together.

Through the rest of the list of objections, RECA lashed out in multiple directions. It named Romanov relatives and others from whom blood samples should have been taken, though in some cases it was unnecessary, and in others permission was denied.

RECA declared that mysterious teeth were recovered from the main site in 1991—teeth from a youth that matched no one in the victim group. But these teeth turned out to belong to the skull identified as that of Grand Duchess Anastasia.

There's reference to "secret police documents" that speak of opening the grave in 1934 and 1946. Yet no one has produced these documents. RECA certainly couldn't do so. It's clear this was another rumor.

RECA cast doubt on the main burial place discovered by Avdonin and Ryabov, implying that it was only a place where remains had been moved to. Soloviev once again reviewed the story of how the two searchers had found the site and added that forensic experts had examined the site closely and found no evidence that anything had been moved. The state of the soil and other factors pointed to this as the original burial site.

Once again, attention was given to the question of decapitation. RECA charged that this issue wasn't addressed by the investigation, though in reality, as Soloviev pointed out, the anthropologists and forensic scientists stated that all these skulls matched their skeletons, and there was no sign of beheading.

RECA cited a newspaper called *Arguments and Facts* that stated the Lenin was presented with the emperor's skull, yet that newspaper could present no evidence to support its assertion, because none has ever been found—only gossip and urban legends.

There were other doubters, if not as loud. A Stanford University scientist tested a finger bone of Alexandra's older sister Elizabeth, who was murdered by the Bolsheviks and thrown down a well in 1918. The mitochondrial DNA from the finger was inconsistent with DNA from the empress's skeleton. RECA cited this, of course, but the forensic science world rallied around the investigation's results. This, they said, was another example of contaminated DNA. If a number of people handle an item, such as the tsar's handkerchief or the sister's finger, the sample's DNA is intermingled with that of other people. Dr. Coble made the point that this is why we look at the entirety of the evidence rather than building a case on one factor.

Japanese scientist Nagai and a Russian scientist, Dr. Vyacheslav Popov, also challenged the Romanov investigation. They tested twenty-five hair samples supposedly from Georgi Romanov, comparing their results to those of the DNA scientists working with the investigative committee. They found the heteroplasmy of Nicholas II, which was discovered earlier, missing.

Dr. Coble reviewed these results, using a translation (the originals were in Japanese), and determined that again, contamination was the issue. Such results, he said, wouldn't have seen the light of day in a respected forensic laboratory. Contamination is the ultimate deal-breaker for DNA analysis, and if a sample hasn't been protected, it's worthless for this kind of study. This is why the handkerchief from Japan was of no help, while the bones, though long under the soil and deteriorated, could still offer DNA evidence—they'd never been handled up to the time they were discovered, and then they were handled with care.

The great thing about science is that there's nothing subjective about it. Scientific enterprise relies upon investigation, evidence, and the checks and counterchecks that make results credible. In the end, good results will withstand all the challenges and remain standing. As years have progressed, this has happened with the careful investigation of the Romanov remains. As Michael Coble put it, "we can finally put the controversies to rest."

But not me—good luck putting me to rest.

Once our results were announced, my mind began to shift toward one final Romanov goal: the location of Mikhail's remains. This brother was all but forgotten. He and his companion were still unaccounted for, and if we could find these eleven others, I believed we could find these two.

23

Searching for the Lost Brother

It was time to turn my thinking to the tsar's brother Grand Duke Mikhail Alexandrovich and his secretary, Nikolai Johnson.

Grand Duke Mikhail Alexandrovich is the forgotten Romanov, and that may be just as he'd want it. Mikhail was the man who would *not* be king. He found himself born into a royal line with tremendous power and even greater responsibilities. But the role of national patriarch was not in his temperament.

Mikhail entered the world as fourth in line to the throne, as his grandfather, Alexander II, was Emperor of All the Russias. His father and then two elder brothers were ahead of him, so it seemed unlikely he would ever be called upon to become the tsar. Then Alexander II was assassinated, and thirteen years later his father Nicholas I died. In 1899 his brother Georgi died, and after all this time, he was the heir presumptive to his brother, Tsar Nicholas II. This was also an era when an assassination was always a possibility, so Mikhail worried about fate thrusting him into a demanding position he never desired.

There was a male heir, of course: Tsarevich Alexei. But he was in poor health, and it was far from a foregone conclusion he'd live to take the helm.

Mikhail pursued romantic relationships and even marriage in such a way that he might remove himself from eligibility to be a Romanov ruler. While his brother married into the highest echelon of European royalty, Mikhail sought unions he knew would fail to meet his country's expectations. He simply wanted a quiet life—which wasn't to say he shied away from military duty. He commanded cavalry in World War I and was well loved and accepted by his men.

When Nicholas abdicated in 1917, it was also decreed that Alexei would be passed over in Mikhail's favor. The fate he dreaded had finally caught up with him. He delayed that ascension, however, in deference to ratification by the proper electors. The truth was that those in power at the moment wanted him in power no more than he wanted it for himself. It was a terrible situation, and he was never confirmed, given the chaos that had ensued in Saint Petersburg by that time. Many viewed his declaration of deference to the provisional government, asking all Russians to do the same, as an act of patriotism. But his brother called it "rubbish."

None of it mattered. The governmental situation remained chaotic, and Mikhail and his personal secretary, Nikolai Johnson, were arrested and eventually sent to Perm. On the evening of June 12, 1918, four men—enemies of the tsar—forged papers, entered Mikhail's room, and demanded the two men accompany them in two horse-drawn carriages. Along the road through the forest near Motovilikha, the men were told to exit the carriages and were shot. Like the tsar's family, Mikhail and Johnson were victims of the local Bolsheviks, the new, supposedly idealistic and honest "party of the people." And again, the bodies were stripped, robbed, and the subject of false rumors about escapes.

Somewhere in the woods near Perm, those bodies lay buried in the earth. But where were they? Living through the first discovery, seeing the victims honored and buried properly, I felt a responsibility to help bring about the same justice for Mikhail and Johnson. I had to be honest with myself: I was no longer a young man. I'd also seen all the heartache that comes from bureaucracy, politics, and the simple inability of some people to work toward a positive goal with others. Was I really ready to embark on a second journey through that terrain? Was I ready to sift through countless acres of dirt, perhaps finding nothing at all?

Then again, I was experienced at this now—particularly in the area of organization. No nonprofit group in the world was better positioned to take up this mission than SEARCH Foundation. The letters of that name stood for Scientific Expedition to Account for the Romanov Children, and Mikhail was one of those children—a "lost boy," an individual murdered only because of the family name into which he was born. He had spent a lifetime disavowing the trappings of royalty, and he was killed for his proximity to it anyway. His death was another crime that went unpunished. He deserved at least the justice of a Christian burial and a national moment of remembrance of his sacrifice.

Yes, I was ready to start sifting.

One thing about searches. They offer long hours of fascinating conversation. You learn a lot about people, because you're working side by side, sweating together, exerting yourself for a common goal. People tend to open up with each other, and you learn a lot about each other. In some cases, you travel with them and spend time in airports. I treasure the relationships I've developed through my Romanov searches. Even if we'd never found a thing, at least we'd have found friendship.

One of these friends was Vladimir Konstantinov, the ground-penetrating radar expert. During the searches for Alexei and his sister, we brought in Vladimir and, like magic, he could tell us all kinds of things about the ground beneath our feet without lifting a shovel. In 2004, during some of our downtime, he talked to me about the murder of Grand Duke Mikhail and how his remains had never been found. I had begun my journey with a lot of information about Nicholas, Alexandra, and their family; not so much about Mikhail and Johnson. Most people don't realize the Bolsheviks murdered a total of eighteen Romanovs—fourteen of those within a period of one month, from mid-June to mid-July of 1918.

Vladimir's words lodged in my mind, and I came to the decision that if we ever completed our work with the Ipatiev House victims, I would begin my search for the remains of the grand duke and his personal secretary. Now, five years later, I called my friend and asked him if he was willing to meet me in Perm for a new search. At the time, my thinking was that it was a good idea for its own sake, but if there was good DNA, it would also help encourage the church to accept the previous remains, and provide a bit more closure for the Russian people on the events of 1917 and 1918. And of course, the victims would receive the burials they deserved. He quickly agreed, and as we got out our calendars, we came to a decision that we'd visit Perm the following July for a preliminary search, mostly to get to know the lay of the land.

I also communicated with Vladimir Soloviev. "Peter," he said, "you're coming to wander through the forest and dig up all our soil again?"

"I sure am," I smiled, "but I need you to wander through the archives and dig up some files."

He promised to send me everything he had on the grand duke's murder. It turned out there were eight versions as to what, how, and when the murders took place and where the bodies were buried. As with the other burials, off the Old Koptiaki Road, it was mostly a local Bolshevik affair with a few witnesses who later gave descriptions, but no organized formal investigation, and no real evidence preserved. We knew the general area where the shootings occurred, but there were different stories as to the distances and directions traveled from Motovilikha.

One story we heard was that in 1921, the Cheka came from Moscow to locate the burial spot, pull the bodies back up, and burn them at the nearby arms factory. Nothing has ever turned up in the archive to support this suggestion; if it had, of course, we would have had no more reason to continue searching. There would be nothing to find.

Upon our arrival in Perm, we heard a variation on that story. A self-proclaimed "witness" claimed that the shots killing Grand Duke Mikhail and his secretary were heard by local people. What we discovered, however, was that no one lived anywhere near the general area where the murders must have occurred. If there were any "ear witnesses" to the gunshots, they'd have to have been travelers passing through. But it's more likely no one outside the executioners heard what happened that night.

For the record, that version of the story went this way: The carriage traveled five to six kilometers on the main road, north of the Motovilikha area of Perm. After crossing the bridge at the Yazovaya River, the party took a right turn and began climbing a hill. Upon coming to a clearing, the two prisoners were told to dismount from the carriage, and they were shot immediately. The sky wasn't yet dark. As it was too late to bury the bodies, however, the plan was to cover the corpses in brush and branches, then return to bury them on the following day. The executioners left.

But the locals had heard the noise, and they came out to investigate, including a little boy who became our witness years later. He was the one who found the bodies hidden under the branches. He ran back and told his family, and his father gathered some men to retrieve the bodies. They brought these bodies to a cemetery in the area and buried them next to a man named Paranomov. They marked the spot of the first grave by carving the letter M (for Mikhail) on one tree and the letter A (Alexandrovich, his surname) on a tree close by.

This fooled the Bolsheviks, who discovered the bodies missing but lied and told the authorities they'd burned the bodies and didn't want to say where. So for all these years, the boy had kept silent on what he knew out of fear of the communists. Then, at age ninety-two, he told his story to a film crew director. Soon afterward, he passed away, at peace because he had kept the secret and lived to deliver the truth about the burial of Mikhail and Johnson.

I listened to this and felt that it could just possibly be true. At least we could check it out. We spoke to the film director, and he took us to the spot where he'd been told the murders took place. This was indeed an open area, a large field in the midst of a pine forest. I groaned inwardly as I thought about the time required to search every square centimeter of such an area. Konstantinov was with me, and he soon had his GPR running, scanning the ground in spots that seemed promising. But it was simply an informal, long-shot attempt to make a quick find.

Based on the story, we retraced the boy's footsteps and ultimately came to two trees. Immediately we saw M on one and A on the other. *Mikhail Alexandrovich*. My hope surged. Could it really be? Why else would these letters be marked on the trees?

Oddly, it would have required a ladder to place those letters. They were about twelve feet (four meters) from the ground. One's first reaction might be that they were placed there many years ago, and the trees grew. But our forensic botanist, Crystal Strouse, confirmed that trees grow out more than up in their mature years. We don't judge the age by the height but by the rings we count in the cross section. So this was hard to explain, but it was still possible someone had placed the letters so high so they wouldn't be disturbed. We continued to check out this site.

Behind the tree we noticed a large oval hole—three feet deep. Clearly it was freshly dug, with the clay still fresh and dry. No plants had been growing inside, as would happen after a while if the hole were older.

Someone had made quite an effort with this hoax.

This false alarm only made me more determined. We were taken to various areas that could be likely burial places for the grand duke and his secretary, so we began to get a better feel for the layout of this section of the Perm area. But the weather became uncooperative. A rain front moved in, and it rained hard enough to make the road leading to the field impassable. Ground-penetrating radars won't operate in wet areas.

We realized our search was over for the time being. We'd leave things as they were and make plans to return next year, hoping for better success. As I flew home, I was thinking, "This isn't going to be the long ordeal that endured at the Old Koptiaki Road. We have the general area pinned down, we have the equipment and a bit of experience, and we'll get this done quickly."

It's a good thing I didn't know at the time that I'd still be working at this task ten years later. Sometimes it's what we don't know that maintains our energy and eagerness. We can always imagine we're one shovel away from a discovery.

Somehow it was 2012 before we made it back to Perm. I'd had cancer twice and four operations in two years. We'd be assisted by the Perm District Government, the Russian Orthodox Church, the Perm Diocese, and the Perm procurator's office. My friend Dr. Sergey A. Nikitin, the Moscow medical examiner, was with me, along with Col. Vladimir Konstantinov and Igor Parfiontsev.

The first thing we did was review all the known facts about the location of the executions.

On the night of June 12, 1918, and into the next morning, the two carriages traveled north of Motovilikha on the Solikhamsky Road for approximately five kilometers. They crossed the Yazovaya River and then turned right. This was a crossover to the Old Solikhamsky Road; both ran north–south, and both led to a railroad intersection. The old road served as a detour while work was being done on the newer road, and the crossover was the detour route. It was lined by small pines and brush, then opened to a large field. People working at the Motovilikha arms factory were given land here for planting grass and making hay for their animals. The Bolsheviks knew this location well, with its hidden gullies, steep hills, hayfields, and forests. The steep hill was called Krasnaya Gorka (Red Hill).

These killers were employees of the arms factory, so they owned plots of land in that field. They held their May Day secret meetings here beginning in 1905, when the peasant revolts were occurring, and when the police came for them, they hid here.

Given what was known about the path of the two carriages, this field seemed like the most probable area to find the remains of the grand duke and his secretary. The local government helped us by having the high grass cut so that Konstantinov and Parfiontsev could get their radars working. Konstantinov found the site very interesting from a topographic point of view, especially the large crevasse. The two GPR operators focused here, but the small trees and heavy bush were forever blocking the information they needed. We spent the time we had and found nothing, but it wasn't as if we'd exhausted the possibilities; we simply hadn't been able to overcome the many physical obstacles. We left with a renewed determination to return in 2013. Sadly, though, in January of 2013, Colonel Konstantinov passed away.

We had to account for tremendous changes in the general areas where the killings and the burials must have occurred. The old roads, never heavy with traffic, had vanished or been superseded. A jail was built in the thirties, between the Solikhamsky tract and the Old Solikhamsky Road. And just north of the jail, a small village had sprung up to support those who worked there.

In the seventies, a large gas pipe and a hot water pipe were run through the field on their way to the village. Our main points of reference, the crossover and the Old Solikhamsky Road, no longer existed. We walked the area, trying to see what had been in the past beneath what had developed, but it was impossible to draw conclusions. We simply needed more information. Something the equivalent of the Yurovsky Note needed to turn up.

Finally, in 2016, we got our hands on copies of the killer's statements. Once again, it turned out they'd felt a sense of their importance and had the foresight to make records for posterity. We were fortunate to receive a good bit of cooperation from the people of Perm, which is now a city of about a million. Nelly Zenkova was the historian who made the biggest difference. A publisher by trade, she had obtained the handwritten testimonies of the murderers from another historian, Vladimir Sergeyevich Kolbas, who worked for the Perm State Archives. These memoirs had been held in Perm, but during the Soviet era, Kolbas had safeguarded them by storing them at his home to ensure they survived an age when records of the worst transgressions of the governing state were being sought out and destroyed. When I think about how fortunate we were to find these almost unknown testimonies—first from Yurovsky and now from those behind the grand duke's execution—I can only shake my head. Historians and researchers know that so many items from history simply vanish without a trace. We have questions that can never be answered. But in this case, the men wrote something down, and almost miraculously, what they wrote lingered into a new century.

I received a typewritten copy of the killers' testimonies and had them translated into English. There were a surprising number of accounts, most from 1924.

Vasily Ivanchenko of the Workers and Peasants Party had been appointed defense commissioner for Perm and was tasked with supervising Grand Duke Mikhail Romanov, his personal secretary, and two bodyguards. He worked from the police headquarters. With the White Army in frightening proximity, he worried constantly about the escape of the Romanov under his watch. When Mikhail went for a walk, Ivanchenko worried. It must be remembered that the Bolsheviks didn't have full and complete control of cities such as Perm.

One night, he began to have more serious thoughts about disposing of the problem once and for all. A woman came to him claiming to be the wife of the grand duke, and she wanted to go on a walk with her husband; she wouldn't say where.

Sooner or later, someone was going to help Mikhail Romanov escape. So Ivanchenko suggested to the executive committee that things would be easier if Mikhail Romanov were disposed of.

He was ignored, but he kept badgering the committee to let him execute the grand duke and his entourage. Finally, when the Urals area was clearly in jeopardy of the advancing Whites, he was told to go ahead and resolve the issue the way he wished.

At a movie theater, he whispered plans with several conspirators. The others had already sketched out a strategy for abducting the grand duke. They forged a document proclaiming that Romanov was to leave Perm under escort, complete with a phony signature. Ivanchenko was concerned; this was a serious step, and it could lead to big problems if an unsympathetic bystander questioned the document.

At ten o'clock on the appointed evening, the men drove up in covered phaetons and went up to get the grand duke. One of the men emerged after a while, in a panic, and said, "It isn't working out—a scandal is arising!" He ran away, but Ivanchenko took charge and insisted to the other man with him that there was no turning back at this point. The other man, Zhuzhgov, again went to the grand duke's room and this time emerged with his prey, along with Johnson, the secretary, who was badgering him with questions.

Ivanchenko showed Mikhail into the carriage and calmed him down. Apparently Ivanchenko was someone he could trust, or so he felt. Johnson was placed in the other carriage. The phaetons drove at full speed toward City Hill. Ivanchenko stepped out to see if anyone had pursued, but it was all clear. Mikhail looked at him and said, "Will I be shot today?"

"No," his captor laughed. "I want to save you because Perm is in danger. Today a rebellion is supposed to occur." He added a good bit of "nonsense," he wrote, and a relieved Mikhail gave him a handshake. He wrote Ivanchenko's name in his memory notebook so he could shower the man with wealth when things turned around.

Then they passed Yazovaya River and drew near to the planned destination, and a voice rang out: "Stop!" The grand duke was told to step out. Ivanchenko knew his horse didn't like gunshots, so he took the reins of the horse and led it away. As he did so, he heard the fatal shots being fired.

He turned his horse back toward the phaeton, lifted his flashlight, and his beam illuminated the two bodies lying on the ground. Zhuzhgov covered the bodies with brush, and the party proceeded to Motovilikha. At the police station, they discussed how to handle the bodies and decided two of them would return to bury the corpses "as deeply as possible" and arrange the surface so as not to attract notice.

Next day, as he entered the police department, he heard the report that Romanov had "escaped." Everyone seemed anxious. There was a bit of complaining about the alarm not being sounded when Mikhail was abducted, about Ivanchenko's assistant Drokin, who had asked questions and made objections in order to delay the mounted police. If this hadn't happened, the police might have caught up with the two phaetons, and the whole group would have been executed.

Now, the word was that Mikhail had been apprehended, and the authorities were allowed to believe that the White Army had captured Romanov.

The following day, Ivanchenko was asked to come to Motovilikha, where the police were meeting about all the Romanov rumors spreading through

Perm. Ivanchenko was to bring Mikhail Romanov's body to stop the rumors, because people were claiming Mikhail was alive and could return as tsar. So dig him up and show everyone he's dead, went the demand. Ivanchenko refused, and he knew the others couldn't produce the body because they didn't know where it was.

Mikhail's bodyguards were arrested for assisting in Romanov's escape. After that, "we all calmed down."

Andrey Markov, one of the conspirators, offered his own perspective. He largely agreed with Ivanchenko's memories, though differing on small details. He had entered the room where Romanov and Johnson were taken, and recalled that Romanov objected strongly to going anywhere. Romanov talked about his illness and physical incapability of traveling, but Markov told him he was going with them whether he liked it or not. The grand duke wasn't allowed to bring any clothes, but Johnson could travel with him; the killers had included Johnson in their plans.

At the proper time, when the group was expected to be outside the city, Ivanchenko's assistant Drokin picked up the phone as planned and officially reported that unidentified individuals had spirited away Mikhail Romanov, and that mounted police should check all the escape routes. All the authorities were given this announcement.

"We were already far away, near the Motovilikha factory," reads the confession at this point. As the two abductees grew nervous and began to ask questions—most of which weren't answered—the party passed "the kerosene store" (also known as the Nobel store) near Motovilikha. No one was around, and the carriages made a sharp right toward the woods. After a short distance, they halted and shouted for the men to emerge.

Markov quickly shot Johnson in the temple as Johnson "fell down swinging." One of the men had a cartridge that jammed. Another only succeeded in wounding the grand duke, who ran toward Markov with his arms spread, begging to say farewell to his closest friend. Markov shot Romanov in the head from short range, so the victim went down quickly. Markov recalled that Ivanchenko's horse panicked and took off for the woods, with Ivanchenko set off running after it.

He wrote that it was Zhuzhgov and Novosyolov, a "reliable policeman," who properly buried the bodies the following evening. The news spread that some officers had abducted the grand duke and secretary, but no one, including Bolshevik party members, knew who.

Zhuzhgov himself offered dramatic recollections of the arrest, in which he had taken the lead. His account reads a bit like one shared later among a group of buddies at a tavern. He said Romanov was sitting at the table with two other men, and a sailor, Romanov's bodyguard, joined them. Upon being given the papers, Mikhail said, "I'm sick and I will not go." Zhuzhgov argued with him, and the other men affirmed their leader was sick and wouldn't allow him to be taken anywhere. After leaving to tell Ivanchenko of the difficulties, he returned with more resolve. He walked right up to Mikhail and said, "Go!"

The others began shouting, and at that point Zhuzhgov pulled out a revolver and pointed it at the grand duke's supporters. "You sit back, don't move, or I will shoot you right here. And Romanov must come with me." Then he grabbed Mikhail by the scruff of the neck and pulled him out of the room.

Later, after the shootings, he observed inscriptions on the grand duke's breast as well as his hands. He had the thought of cutting off the head and hands for burial elsewhere, but another man urged him not to do it, and he abstained.

Militiaman I. G. Novosyolov was a particularly interesting conspirator. He seems to have spent much of the rest of his life insisting upon his participation in the murder and burial of the two bodies, having fallen on hard times. He felt that that if his place in history were recognized, perhaps a job would materialize. It seemed that the other conspirators would only vouch for his involvement in the burial on the second day. He wanted it known he had fired shots and helped to kill the grand duke and his English associate.

He wrote the government, he wrote party historical commissions in various cities, and he even wrote the newspaper *Pravda*, boasting of his guilt in the murder plot. He also shared details the other conspirators left out—namely, how the personal possessions of the two murdered men were divvied up. There were agreements about who would keep what possessions of the victims.

Ivanchenko, he said, had done the job "only for the watch," which he described as a "golden six-sided watch made of rose gold, from the executed Mikhail

Romanov." He said it was a valuable watch that should be in a museum, but Ivanchenko was keeping it. He also claimed to have marked a series of initials on a tree near where the shootings took place.

It was clear to us that the statements of the murderers contained lies and omissions. Their accounts of the locations of the murders and burials were maddeningly vague and inconsistent. We gave all the accounts of the conspirators to a forensic psychologist, who analyzed the statements and told us which one was most likely to be truthful. It was Novosyolov's—ironically, given that he was the one the others accused of spinning fictions when he described in detail his presence at the murders and then his assistance in the burials. When he offered his various confessions, he seemed to be a man with nothing left to lose, he was very careful in establishing verbal proofs he was there, and he was more than willing to expose the petty thievery of the other men.

All of this was fascinating, particularly in comparing and contrasting the memories of several participants from the same criminal act. Each told the story a different way. But I scanned each report for the details of where. Where had the murder taken place? And particularly, where were the bodies finally deposited? All the descriptions were vague, simply because there weren't many landmarks. Nobody buries a murder victim in a crowded, busy area.

All we could do was continue our search, but with such a wide range of possible sites, we had to decide on the most promising and focus there. Over the years, many more trips were to come. We learned a great deal about the area. We found evidence of the old roads traveled by the phaetons. We built wonderful relationships with the local authorities of Perm, and as always, I enjoyed my friendships with search partners, including my associates from NecroSearch.

The Yazovaya River and the foot of Red Hill became major points of focus for us. Local lore says that the two bodies were buried in that valley, and several factors point in that direction.

There's a chapel dedicated to Grand Duke Mikhail on Red Hill, overlooking the valley where we've searched. The Russian Orthodox Church holds processions there each year, and we've heard references implying that the chapel's location is no coincidence.

Artists have always used the foot of Red Hill as their backdrop when illustrating the crime. One such painting was crafted in 1920—just two years after the fact. What had the painter heard? Why did he choose the site he did?

We're aware that within a century, a river will change its course. The relative positions of the burials, therefore, would have changed too. We have to read the witness accounts with that in mind.

I made a total of ten trips to Perm for searches, and we covered a lot of ground with volunteers, technology, and even cadaver dogs. Americans, Russians, and citizens of the United Kingdom have taken part. We've interviewed local people who may have family lore to share, a word or two from a grandparent or great-grandparent. We've concentrated on the vicinity of the valley through which the Yazovaya River flows from Ulitsa Lyangasova to the Solikhamsky Tract.

On the final day of our 2018 search trip, I thought to myself, "Another year, no remains." It was difficult not to feel a little disappointment, though I'm a patient man. Then Crystal Strouse and Steven Jackson asked me to walk with them into the forest. These were our forensic botanist and our historian, respectively.

We followed a trail that took us to the top of Red Hill, to the open grassy field we knew so well by now. We came upon three large scotch pines. Crystal turned to me and said, "That's the Trinity"—the nickname for the oldest trees in the area. These three were grandmothers to the young pines all around them. As we walked in that direction, my two companions shifted toward what appeared to be the scraggliest tree around. It had reddish bark and a square top. People had chopped bark for the campfires they made beside this tree.

Crystal and Steven pointed to the other side of the tree and I stepped over to take a look. The initials M and P (the Russian R, for Romanov) had been carved there, deeply, apparently many years ago. Could the killer Novosyolov have left them there? Could he have remembered incorrectly, adding the other two letters in his imagination?

Nearby, a farmer was tending his cows. Steve walked over to him and asked if there had been a road climbing this hill. Yes, there had, agreed the man. He pointed to a washed-out road. He said people were using it thirty years ago; we'd first found it in 2013. But if the tree wasn't another hoax, then this road would fit nicely into the scenario: the cart road that the phaetons couldn't handle, the reason for stopping, the shots, and the carving of the grand duke's initials.

Our tenth trip came in September 2021. I was accompanied once again by Russian and American forensic experts, historians and archivists, and members of Mountain Shield, the group that finally found the last two children. One reason for continuing to return is that, as our trips continue to be noticed and talked about in the area of Perm, we receive new information. On this occasion, we were interviewed on local radio, and as always, we asked for people to come forward if they had any knowledge that might help us. And we were always receiving it.

Perhaps the information is rumor or legend. Perhaps it's simply wrong. But we're willing to check into any credible tip, knowing just three generations or so separate the local folks from the events. Sometimes people remember things.

Natalya Alekseevna Pashkova was one of those. She confessed to a priest that her mother took her swimming when she was seven where the Gaiva River flows into the western side of the Kama. During their outing, her mother took her aside and confided a secret—one she warned was dangerous. She would only have spoken it in a secluded spot like this one. Her secret: "The king is buried here."

Pashkova's grandfather, we were told, was a factory watchman. A colleague who lived by himself in a hut was supposedly involved in the burial that occurred in 1918. Two Red Guards showed up at the hut and demanded that he eviscerate the body parts and stuff them into a large porcelain container. The grandfather's colleague said that he did as he was told, took the container and its contents across the river, and buried it in a pre-dug grave.

This was the first time we'd received information pinpointing a burial place. So we hurried to that spot, found anomalies through radar, and dug, but there were no signs of a grave. Pashkova was with us and suggested perhaps the site was closer to the river's edge. The problem was, we'd have to contend with cement and large tree trunks. But our equipment did tell us there was a fairly large anomaly, 4 by 2 meters at a depth of 1.4 meters of disturbed soil. We've yet to take that on.

Then, on the same trip, two other people came forward to tell us they'd seen two crosses put up by locals, supposedly marking the graves we were seeking.

We're looking forward to checking those, too, but September weather cut short our investigation time.

When I think of those helping us—NecroSearch; various officials in Perm; Russian forensic scientists and archaeologists; His Eminence Methodius, the metropolitan of Perm and Kungur; the Russian Nobility Association of the USA; and Mrs. Nadja von Lowenstein, to name only a few—I feel deep gratitude and encouragement to persevere.

We will find these two men and see them buried with dignity and honor.

24

The Church Moves in Mysterious Ways

The Eastern Orthodox Church exists in the blind spot of Western Christians. If asked to name the main sectors of Christianity, an American or a Western European is likely to think of Roman Catholicism and Protestantism.

Yet the Orthodox Church is the second-largest branch of Christianity, claiming 120 million adherents. The Russian Orthodox Church accounts for half of those. And since the diaspora of Russian Revolution, fleeing Russians have brought their church to many other nations. The Russian Church Outside of Russia, established as an independent entity in 1920, has nearly thirty thousand members. It's also referred to as the Russian Church Abroad.

Orthodoxy is a powerful, vital, and vast tradition, regardless of who notices it in the West. It remains close to the hearts of its adherents. The Russian church, in particular, has followed a winding and often treacherous path in its history. With all it has been through, with the forces of modernism, with attempts to snuff it out, it's managed to show a strong resurgence since the fall of the Soviet Union. One must know at least a little about its life and times to understand its puzzling relationship to the discovery and authentication of the Romanov remains.

Before 1917, church and state were closely intertwined. By definition, there would always be issues of corruption and control. But when the revolution came and the Russian empire began to fall apart, the government lost control of the church along with everything else. The civil war put the Russian Orthodox Church in a tenuous position; the church sought to remain neutral, but this was an impossible stance as the Bolsheviks included churches and bishops in their list of enemies of the people. Written into their ideals was the idea of eliminating religious bodies entirely.

In 1918 the Soviets passed a law separating church and state but also stripped the church of the right to own property. The church was limited to what happened inside a church sanctuary. Over the next five years, twenty-eight bishops and 1,200 priests were executed. Beginning in 1922, the state openly aimed to rid the nation of religion. For generations, a call to the priesthood didn't offer a promising future, and those who did serve had to do so with extreme care. All the same, Christianity has a history of flourishing under persecution. Resentment toward heavy-handed Soviet government often drove people toward the acceptance and community offered by the church.

There was also the problem of the state infiltrating the church, regardless of supposed separation of church and state. New sects were created for the purpose of causing divisions and in-fighting. And as the Russian Orthodox Church was brought into obedience with communism, this caused a split with the Russian Orthodox Church Outside of Russia.

Joseph Stalin actually attempted to boost the Russian Orthodox Church once World War II began. It was little more than a ploy to wrap patriotism in priestly vestments to increase support for the war. Once-secret documents from the period show that the government was actively working to control the church by placing its own agents in leadership positions. Ultimately, all these things had the effect of increasing people's skepticism about the Russian Orthodox Church. Could it be trusted? How much of its guidance was coming from the Kremlin rather than heaven? White Russians in the United States and other countries learned to be highly skeptical of religious pronouncements coming from Moscow rather than New York City, where the Russian Orthodox Church Outside of Russia was based. Realistically, bishops had little chance of functioning unless they cooperated with the KGB.

In 1990, after Soviet communism collapsed, Metropolitan Alexy began his patriarchal tenure and worked to restore Russian Orthodoxy to its pre-1918 status. Closed churches were reopened; new ones were built. But it would have been naive to think a pure transformation could happen quickly, if at all. For too long, the church had been under state control. Just as much of the

KGB remained just as it had been, the church, too, was still led by much of the same hierarchy, and people knew it. The new government continued to have its hand in church affairs.

Patriarch Kirill supported the election of Vladimir Putin in 2012 and called Putin's leadership "God's miracle." That was the official line, but some church insiders felt the relationship between church and state leaders grew worse and worse. This is how things have been in Russia for the last century—there's what is said officially and what is said behind closed doors. Leaders are secretive because it's required for survival. The church in particular is always in some form of crisis, because the nation itself remains in various kinds of turmoil.

Russia invades a country, and that forces the church to either bless or condemn the act. The church must be very careful what is said. If it speaks out too openly against government policy, it faces trouble from the state. If it fails to speak out, it faces trouble from the people who look to the church for moral guidance. Sometimes the church looks at its options and decides not to speak at all.

That may explain why the church is so cautious about taking official stances of any kind—even if it's the recognition of a few bones unearthed in a forest near Yekaterinburg. What do the bones symbolize? They symbolize the old times, the days of monarchy. They also speak of the brutality of the Bolsheviks and the hypocrisy of their revolution. The bones themselves were one more Russian secret that robbed the people of closure for an entire history of a tsardom. When we're unsure whether someone is dead or alive, we can't grieve, and grief is a necessary part of moving on with life. The Russians felt this, and the matter of unearthing the bones and answering the questions became one fraught with deep emotions.

Putting those questions to rest would bring rest for the mind and soul. But what if it was just more lies? What if Yeltsin, who came from around Yekaterinburg, had some ulterior motive to produce a dog-and-pony show about solving the old mystery? What if the KGB stage-managed the whole operation to create sympathy for the new leaders? The timing of the announcement was suspicious, but the substance of the announcement would have invited skepticism at any time. A century of lies has made people—Russian and non-Russian—exceedingly slow to accept such assertions.

One other factor may be at work, and it's by no means exclusive to the Russians: an age of conspiracy theories. In recent years, nearly every large news event is greeted with one or several spectacular assertions that what has been seen cannot be believed. Thus the 9/11 attack on the World Trade Center is fervently believed by some to have been an "inside job." A school shooting is said to have been staged by anti-gun advocates using "crisis actors." An entire American election is believed by a large portion of the population to be rigged, even when no actual evidence can be found to support the idea.

What, then, is to stop people from believing a few bones could have been placed in the ground? Is it any more outrageous an idea?

There were rumors, of course, from the very beginning. The communists themselves spread a few. The Romanovs are still alive. Or the family is still alive, but Nicholas was executed for trying to escape. Then, of course, rumors began sprouting everywhere. One was that Nicholas had somehow survived and lived in the Urals. There were plenty of claimants for a still living tsarevich, and of course the Anastasia rumors continued. As a matter of fact, even those who accepted that the bones dug up off the Old Koptiaki Road were the Romanovs and servants had to wonder about the two missing children. Could they have survived after all?

In 1976 two British journalists published *File on the Tsar*, which purported to contain evidence that one or more Romanovs had been helped to safety in Perm. And so, just as two searchers were uncovering the real skulls, rumors were starting up all over again.

A number of White Russians had been taken in by the long-running mystery of Anna Anderson. When the DNA proved conclusively she was just what some claimed—a factory girl from Poland with mental health issues—it was difficult for people to believe they'd been so thoroughly fooled.

And now, this issue with old bones.

In the 1990s, when news spread about what had been uncovered, the church took no stance and immediately showed a reluctance to speak on the matter. But in 1995 the Russian Orthodox Church formally submitted ten questions to the government commission that set out to investigate the remains. The question that loomed largest asked whether the Romanov murder had been a ritual killing. The church indicated it would like to rule that out, but it seemed very reluctant to let go of the idea. It was held by certain groups that were applying tremendous pressure to the church not to recognize the Romanov remains. The government commission found no evidence for a ritual killing.

The underlying tension was that "ritual killing" is a phrase that has long been a part of antisemitic rhetoric. The last thing an already controversial issue needed was the world accusing it of antisemitism. But a large number of the skeptic group embraced that theory. Where did it come from?

Robert Wilton, the British journalist, wrote an early book, *The Last Days of the Romanovs*, that contained references to occult messages sketched on the walls of the basement room where the executions happened. Wilton was known for antisemitic conspiracy theories, and "ritual killings" seem to have been one of his specialties.

Then there were the rumors about beheadings. The rumor went that after the Romanovs and servants were shot, they were all beheaded. Their bodies were burned or disposed of in some way, then the heads were taken in a bag to display before Lenin. Presumably beheading would have been part of the ritual. The problem, of course, is that the skeletons show no sign of beheading. While the bones themselves are separated, beheadings would have severed spines and the evidence would still be there. While there's clear evidence of bullet holes, no one seems to have been beheaded.

As late as 2017, Bishop Tikhon Shevkunov, known for his closeness to Vladimir Putin, claimed the ritual killing story is widely accepted among members of a church commission that was investigating the murder. He said, "For a significant part of the church commission, there's no doubt that that is what happened." Part of the theory is that Lenin himself ordered the murders as a ritual, but scholars agree that all the leaders of the Bolshevik Revolution were avowed atheists, interested in superseding religion entirely. The idea they'd be trafficking in odd Jewish rituals doesn't add up. But it's the myth that refuses to die.

During the period of the DNA tests and forensic examinations, the church continued to seem unimpressed. The general reason given was that "all the questions haven't been answered." Independent DNA tests confirmed beyond any shadow of a doubt that these were the remains of the imperial family and servants, but the church, which is generally in the business of giving answers, could only offer questions.

We continued to speak to our connections within the church, offering research, insights, and information. But at the same time, other voices were pitched much louder, telling the ecclesiastical leaders not to dare acknowledge those remains as legitimate. So it was a no-win situation for the church. It could either keep the angry naysayers happy and appear hostile to science to the rest of the world, or it could listen to the science and have to deal with the fury of some very influential Orthodox Christians. The only solution was to appear continually open but still undecided. That held both sides at bay.

But as I continued my searches and my lobbying attempts to get help from the FBI and others, this wasn't enough for me. Closure was the ultimate goal, and there could be no closure if the church of the Russian people didn't validate what we were doing.

In 1998, on the eightieth anniversary of the executions, nine small coffins—just large enough for the bones—were interred in the crypt at Saint Peter and Saint Paul Cathedral, in the Saint Catherine Chapel, where Russian emperors have been laid to rest since Peter the Great. Boris Yeltsin said, "Today is a historic day for Russia. For many years, we kept quiet about this monstrous crime, but the truth has to be spoken."

If only it were that simple. At first Yeltsin had declined to attend the ceremony, worried about his relationship with the Russian Orthodox Church. But he changed his mind, attended, and spoke at the ceremony, asking for a time of repentance for crimes of the past. Patriarch Alexy II was not present, and no church representatives above junior clerics were permitted to attend. I couldn't help but feel sorrow over the fact that after eight decades, on the day when the imperial family received the sanctity of a church burial, the church itself would cast a shadow over the event. The presiding priest offered a blessing for the bodies without acknowledging who the bodies were. "God knows their identities," he said, in one of the most awkward blessings ever.

Two years later, the Romanovs were canonized by the church. Tsar Nicholas II was honored for his "humbleness, patience, and meekness." This was an action the church could take without regard to their remains. The Romanovs had undeniably been the last imperial family, and because of their manner of death, they should be canonized—on that, everyone could agree. Or could they?

Some blamed Nicholas for the Russian Revolution—too much "humbleness, patience, and meekness" to take strong action and avoid the chaos that brought in communism. It was pointed out that the victims did not die for their faith, as martyrs normally do—unless, of course, the killings were ritual murders. That debate began all over again. Was the church trying to use canonization as a subtle way to suggest Jewish conspiracies?

The Russian Orthodox Church designated them as "passion bearers," which is distinct from martyrdom. If they did not die for their faith, they endured suffering and death in a Christlike way. Anyone who reads the diaries they left behind in Ipatiev House would have to agree, at least, with that. The Romanovs were pious and sincere in their devotion, consistent in their Bible readings, and unfailing in their attendance at worship and mass.

And certainly, the church remained immovable. Vsevolod Chaplin, speaking for the Russian Orthodox Church, said there needed to be further testing—of all the remains, including those now buried in Saint Peter and Saint Paul Cathedral. He argued that previous investigations were "opaque." He said, "People have questions. We want further investigation so that any tests are done in the presence of church officials. These people have been canonized, and if their remains are found, they will be considered holy relics that believers will pray to. For this reason, it's very important to make sure." I could only wonder, how many times must Soloviev answer these questions? The church was kept abreast of all investigations yet showed no interest in being present during testing.

How does this generation of Romanovs feel about the matter? Nicholas II's great-great-niece, Grand Duchess Maria Vladimirovna, affirms the church's stance. But many other Romanovs do not. Prince Dmitry Romanovich doesn't consider Maria Vladimirovna to be the rightful heir to the Romanov name, and this branch spoke in favor of burying the last two children found.

This last item—what to do with the tsarevich and his sister—became the new debate. Other than full acknowledgment of the remains by the church, this one final thing had to be done: reunite the family. Bury the last two children.

In October of 2015 a funeral was scheduled for Alexei and his sister, but the Russian Orthodox Church spoke out, once again questioning whether the remains were authentic. That got the funeral postponed. The church reopened the investigation, and the subject disappeared again behind a veil of secrecy.

There was an outburst of indignant anger, of course, but spokesmen for the church continued to shrug and say, "We must be certain. We need more testing."

Bishop Tikhon, thought to be Putin's confessor, was the main voice expressing doubts at strategic times, and he seemed in favor of stretching out the church's own investigation into perpetuity. On state television, he affirmed that scientists would have all the time they could need. He suggested two or three more years of tests. What kinds of tests? Who would perform these tests? He gave no specifics.

The church seems to be saying, "Nothing to see here. Move along. We'll let you know if anything turns up."

Just the same, Russia's prime minister, Dmitri Medvedev, responded to pressure from the Romanov family and others to release an official state ruling that same year: the remains are authentic. This was just prior to the canceled funeral, so this indicated some divergence between church and state. Patriarch Kirill cast aspersions on the Yeltsin-era commission and promised that Vladimir Putin would give us the true investigation.

The 2015 commission was headed by Metropolitan Tikhon Shevkunov of the Russian Orthodox Church and Col. Marina Molodsova from the investigative committee.

Of course, in the category of "reinventing the wheel," the commission announced it would re-perform all the tests that had already been done. But how could that be done, when the remains had been buried? The church was willing to disinter them once again. And while they were at it, Alexander III, the previous tsar and father of Nicholas II, would also be exhumed. The DNA of the long-buried Romanov could be compared to the Romanovs buried along Koptiaki Road.

It concerned me, of course, that the church had total control this time. Its officials had been building the case for flawed earlier investigations, and if they now produced their own results, saying these remains were not genuine, they could say they'd been right all along. On the other hand, I knew that Marina

Molodsova was involved, and I knew she was a woman of high integrity. I'd been impressed in my dealings with her.

All the labs received matching results.

I was able to be of assistance on several occasions. When I first met Molodsova, I asked if she had the information from our DNA studies of 2007 and 2008. She told me those studies weren't in their records, amazingly enough. Most of our other tests and research also weren't there. On my next trip to Russia, I presented her with all the records from the Maples work, plus the full DNA reports from AFDIL, the University of Innsbruck, and the Yekaterinburg Bureau of Forensic Medicine.

Now she had the full and complete research, and all of it together added up to a strong testimony.

I also helped obtain full volumes of the Sokolov investigation. Most people don't realize his report worked out to seven volumes, all held at Harvard University's Houghton Laboratory and not freely available. The committee had only four volumes, and they were nearly unreadable. Having a clear copy made electronically was expensive, but I eagerly provided this to the investigation. Molodsova was appreciative.

One of the more interesting projects came about when Molodsova asked me to help obtain a plastic 3D casting of Dr. Botkin's famous dentures. His lack of original teeth made his skull the easiest to identify. Sokolov found two sets of Botkin's dentures—one at the Four Brothers area, which disappeared, and another on the second floor of Ipatiev House, which are in possession of the Russian History Museum in Jordanville, New York. I called my friend forensic odontologist Lowell Levine from the New York State Police Crime Laboratory. He introduced me to Dr. Douglas Smail, a maxillofacial surgeon who was able to arrange for a 3D facsimile to be created. The resulting cast came to me by mail, and I sent it, with the 3D computer file, to the Russian scientists. It fit the skull perfectly.

The committee searched an impressive number of archives and made a number of other compelling investigations, including a number designed to destroy some of the persisting myths about the executions and burials. They proved a room the precise size of the basement room in Ipatiev House could have allowed for eleven individuals to be executed (some insisted it couldn't). They showed that the bodies couldn't have had acid thrown on them, then been burned to ashes. Acid, they demonstrated, actually retards the burning process. The committee sought to identify the authors of the wallpaper graffiti.

On July 17, 2018, the Russian investigative committee announced they had accepted all the DNA tests. It was announced once more—hopefully once and for *all*—that the remains found at Pig's Meadow, along the Koptiaki Road, are those of the Romanovs and faithful servants.

Still, however, there was to be an announcement along those lines from the Bishops' Council of 2020. This would be the formal, for-the-record Russian Orthodox Church pronouncement on this matter. But in March of 2020, COVID-19 suddenly blew up into an international pandemic, the worst in more than a century. The Holy Synod of the Russian Orthodox Church announced that the Bishops' Council would be postponed until the end of 2022. This was certainly understandable.

It was also understandable in 2022 that the Bishops' Council would be once again postponed—this time because of the invasion of Ukraine. Now the nation was in crisis, and the church also had to worry about its relationship with Ukraine's Orthodox Church, which split with the main body over the war.

Whenever the synod finally meets, one of the main areas of discussion is scheduled, as of this writing, to be a final, definitive decision on whether to accept the Yekaterinburg remains as holy relics. The longer the war drags on, the longer this issue will be unresolved.

Meanwhile, I continue to speak to my various friends in the ministry, updating them on our work, explaining all the various investigations and DNA tests, all the politics, all the twists and turns from this story—because there are still plenty of questions out there. Some people, I find, are confused; others have only heard the news releases in bits and pieces, and they're trying to put the whole picture together. A few aren't sure why this is so important. And many are still hostile toward the truth of the matter.

A bishop from Canada asked me to speak to a gathering of Russian Orthodox Church Outside of Russia bishops about all these things and to answer their questions. I told him I'd be happy to do that. Telling this story has become second nature by now, and my passion for it hasn't subsided in the least.

The bishop thanked me, then, with a slight frown, said, "You know, we're inundated with emails and letters attacking those remains. They still don't believe they're real."

These bishops will eventually travel to Moscow for their synod, and they'll be called upon to vote. This is why I take every opportunity to speak, to tell our story, and to raise awareness that we're facing another example of the modern world's refusal to accept science over personal agenda.

The opposition is strong. It comes from a few, but they know quite well how to amplify it.

We must be stronger still.

Epilogue

THE LOCKET AND THE FRAME

Sometimes we find the evidence; sometimes the evidence finds us.

Nikolai Bachmakov is a jeweler and conservator of the works of Peter Carl Fabergé. One of the most trustworthy and knowledgeable dealers of Russian art, he advises collectors, museums, and institutions.

One day, Bachmakov acquired a Fabergé locket that contained a photograph of Empress Alexandra Fyodorovna—a gift to Grand Duchess Xenia on the birth of the Tsarevich Alexei. The grand duchess was the sister of Nicholas II, and therefore sister-in-law to the empress. Alexei was an heir long-awaited as four older sisters had preceded him, so his birth was, of course, a big event for all the Romanovs. Special gifts and commemorations would have been the order of the day.

When Bachmakov carefully opened the locket for cleaning and restoration, he caught his breath to see a small lock of hair inside. Logically, this would be hair from the infant tsarevich. Instantly, his view of the piece shifted from Fabergé-related considerations to historical significance.

I came into the picture in March 2017, when my friend Nicholas B. A. Nicholson wrote to pass on the news of this locket being found. He said Bachmakov had approached DNA labs about testing the hair but hadn't had good experiences, and he needed advice on how to test this hair so that it could be authorized. This was no longer a jewelry issue, Bachmakov had said—this was a relic to be treated appropriately.

If only this piece had come to light a few years earlier. Hair is reliable as forensic evidence, and it does provide DNA in good conditions. The hair would have made a nice addition to our past testing, but it was too late for the commission's investigation that was now in progress in Russia. Five DNA labs were hard at work. Just the same, I'd speak to Col. Marina Molodsova, head of the commission, and tell her my plans, which were to contact the FBI's DNA lab. Dr. Odile Loreille and Dr. Jodi Irwin were my contacts in Quantico, Virginia.

I'd been working with Loreille to identify the remains of three skeletons found at the Convent of the Assumption in Vladimir, Russia. The founder of that convent, Saint Maria Shvarnovna, was my distant great-aunt.

I also knew Loreille from her days at AFDIL, when she'd worked with us on the Romanov case. Would she be interested in doing so again? I described what had been found in the locket. She immediately expressed excitement at this piece of serendipity and requested a photograph or at least a good description, and suggested that nobody touch the hair from then onward without wearing gloves.

In reply, Bachmakov offered a description: "Shaped as a heart, decorated with wreath, two diamonds and ruby on one side, and with Empress Alexandra Fyodorovna's monogram on the other side." He had recognized certain marks that left no doubt in his mind the piece was genuine, but at the time of purchase he couldn't open it without special tools. Once he did, underneath the silk he found the sample of light, thin hair. The hair of babies is always very fine. He knew that something very special had come into his hands.

From there, he'd traveled to Virginia and presented two hairs to a DNA lab, but the lab reported they hadn't been able to get a reading from such a small sample. They wanted the rest of the hairs, and naturally, Bachmakov declined. He was eager to have proof of the authenticity of this locket and the hair, though he knew in his heart it was the real thing. If any of it had to be destroyed simply for identification, he wanted to lose as little of it as possible.

My friend Nicholson, who was part of the correspondence, made a valid point. Since the locket itself was pre-1899, the hair could belong to Olga or Tatiana, the two older daughters. And Nicholson personally felt the hair belonged to the empress, since she was shown in the picture. The picture was taken in 1896, so this could have been a wedding or coronation gift. Later, Colonel Molodsova suggested we could even be dealing with hair from Nicholas II himself—in examining the files and evidence, she'd come across an envelope belonging to Alexandra, and it contained the tsar's hair from the age of three.

I felt that Bachmakov had it right: this must be Alexei's hair, in keeping with the occasion of his birth. But who knew? Only DNA would reveal, or at least suggest, the solution. Loreille reminded me that if the hair sample contained no root, then mitochondrial DNA would be the only type that could be gathered—and that meant we wouldn't know which Romanov child it might be, assuming it was one of them. They shared the same DNA sequence as their mother in mitochondrial DNA. If this was their father's hair, that was a different matter.

Later, Bachmakov produced a hair belonging to Empress Maria Fyodorovna's mother—maybe that could help, he suggested. I agreed to pass that on to Loreille.

Loreille's supervisor wrote me a note that was a bit discouraging. She wanted us to know up front that differentiating siblings from one another in modern hair is nearly impossible; with century-old hair, the chances are virtually nonexistent. Not only that, but she felt there might not have been enough DNA to extract from this sample, unless there was a root or root tissue.

We made plans for the hair sample to be sent to me so that I could deliver it to Quantico. Bachmakov provided a letter giving me full custody of some of the hairs found in the locket, and some hair samples from Queen Louise of Denmark, the maternal grandmother of Nicholas II.

By this time, Bachmakov was fascinated with the subject. He'd handled Romanov articles in the past, but he was now engaged with searching for anything to bolster the DNA evidence, and he was corresponding with members of the Romanov family who might have mementos. He'd purchased a metal picture frame from one of them. It wasn't Fabergé, but it held a photo of Queen Louise of Hesse-Kassel—and sure enough, as he inspected the frame, a lock of thick hair appeared. He carefully extracted it and sent the lock directly to Loreille.

In October of 2017 Loreille emailed us with preliminary results on the queen of Denmark's picture frame. The lab had tested it first because it was a better subject; it had more hairs. With DNA, the more, the better. They began with mitochondrial DNA, which, if genuine, would match the published results from Nicholas II—this was all on the maternal side.

It was a perfect match.

Again, the validity of the earlier DNA from our testing was bolstered. If our labs had conspired to fake the results, what were the chances a picture frame of the maternal grandmother would surface, and then, years later, a different lab would be able to match the DNA sequence? We already knew our DNA of Nicholas II was legitimate, but this reinforcement felt good anyway. It was one more glowing validation that the remains found off the Old Koptiaki Road were exactly what we said they were.

For the record, the frame's hair could have come from the queen or a maternal relative from one of her six children, or even the children of her daughters. At least, that's what can be derived from mitochondrial DNA. All the information is related to the maternal side.

But there was more. Nuclear DNA had been successfully extracted too. While the results were preliminary and awaited confirmation, they could determine that the hairs had come from a female, perhaps the queen. Loreille was excited because she hadn't expected any DNA results at all, yet they'd established the identity with the Romanov family and a female member.

During this period, the Russian commission was proceeding with its own investigation and DNA research through five labs. These labs were redoing all the work we had done in 2008, plus some new tests. But I knew that working with ancient DNA was just a bit beyond the capabilities of Russian labs in their current stage.

It was all the more dispiriting that our results had disappeared from the Russian records. That was the entire argument for redoing everything—they claimed they had nothing in their files about all the work that had been done in 2008, even though I could (and did) simply give them copies of what our labs had done.

As Loreille put it, there was no law against running the tests as many times as they liked, but it was a shame to consume portions of the human remains, as tests do, unnecessarily. Soon I found new information. Only two of the Russian-appointed labs had gotten results.

In February 2018 Loreille reported some good news. There was good DNA in the locket hair, and it matched the empress one hundred percent—again indicating someone maternally related to Alexandra Romanov. To help explain the result to anyone new to the subject, she attached a slide from previous work she'd done with Dr. Michael Coble. It showed the family tree with those who had the same mitochondrial profile as Nicholas II in red, and those who matched Alexandra in blue. The Queen Louise DNA had matched the red sequence; the hairs from the Fabergé locket matched the blue.

I communicated with Colonel Molodsova and explained what we'd done with the locket and the frame, and the DNA results we'd received. She said that once the results were published, she'd enter the paper with translation into the official Russian case record. She also asked for two other things: first, to stop in Moscow for a day when I could, to be interviewed by Russia TV-1; and second, to write about my twenty-five years of involvement with this case—something that could be published in the church's newspaper.

I did make that stop in Moscow, and in sitting down at the TV studio, telling the story of what I'd done to help bring closure to the Romanov case, I was taken on a trip through those years. I couldn't help but feel relief that we were near the end of this road.

It all began with my grandmother Anna, and her stories from another world, another time. She described such an exciting, frightening world compared to the one around me, where I had so many good things, so much safety, security, and provision. Hearing her experiences was like something from an adventure book.

Then there was my mother, Anastasia, who told me, "Peter, once you start these things, you must finish, for the honor of our family." She was a Naryshkin.

In 1991, after hearing that the remains of the imperial family had been found, and after coming to believe they were real, I knew I had to find some way to get involved, because I didn't want my grandmother's story to be forgotten. Her courage was an inspiration for my life, and I couldn't stand to think about it fading into the dust of dying memories. I wanted the world to know about Anna's adventures and accomplishments.

So I jumped in headfirst. Those remains, found and unfound, became my life. At times, I must have bored all those around me with my inability to talk about any other subject. On my ships, some of the crew became interested and wanted to hear all about it. I made Russian history enthusiasts of some of them. Others must have thought I was obsessed and needed to get a life of my own and start living in the present.

Then there was Masha, my wife. Perhaps there were moments when she secretly wished I wasn't so absorbed in this one subject, though her family history was caught up in it too. But she loved me, she supported what was important to me, and I'm eternally grateful to have had her with me on the whole journey. I can't imagine it otherwise.

Most of all, I think about those characters from history, those real people whom I never met but who feel like old, familiar friends. Tsar Nicholas II, Empress Alexandra, their children—Grand Duchesses Olga, Tatiana, Maria, and Anastasia and Tsarevich Alexei—and of course, their small team of devoted, unfortunate helpers. None of these were perfect people. Like everyone else, they had their flaws and their virtues. But they didn't deserve to be imprisoned on the sole basis of their name and status; to be herded into a little basement room and to be shot, stabbed, and beaten with gun stocks; and then, finally, to have their bodies thrown into carts like so much rubbish, stripped, burned, and mass-buried in a desolate forest, with no markers, no honor, no sanctification.

This was a matter of historic injustice, and I was determined to give these people the dignified and honorable burial they deserved—including Grand Duke Mikhail Romanov and his secretary Nikolai Johnson.

The fruit of pursuing these things was not just achieving the goal itself but a great many new and wonderful friendships, the kind that are only possible when we work together with someone over time and across continents for a common goal. Some of these friends are in one country, some in another, but I'll never forget working with them. And I hope that what we accomplished together—the scientists, the diggers, the public servants, the ordinary men and women like me—won't be forgotten.

One thing is certain: our relationships have had some positive effects in this world, particularly in Russia. We brought forensic experts from the United States and the United Kingdom to work with Russian scientists, and they had an exchange of ideas and methods, all in a friendly manner (with the one exception I've documented). This wouldn't have been possible without the duty we all felt to history and the allegiance we had to science. Across the old boundaries of international rivalry, nations found a way to cooperate, to everyone's benefit.

We bought radar and special equipment for use in searches, and then trained Russian police to find remains in the most efficient way possible. Instead of sending one hundred soldiers to dig up an entire football field, a few searchers with the right technology can now locate remains in Russia.

The U.S. Army and the University of Innsbruck helped train Yekaterinburg scientists in DNA analysis. This was an invaluable new tool. When a plane crashed near Perm and all eighty passengers died, the authorities were able to identify all the remains and provide closure to the families. Before this, Moscow had a monopoly on DNA work in the nation, so that if someone committed a murder in Siberia, and the investigation needed DNA identification, they might wait many months to receive lab results from Moscow. But because of what we were able to share in our joint work, DNA labs sprouted up in every major city in Russia. This was a quantum leap for solving crimes in that country.

Even in this recent case of the locket and the frame, both containing hair with DNA, new protocols were developed because of the Romanov investigation. Dr. Loreille had to develop brand-new approaches and standards to extract DNA from hundred-year-old hair. That was all new. As important as DNA analysis is to our times, it feels good to know that the Romanov search played a large part in pushing the science forward.

This quest certainly stretched me as a person, put me in situations I never could have predicted, and forced me to be more outgoing and organized. And even now, I'm involved with non-Romanov searches, both in Russia and in the United States. I can't begin to imagine what my life might have been without this work, as much as I loved my career on the high seas.

I think of the long years of patience, when it seemed as if little was happening, and I recall how it felt to complete yet another search without finding the remains we were seeking—then I realize that, in reality, lots of good things had come from our work, even when we didn't see results. Good work has a way of multiplying itself, causing chain reactions of other good things. I'm grateful for that.

So, as I think of the past, my thoughts stretch also to the future. I hope my grandchildren cherish this book, long after I'm gone, and pass it on to their children.

In that way, what Anna began, a century ago, will move forward, generation by generation, and perhaps we'll care more about justice, more about our history, and more about the kind of place the world needs to be.

Appendix

YUROVSKY'S NOTE

Yakov Yurovsky was a watchmaker, a member of the Cheka (the Soviet secret police), and an operative in the Russian Revolution. In early July 1918 he was placed in charge of Ipatiev House and, weeks later, the execution of the Romanov family and attendants. In 1920 he offered in writing his initial account of his actions, answering many questions that lingered and were the subject of controversy until his note came to light in the 1990s, provided by his son. In particular, Yurovsky described the burial and reburial of the bodies.

The Note of the Commandant of the Ipatiev House Yakov M. Yurovsky about the Execution of the Imperial Family and the Attempts to Hide the Corpses [1920]

A telegram using conventional language was received from Perm on 16/VII/1918, which contained an order about the extermination of the Romanovs. Initially it was proposed to prosecute Nikolai (in May)—this was prevented by the advance of the Whites.

On 16th at 6 o'clock in the evening, Philipp Goleschekin ordered the execution. By 12 o'clock at night a car should have arrived to remove the corpses.

At 6 o'clock the boy . . .[1] was led away, which really bothered the Romanovs and their people. Doctor Botkin came to ask what caused this? It was announced that the boy's uncle who had been arrested and later fled, has now returned, and wants to see his nephew. The next day, the boy was sent to his homeland (maybe in the Tula Province). The truck did not arrive at 12 o'clock, and instead arrived at 2.30. This delayed the execution of the order. In the meantime, all preparations were made: 12 men were chosen (including 6 Latvians) with Nagants [revolvers], who were to carry out the sentence, although 2 Latvians refused to shoot the girls.

When the automobile arrived, everyone was sleeping. Woke up Botkin and he [woke] all the others. This is the given explanation: "Because there was unrest in the city it was important to transfer the Romanov family from the top to the lower floor." They were dressed after ½ hour. A room had been chosen downstairs with a plastered wooden partition (to avoid ricochets), from which all furniture had been removed. The team was on standby in the next room. The Romanovs had no idea. The commandant[2] went after them personally and led them down the staircase into the lower room. Nikolai carried Alexei in his arms, the others carried pillows and various other small items.

Entering the empty room, Alexandra Fyodorovna asked: "What, there is no chair? Can't we sit?" The commandant ordered two chairs to be brought in. Nikolai seated Alexei on one, Alexandra Fyodorovna sat on the other. As for the others, the commandant ordered them to stand in line. When they did so, the team was called in. After the team had entered, the commandant told the Romanovs, because their relatives in Europe continue attacks on Soviet Russia, the Ural Executive Committee ordered them to be shot. Nikolai turned his back to the team, faced the family, then as though coming to his senses, turned around to the commandant with the question: "What? What?" The commandant hastily repeated then ordered the team to prepare. The team was told in advance as to who would shoot whom and ordered them to aim straight into the heart to avoid a lot of blood and end it sooner. Nikolai did not say anything more, again turning to his family, the others made several incoherent exclamations, everything took a few seconds. Then the shooting began, lasting two [to] three minutes. Nikolai was killed instantly by the commandant. Then Alexandra Fyodorovna and the Romanov people died immediately (altogether there were 12 people shot:[3] Nikolai, Alexandra Fyodorovna, four daughters—Tatiana, Olga, Maria and Anastasia[—]Doctor Botkin, the lackey Trupp, the cook Tikhomirov,[4] another cook[5] and a freilina[6] whose name the commandant forgot).

Alexei, three of his sisters, the freilina and Botkin were still alive. They had to be shot again. This surprised the commandant because they aimed straight at the heart, it was amazing that the bullets from the Nagants bounced off from something and leaped around the room like hail. When one of the girls was stabbed with a bayonet, the bayonet was unable to penetrate the corset. Thanks to this, the entire process including the check-up (feeling for a pulse etc.) took minutes. Then they began to take away the corpses and stack them in the car that had been lined with cloth to prevent the seepage of blood. This is when the thieving began: had to place reliable comrades to guard the corpses, while the transfer continued (the corpses were carried out one by one). Under the threat of being shot, everything that was stolen was returned (gold watches, a cigarette case with diamonds etc.).

The commandant was only ordered to carry out the sentence, the removal of corpses etc. was comrade Ermakov's (a worker from the Verkh-Isetsk factory, party comrade, former convict) duty. He should have arrived with the automobile and was allowed to enter using the conditional password "trubochist" [chimney sweep]. The automobile's delay caused the commandant to doubt Ermakov's punctuality, therefore the commandant decided to check the operation until the end. Around 6 o'clock in the morning we left for the place (behind the Verkh-Isetsk factory) that Ermakov should have prepared. At first the corpses were meant to be taken by an automobile then from a known point, on horses because the automobile was unable to go further. The place chosen was an abandoned mine. Having passed the Verkh-Isetsk factory 5 versts [3.3 miles], we stumbled upon a camp of 25 people, on horseback with carts etc. These were the workers (members of the Soviet, the executive committee etc.) that Ermakov had prepared. The first thing they yelled: "What you did not bring them to us alive?!" They thought the execution of the Romanovs would be entrusted to them.

We began to unload the corpses into the carts, as they would be needed [later]. This was very inconvenient. Straight away they began to empty the pockets—I had to threaten to shoot immediately and place guards. Here it was discovered that Tatiana, Olga and Anastasia were wearing some sort of special corsets. Decided to undress the corpses, not here but at the burial place. However, it turned out that nobody knew where the designated mine was for this. Crack of dawn. The commandant sent the horse riders to find the place, but no one found anything. It became clear that nothing had been prepared: there were no shovels and the like. As the car got stuck between 2 trees, it was abandoned, having covered the corpses with cloth, we proceeded on rail carts.

[The corpses] were driven 16½ versts [10.9 miles] out from Yekaterinburg, stopping 11 versts [7.3 miles] from Koptiaki village; this was [about] 6–7 o'clock in the morning. We found an abandoned artisanal mineshaft, once mined for gold, [it was] 3½ arshin [8.2 feet] deep. The mineshaft had 1 arshin [2.3 feet] of water. The commandant gave the order to undress the corpses and make a fire to burn everything. Men on horseback were positioned all around, to drive away all passersby. Once the undressing of one of the girls began, we saw in the holes of the corset that was in parts shredded by bullets—diamonds. The eyes of the crowd were clearly on fire. The commandant decided to disband all the workmen, leaving behind several horseback riders and 5 team members. The others had dispersed. The team began the stripping and burning. Alexandra Fyodorovna turned out to have a pearl belt, made from several necklaces, sewn into the fabric. On the necks of all the girls there was a portrait of Rasputin with the text of his prayer, sewn into an amulet. The diamonds immediately fell out. The accumulated weight (that is, the diamonds) was about ½ pud [18 pounds]. These were buried underground in a small house at the Alapaevsk factory; in 1919 they were dug up and brought to Moscow. Putting all the valuables in bags, the rest of what was found on the corpses was burned, while the corpses were lowered into the mineshaft. During this, some of the valuable items (someone's brooch and Botkin's dentures) had dropped out and while trying to fill in the mineshaft with hand grenades, apparently the corpses were damaged, from which several parts had blown off—with this the commandant explains that when the Whites found this place (that they later opened) they found a severed finger and the like. However, the Romanovs were not supposed to be left here—the mineshaft was only intended to be a temporary burial place.

Finishing the operation and leaving guards, at 10 o'clock in the morning (already July 17th) the commandant went to the Ural Executive Committee with a report, where he found Safarov and Beloborodov. The commandant explained what was found and expressed regret that he was not allowed to search the Romanovs. From Chutskaev (the city executive committee president), the commandant found out that 9 versts [6 miles] along the Moskovskii Track there are "very deep abandoned mineshafts suitable burying the Romanovs." The commandant headed there but failed to reach the place due to a car breakdown. Reaching the mineshaft on foot, he did indeed find three very deep mineshafts filled with water, where he decided to drown the corpses by tying rocks to them. Since guards were there, who would be awkward witnesses, it was decided that simultaneously with the truck that would bring the corpses, an automobile with Chekists would also arrive, who under the pretext of a search, would arrest all the individuals. On the way back, the commandant had by chance caught up with a detained couple.

The delaying incidents continued further. Having gone with one of the Chekists to the place on horseback to organize the entire matter, the commandant fell off his horse and was badly injured (soon after the chekist also fell). In case the mineshaft plan did not work out, it was decided to either burn or bury the corpses in clay pits, filled with water, beforehand the mutilated corpses were made unrecognizable using sulfuric acid.

Finally returning to the city at 8 o'clock in the evening (on the 17th), we began to get everything that was needed—kerosine, sulfuric acid. Carts with horses without coachmen were taken from the prison. An incident with the Chekists had delayed the planned departure for 11 o'clock at night, and so to the mineshaft with ropes to pull out the corpses etc., we only departed at night of 17 to 18th [July]. To isolate the mineshaft (the first artisanal) during the time of the operation, the announcement in Koptiaki village [said] that the Czechs were hiding in the forest, the forest will be searched, hence nobody is to leave the village under any circumstance. The order came that anyone who breaks into the cordoned area will be shot on the spot. Meanwhile it had dawned (this was already the third day[,] the 18th). The thought arose that some of the corpses be buried right here next to the mineshaft, they began to dig the holes, and almost finished digging. But at this time Ermakov's peasant acquaintance drove up and it became apparent that he could see the hole.

The matter had to be dropped. It was decided to take the corpses to the deeper mineshafts. Since the carts proved unstable, falling apart, the commandant headed to the city for vehicles (a truck and two lighter vehicles for the Chekists). The carts broke at the outset, the vehicles were needed to be taken into the deeper mineshafts, moreover the vehicles were unable to reach the temporary burial place, hence the carts still had to be used. When the vehicles arrived, the carts were already moving—the vehicles met them ½ verst [0.3 miles] closer to Koptiaki. We were only able to set out at 9 o'clock in the evening. [We] crossed the railway line, at half a verst and reloaded the corpses into the truck. Drove with difficulty, paving dangerous places with sleepers, although got stuck a few times. Around 4.30 in the morning of the 19th [July] the vehicle got struck completely; left with, not reaching the mineshafts, to bury or burn. The latter, one comrade whose surname the commandant forgot, had promised to take it on, but he left without fulfilling his promise.

Wanted to burn Alexei and Alexandra Fyodorovna, [but] by mistake instead of the latter, burned the freilna with Alexei instead. Then we buried the remains right here under the fire and relit the fire, which completely covered [any] traces of digging. In the meantime, we dug up a mass grave for the others. Toward 7 o'clock in the morning, the hole, 2½ arshin [5.8 feet] deep, 3-½ [arshin, 8.2 feet] square was ready. The corpses were piled into the hole, the faces and all the bodies were in general doused with sulfuric acid, both for unrecognizability and to prevent the stench from decomposition (the hole was not deep). After throwing earth and brushwood, sleepers were placed on top and [then] driven over a few times—leaving no traces of the mineshaft. The secret was kept well—the Whites did not find this burial [site].

Koptiaki is [located] 18 versts [11.9 miles] from Yekaterinburg. To the northwest, the railway line passes at the 9th verst [5.96 miles], between Koptiaki and the Verkh-Isetsk factory. At the intersection with the railway line, the buried [corpses] are 100 sazhen [700 feet] closer toward the Verkh-Isetsk factory.

[One original copy of this document is held at the Russian State Archive of Socio-Political History, F. 588, Op. 3s. D. 11. L. 1-7.]

Translated by Margarita Nelipa[7]

NOTES

1. Editor V. Khrustalev states (236n3): the discussion here is about Leonid Sednev.
2. Editor V. Khrustalev states (236n1): Yurovsky calls himself the commandant.
3. Editor V. Khrustalev states (237n1): in fact, eleven persons were shot.
4. Editor V. Khrustalev states (237n2): the document contains an error, meant to be the young cook, Kharitonov.
5. Editor V. Khrustalev states (237n3): Yurovsky was inaccurate. The cook was Leonid Sednev who on the eve of the sentencing was isolated from the imperial family.

6. Editor V. Khrustalev states (237n4): Yurovsky is referring to the room maid, Anna Demidova.
7. Translator's reference: Document No. 186 in *Arkhiv Noveishei Istorii Rossii*, vol. 3, *Skorbnii Put' Romanovikh 1917–1918*, edited by V. M. Khrustalev (Moscow: ROSSPEN, 2001), 236–39.

Bibliography

Avdonin, Alexander. *Delo zhizny sudevnogo sledovatilya Nikolaya Sokolova*. Yekaterinburg: Yava, 2000.

———. *History of the Search for the Imperial Family, Ganina Yama*. Yekaterinburg: Real Media, 2003.

———. *Secrets of the Imperial Remains*. Yekaterinburg: Mid-Ural, 1994.

Bever, M. I. *Life and Death of Nicholas Sokolov (1882–1924)*. Yekaterinburg: Derzhavnoe Nasledie, 2000.

Bulygin, Pavel. *Murder of the Romanovs*. Moscow: Moscow Academia, 2000.

Crawford, Donald. *The Last Tsar: Emperor Michael II*. New York: Scribner, 2015.

Diterikhs, M. K. *Murder of the Imperial Family and Members of the House of Romanov in the Urals*. Vladivostok: Military Academy 36th Regiment, 1922.

Ford, Corey. *Donovan of OSS*. Boston: Little, Brown, 1970.

Gibbes, George, and J. C. Trewin. *The House of Special Purpose: An Intimate Portrait of the Last Days of the Russian Imperial Family*. New York: Stein and Day, 1975.

Graves, William S. *America's Siberian Adventure, 1918–1920*. New York: Peter Smith, 1941.

Halliburton, Richard. *The Famous Adventures of Richard Halliburton*. New York: Bobbs Merrill, 1940.

Lykova, L. A. *The Murder of Emperor Nicholas II*. Moscow: Russian Federal Archives, Russian Forensic Processes, 2015.

Massie, Robert K. *The Romanovs: The Final Chapter*. New York: Random House, 1995.

Rodzianko, Michael V. *The Reign of Rasputin*. Gulf Breeze FL: Academic International Press, 1973.

Sokolov, Nikolai. *The Murder of the Imperial Family*. Buenos Aires: Vervo Ruso, 1978.

Soloviev, Vladimir. *Secrets of the Old Koptikovsky Road.* Moscow: Dostoinstvo, 2010.

Summers, Anthony, and Tom Mangold. *The File on the Tsar.* New York: Harper & Row, 1976.

Von Rathlef-Keilmann, Harriet. *Anastasia.* New York: Pyson and Clark, 1928.

Youssoupoff, Felix. *Lost Splendor.* New York: Helen Mark, 2003.

Index